DENNY DAY

Also by Terry Smyth

Australian Confederates

DENNY DAY

THE LIFE AND TIMES OF AUSTRALIA'S GREATEST LAWMAN

—

THE FORGOTTEN HERO OF THE MYALL CREEK MASSACRE

TERRY SMYTH

EBURY
PRESS

An Ebury Press book
Published by Penguin Random House Australia Pty Ltd
Level 3, 100 Pacific Highway, North Sydney NSW 2060
www.penguin.com.au

Penguin
Random House
Australia

First published by Ebury Press in 2016

Addresses for the Penguin Random House group of companies can be found at global.penguinrandomhouse.com/offices.

National Library of Australia
Cataloguing-in-Publication entry

Smyth, Terry, author
Denny Day: the life and times of Australia's greatest lawman – the forgotten hero of the Myall Creek Massacre / Terry Smyth

ISBN 978 0 85798 682 5 (paperback)

Day, Edward Denny
Myall Creek Massacre, 1838
Police – New South Wales – Biography
Trials – New South Wales – Myall Creek
Justice, Administration of – New South Wales – 19th century
Equality before the law – New South Wales – 19th century
Aboriginal Australians – Crimes against – New South Wales – Myall Creek
Massacres – New South Wales – Myall Creek
Myall Creek (N.S.W.) – History – 19th century

305.89915

Cover design by Blue Cork
Cover images: battle scene courtesy the Calvert Collection, Mitchell Library, State Library of New South Wales; Denny Day portrait courtesy the *Maitland Mercury*; photo of spear courtesy Lindsey Horton; landscape by Luke Causby
Internal design and typesetting by Midland Typesetters, Australia
Printed in Australia by Griffin Press, an accredited ISO AS/NZS 14001:2004 Environmental Management System printer

Penguin Random House Australia uses papers that are natural, renewable and recyclable products and made from wood grown in sustainable forests. The logging and manufacturing processes are expected to conform to the environmental regulations of the country of origin.

For Kate, Ben, Sophie and Acky, from the man upstairs
And for my brother Dan

Contents

'To no man will we sell, or deny, or delay, right or justice.'
– Magna Carta, 1215, clause 40

Foreword

It was some years ago now that my brother Dan and I climbed over a stile and followed a muddy track down the fence line to the base of a hill. It was a winter's afternoon, the ground was sodden, the wind was bitter and we weren't dressed for the weather.

'This is the Old Glebe Burial Ground,' Dan told me as we trudged uphill through the long yellow grass. Like eddies in a shallow sea, the swirling west wind gave us glimpses of headstones and vaults hidden in the grass. Closer now, we could see that neglect, vandalism and rabbit burrows had left many of the tombstones toppled and vaults collapsed.

'What are we doing here?' I asked. 'What was it you wanted to show me?'

He led me to a grave halfway up the hill, choked by grass and weeds, surrounded by a rusted iron fence. On the simple sandstone headstone, still standing but badly weathered, I could just make out a name but little else, so again I asked, 'What are we doing here?'

My brother told me a story then. It was a tale that deserved to be told, related to him by an old-timer who had learnt it from another old-timer who, like others before him, had preserved the legend of a man who brought law with justice to Australia's wild frontier, from the Big River to the sea.

This is the story of Denny Day.

– Terry Smyth, January 2016

Introduction

The wilderness

Sydney sits cowering in its cove, its face turned seaward, lying back and thinking of England. In the 1830s there is no place on Earth where a European might feel further from home. The voyage out is long and perilous and for many there is little or no hope of return. The seasons are topsy-turvy, the stars alien, the native animals jokes of nature, the native people turbulent and beyond understanding, the land itself scarcely green and anything but pleasant, and mail from Europe can take up to six months to arrive, if it arrives at all.

Notionally, New South Wales includes almost the entire eastern half of the Australian continent, as well as most of New Zealand. Van Diemen's Land (Tasmania) has been a separate colony since 1825, and the Swan River colony, in Western Australia, since 1831. South Australia will be next to separate from the mother colony, in 1836, followed by New Zealand in 1841, Victoria in 1851 and Queensland in 1859.

Presently, though, the term *terra incognita* – 'unknown land' – still very much applies. New South Wales might as well be another planet.

Isolation in the Antipodes is compounded by insecurity. Since the arrival of the First Fleet from England, in 1788, the Sydney settlement has been constantly on the edge of disaster, barely managing to survive. Now, it is in the grip of drought and a floundering economy, forced to import wheat from Chile. The only growth industries are smuggling, particularly of rum and brandy, and bushranging, increasingly the career of choice for escaped convicts and sons of convicts.

The colony's most debilitating affliction, though, is an abiding dread of the wilderness beyond the settlement. The map of New South Wales divides the land into 19 settled counties, marked more by speculation than exploration. On the east coast, rivers flowing inland have been partly mapped but their destinations remain a mystery, and many people believe the rivers flow into a vast inland sea. Along the Great Dividing Range – the spine stretching 3500 kilometres down the east coast – most of the mountains and valleys are as yet unnamed and unexplored by white men. To the south, only one route – to the upper reaches of the Murray River – has been mapped, and much of the southern coastline is only sketchily charted and a hazard to shipping. Explorers have blazed trails into lands outside the 19 counties, but only the brave or desperate have followed. To the European mind, out there is a terrible fastness where the cries in the night of unknown creatures chill the blood, and where fearsome dark men lie in wait to fall upon any who dare to venture beyond the pale.

'Myalls', the white men call them. Originally the Dharug word for 'stranger', it has been adopted by Europeans to mean wild or uncivilised, particularly describing Aborigines from beyond the limits of settlement.

In his memoirs, a settler named Thomas Browne, better known as the novelist Rolf Boldrewood, author of *Robbery Under Arms*, captures the colonial consternation. Browne recalls that while making his way along a lonely track, 'I began to think about the blacks, and whether they might attack us in force. At that moment I heard a wild shrill cry, which considerably accelerated the circulatory system. I sprang to my gun.'[1] Luckily for Browne, that 'wild shrill cry' came not from a black man but a black swan.

In this wilderness, where vast forests of tall timber and rich black-soil plains are yet to feel the bite of axes and ploughs, the warlike inland nations stand ready to resist the curious strangers determined to cut a path through a continent. Out there, on the edge of nowhere, is Australia's frontier – a forbidding yet seductive place that makes no promises and gives no quarter.

In the early years of white settlement, no free person could enter the colony without British government approval, and no one, whether free settler or felon, could venture beyond the limits of settlement without official permission. Inevitably, as the restrictions eased and the number of free immigrants grew, along with the numbers of native-born colonists and convicts freed after serving their time, European settlement spread from Sydney north to the Hawkesbury River, then further north to Hunter's River and west across the Great Divide to the Liverpool Plains.

*

In the first census of New South Wales, in 1828, the white population was 36,598, of which 20,870 were free and 15,728 were convicts.[2]

In the bush, where there were more than 30 white men to every white woman, sexual abuse and exploitation of Aboriginal women was widespread. On outlying pastoral stations, black women were victims of routine abuse by overseers, stockmen, station hands, cooks – in fact, any white male – and the men had a name for such abuse. 'Black velvet', they called it. Not that they considered it abuse or exploitation. By their reckoning it was nature's way; a white man's right; a perquisite of Manifest Destiny. Some even claimed it had God's blessing, reasoning that because black women could be found wherever pioneers went, clearly it was part of the Almighty's great purpose.

By 1838, more than 80,000 convicts had been transported from Britain to New South Wales. In that year, a British parliamentary inquiry into the social consequences of the convict transportation system concluded that the system not only failed to reform criminals but had created a society 'most thoroughly depraved, as respects both the character and degree of their vicious propensities', and that Australia displayed 'a state of morality worse than that of any other community in the world'.[3]

Many of the pioneers pushing further and further inland were not – as the colonial authorities had first imagined – God-fearing yeoman farmers dedicated to creating an Antipodean replica of Merrie Olde England, complete with due deference and noblesse oblige. Granted, some among the freeborn – and among the felons, too – took decency and even gentility with them into the wilderness. For the most part, though, the early pioneers were adventurers and chancers, misfits and miscreants. Into the black man's society came white men made bitter by a world that had treated them with scorn; desperate for a chance to spit in the master's eye, and to find someone to be better than. And with the white man's axes and ploughs came guns and swords.

In the ancestral lands of the Awabakal, Darkinjung, Dharug, Wonnarua, Worimi, Geawegal and Kamilaroi, the custodians watched with rising anger as the ranges and plains were cleared for homesteads, crops, cattle and sheep, and ancient stands of cedar were felled for ships and building. For the whites, firm in the belief that freedom and prosperity in a new land was worth the toil and danger, there was no going back. For the inland nations, now aliens in their own country, there was no choice but to resist.

The immediate impact of white incursion into black lands was not its effect on traditional hunting grounds. Kangaroo and wallaby were still abundant, and possum ever more so as the settlers killed off the dingoes that kept possum numbers in check. Plains turkey remained plentiful, emu eggs were still easy pickings, to be baked in hot ashes, and the streams were alive with perch and mullet to be speared, netted or hooked on lines spun from fur or human hair. There were yams and other edible roots to dig from the ground, witchetty grubs to pluck from dead timber, honey from native bees, fruits and berries to pick, grass seeds to be ground into flour. In fact, with access to trade goods such as steel tomahawks, hoop iron, fish hooks and metal tools, hunting and gathering was easier than it had been before the coming of the white man.

It was not hunger that lit the fire. It was contempt. To the watching blacks, the whites invading their country were perverse creatures at war with the natural world, determined to bend it to their will, even if that meant destroying it. The ring of the white man's axe was the sound of profanity. The furrows dug by his plough were wounds in the martyred earth.

Chapter 1

A vicar's son

His was a noble lineage, being a descendant, on his mother's side, of the man whose job it was to wipe the king's arse. Denny Day's illustrious ancestor, Sir Anthony Denny, proudly bore the title of Groom of the Stool to King Henry VIII. The role, in its original form, involved nothing more than assisting the monarch in the performance of the royal bowel movement, but by Tudor times it had evolved into a much sought-after position. Proximity to the king's backside meant proximity to the king's ear, and the Groom of the Stool, being singularly honoured by access to the king's Privy Chamber, was thus privy to royal secrets, gossip and vital information. As such, he was the most powerful – and the most feared – courtier in England.

Sir Anthony Denny made the most of his position, using his influence on the dealings of the royal purse to enrich himself. By late in Henry's reign, his majesty's loyal Groom of the Stool had secured the use of the stamp of the king's signature, and could boast a property portfolio that included several grand manors, as well as former Catholic monasteries forcibly appropriated by Henry after his split with Rome.

Shakespeare immortalised Sir Anthony in *The Famous History of King Henry the Eighth*, albeit with one brief appearance and just three lines. Act five, scene one, finds the king in a gallery in the palace. It's past midnight and Henry is tired and emotional, not because he's just been informed that his queen, Anne Boleyn, is having a difficult childbirth and may die, but because he has been playing cards with the Duke of Suffolk and lost. Enter Sir Anthony Denny.

Henry: Well sir, what follows?
Denny: Sir, I have brought my lord the archbishop, as you commanded me.
Henry: Ha! Canterbury?
Denny: Ay, my good lord.
Henry: 'Tis true. Where is he, Denny?
Denny: He attends your highness' pleasure.
Henry: Bring him to us.

Sir Anthony exits, re-enters with the archbishop, then exits again without another word.

Still, while Shakespeare granted him only a walk-on part, in real life Sir Anthony was Henry's best supporting courtier. It was Sir Anthony in whom Henry confided that he doubted Anne of Cleves' virginity because her breasts were 'so slacke'.[1] It was in Sir Anthony that Henry confided almost exclusively in his latter years when, due to failing health, he spent more and more time in the Privy Chamber. Sir Anthony was executor of the king's will, and it was he who told Henry to prepare to meet his maker and attended him on his death bed. The king was so impressed that Sir Anthony was the only one of his courtiers brave enough to tell him his time was up that he presented him with a pair of gloves – which, given Sir Anthony's job description, suggests that the dying king hadn't lost his wicked sense of humour.

Sir Anthony Denny married Joan Champernowne, a lady-in-waiting to Henry's sixth wife, Catherine Parr. They had 12 children, including Sir Edward Denny. The first of several Denny men of that name, Sir Edward was a soldier and swashbuckling privateer – that is, a pirate commissioned by Queen Elizabeth I to capture and plunder Spanish ships. It was Sir Edward who established the family's Irish connection when in 1580 he and his cousin and fellow privateer, Sir Walter Raleigh, joined an English campaign to put down a rebellion in Ireland led by Gerald FitzGerald, Earl of Desmond, and allied Catholic Spanish and Italian forces.

Sir Edward led a company at the Siege of Smerwick (now Ard na Caithne) in County Kerry, in which the Spanish and Italian garrison surrendered after being promised their lives would be spared. His cousin Raleigh commanded troops in the ensuing massacre that dishonoured the English promise. Over two days, more than 500 prisoners of war were executed. Most were beheaded and their bodies thrown into the sea. Sir Edward reputedly captured the Earl of Desmond in battle, but it's not known whether or not he played any part in the slaughter.

For his services to the Crown, Sir Edward was granted the rebel earl's castle and vast estates in Kerry. Queen Elizabeth made him a baronet and a gentleman of the Privy Chamber. And while that was an honorary rather than a hands-on position, the gift the Queen gave him would surely have made Sir Anthony's ghost chuckle. It was a pair of gloves.

Sir Edward Denny and his wife Margaret had ten children, who in time came to see themselves as Anglo-Irish – literally and culturally a hyphenated people: English in Ireland, Irish in England.

Yet by the early nineteenth century, many descendants of English settlers in Ireland had distanced themselves from their origins in the conquest and subjugation of Ireland. To varying degrees, the Anglo-Irish had become assimilated into the native culture, albeit with strict lines of demarcation; in particular their Protestant religion, high social status and the English language – the language of law, education, commerce and advancement.

With notable exceptions, such as some among the landed gentry who preferred to live within their walls in a world of their own making, with Ireland outside the gates, many of the Sasanaigh (Saxons) now dropped the hyphen and declared themselves Irish. And while the inequities of English rule continued to deny the native Irish liberty in their own country, great Irish revolutionary leaders of the day included descendants of English settlers – Theobald Wolfe Tone, Robert Emmet, James 'Jemmy' Hope and John Mitchell.

The fortunes of the Dennys of Tralee Castle waxed and waned over the centuries. Some, through political connections, blind luck and inherited talent as land buccaneers, increased the family's wealth and estates. The family motto, after all, was *Et mea messis erit*, meaning 'The harvest also shall be mine.'[2] Others, through mismanagement, misfortune and a tendency to reckless behaviour – another family trait – lost land, money and influence. One such was Sir Barry Denny, a militia colonel whose adventurous spirit led him off to fight for Britain in the American Revolutionary War, meanwhile amassing debts he couldn't or wouldn't pay, whereby parts of the estate had to be sold.

Sir Barry's son, also named Barry, had only recently married when he was challenged to a duel by his cousin, Colonel John Gustavus Crosbie, a rival in an election campaign. Early on the morning of 20 October 1794, at Oak Park, Tralee, Colonel Crosbie, who had never fired a pistol in his life, shakily took aim at the luckless Denny and shot him dead.

The colonel won the election but a year or so later he, too, was dead. Riding home one night, he was thrown from his horse and killed. Some muttered darkly that he had been poisoned by the dreaded Dennys of Tralee Castle. Others whispered that his horse had been spooked by the vengeful ghost of Barry Denny.

On his father's side, Denny Day's family tree was heavy with Protestant clergymen – the notable exception being Judge Robert Day, famed for his humanity and incorruptibility on the bench. While the Days, being an old Anglo-Irish settler family, were staunchly Protestant, Robert, for the first seven years of his life, was raised by a Catholic tenant farmer on his family's estate. On returning home he could speak only Irish and never lost his affiliation with the native Irish. He remained a fearless advocate for the civil rights of Catholics and fierce in his condemnation of corrupt and prejudiced magistrates and landlords.

Denny Day, who as a boy would have known the judge, must surely have found him inspirational. The judge, too, was the son of a clergyman, and, being the father-in-law of a Denny, provided the first link between the two families. The next came in 1796 when Denny Day's father, Reverend John Day, married Charlotte Denny, daughter of Sir Barry Denny Snr.

Reverend John Day was the rector of the Church of Ireland diocese of Ardfert and Aghadoe, in Tralee, and, thanks to inheritance, a major landlord in the district.

Denny Day was born, at his father's vicarage, in 1801. Edward Denny Day was the name his parents gave him, but, informally at least, posterity would know him by his middle name – Denny.

The year of his birth was the year the Act of Union came into force, whereby the separate kingdom of Ireland was merged with England and Scotland to form the United Kingdom of Great Britain and Ireland. Apart from the addition of the Cross of St Patrick to the Union flag, there was little apparent change. The British were still overlords, as they had been for hundreds of years, and, for the disenfranchised Catholic majority, life would have gone on much as it had before but for growing resentment over the forced payment of tithes for the upkeep of the established church – the Church of Ireland. There had been high hopes, particularly among poor tenant farmers, that the payment of tithes, in cash or kind, enforced since the Reformation, would be abolished under the Act of Union. It wasn't, and the festering resentment erupted into civil disobedience.

In Reverend John Day's diocese of Ardfert and Aghadoe, which covered most of County Kerry, the population was 304,687, of whom 297,131 were Catholic, 7529 were Church of Ireland, and just 27 were Protestant Dissenters.[3]

In Denny Day's childhood, the seeds of an organised campaign of non-violent resistance were being sown in the fields surrounding his father's vicarage. Catholics no longer willing to support the church of the Protestant minority defied the law by defaulting on their tithes, with a resulting loss of income for Church of Ireland clergy.

In time, when constables took to seizing the stock and produce of defaulters at markets and fairs, the resistance would turn violent. In what would come to be called the Tithe Wars, hundreds would lose their lives in pitched battles, riots and burnings.

In 1826, it had not yet come to that, but the strain on relationships between Protestant clergy and their Catholic neighbours made life at the vicarage uncomfortable, to say the least. That may be one reason why Denny Day decided that year not to become a man of the cloth like his father, his uncles and his cousins. Instead, he joined the British Army.

It's likely also that he was inspired by the stellar career of another Anglo-Irishman – Arthur Wellesley, the Duke of Wellington. To a young man with some of that old Denny adventurism in his blood, there was great appeal in joining the ranks of the hero who beat Napoleon. Although it had been eleven years since Waterloo, the British world was still basking in reflected glory.

It's possible, too, that he was at last free to follow a different drum without disappointing his mother. Charlotte Day died earlier that year.

Chapter 2

Blood for blood

Smashem Smith lived to tell the tale. The recollections of Hawkesbury settler and former convict Joseph 'Smashem' Smith, as recorded in 1845 by the great social reformer and champion of immigration Caroline Chisholm, provide graphic details of the brutal reality of early frontier life. Smith, who arrived in New South Wales in 1790, was just 14 years old when sentenced to seven years' transportation for stealing two linen shirts, two linen handkerchiefs, three pairs of cotton stockings and a waistcoat.

Nicknamed 'Smashem' due to his tendency to speak his mind without fear or favour, Smith – a large, handsome old man resplendent in a red flannel shirt, black bandana and blue coat with gilt buttons – told Caroline Chisholm:

'Myself and 18 others laid in a hollow tree for 17 weeks, and cooked out of a kettle with a wooden bottom. We used to stick it in a hole in the ground and make a fire around it. I was seven years in bondage and then started working for a living wherever I could get it.

'There was plenty of hardship then. I have often taken grass, pounded it, and made soup from a native dog. I would eat anything then. For 17 weeks I had only five ounces of flour a day. We never got a full ration except when the ship was in harbour. The motto was "Kill them or work them, their provision will be in store."

'Many a time I have been yoked like a bullock with 20 or 30 others to drag along timber. About 800 died in six months at a place called Toongabbie, or Constitution Hill [a notorious secondary punishment station west of Sydney]. I knew a man so weak he was thrown into the grave. When he said, "Don't cover me up! I'm not dead! For God's sake, don't cover me up!" the overseer answered, "Damn your eyes! You'll die tonight, and we shall have the trouble to come back again."

'The man recovered. His name is James Glasshouse and he is now alive at Richmond.

'They used to have a large hole for the dead. Once a day, men were sent down to collect the corpses of prisoners and throw them in without any ceremony or service. The native dogs used to come down at night and fight and howl in packs, gnawing the poor dead bodies.

'The Governor would order the lash at the rate of five hundred, six hundred or eight hundred, and if the men could have stood it they would have had more. I knew a man hung there and then for stealing a few biscuits, and another for stealing a duck frock [a heavy cotton shirt]. The overseers were allowed to flog the men in the fields. Often have men been taken from the gang, had fifty, and sent back to work.

'Any man would have committed murder for a month's provisions. I would have committed three murders for a week's provisions. I was chained seven weeks on my back for being out there getting greens, wild herbs.

'Old Jones [an overseer] killed three men in a fortnight at the saw by overwork. We used to be taken in large parties to raise a tree. When the body of the tree was raised, Old Jones would call some men away, then more. The men were bent double. They could not bear it – they fell – the tree on one or two, killed on the spot. "Take him away! Put him in the ground!" There was no more about it.'[1]

Smith's wife Margaret had been sent to New South Wales for stealing 14 yards of calico. Now blind, she wept as she told Caroline Chisholm of horrors witnessed in her youth.

'The laws were bad then,' Margaret said. 'If a gentleman wanted a man's wife, he would send the husband to Norfolk Island [penal colony]. I have seen a man flogged for pulling six turnips instead of five.

'One Defrey was overseer, the biggest villain that ever lived, delighted in torment. He used to walk up and down and rub his hands when the blood ran. When he walked out, the flogger walked behind him. He died a miserable death. Maggots ate him up. Not a man could be found to bury him.

'I have seen six men executed for stealing 21 pounds of flour. I have seen a man struck when at work with a handspike, and killed on the spot.'[2]

Freed after serving his sentence, Joseph 'Smashem' Smith worked on the Hawkesbury River until he had saved enough to buy a 40-acre farm. By 1845, when Caroline Chisholm paid him a visit, he was a wealthy man, with four farms and some 500 head of cattle. 'We are never without a chest of tea in the house,' he boasted. 'Tea is a great comfort.'

Besides tea and comfort, he offered Chisholm a souvenir of the occasion – a loaded pistol he pulled from his belt. 'You may depend on it,' he said.[3]

Pemulwuy's war was over. The Bidjigal leader – the William Wallace of Australia – led a band of warriors in a 12-year war of resistance after the arrival of the First Fleet in 1788.

A legend in his lifetime and since immortalised as an Indigenous hero, Pemulwuy was said to have killed more than 30 white men in attacks on the fledgling colony, all but halting the spread of settlement beyond Sydney Cove. The mercurial leader had escaped captivity several times, and had been wounded in battle so many times that his followers – and many among the whites – believed he could not be killed by gunfire.

In December 1790, 52 officers and men of the New South Wales Corps, led by Captain Watkin Tench, marched south from Sydney to avenge attacks by Pemulwuy's guerrillas. Their orders, Tench recalled in his memoir, were 'to proceed to the peninsula at the head of Botany Bay; and thence, or from any part of the north arm of the bay, we were, if practicable, to bring away two natives as prisoners: and to put to death ten; that we were to destroy all weapons of war, but nothing else; that no hut was to be burned; that all women and children were to remain uninjured, not being comprehended within the scope of the order; that our operations were to be directed, either by surprise or open force; that after we had made any prisoners, all communication, even with those natives with whom we were in habits of intercourse, was to be avoided, and none of them suffered to approach us; that we were to cut off, and bring in the heads of the slain, for which purpose, hatchets and bags would be furnished.'[4]

A few days of tramping through the bush later, the troopers returned to Sydney with nothing to show for their efforts but mosquito bites and blisters. Tench wrote that the soldiers came upon and pursued a party of five warriors but that 'a contest between heavy-armed Europeans, fettered by ligatures, and naked unencumbered Indians, was too unequal to last long. They darted into the woods and disappeared.'[5]

A second expedition was abandoned after Tench and some of his troopers got stuck in the mud when crossing a creek and had to be hauled out with ropes. A third expedition, also led by Tench, came upon a group of Bidjigal huts. At dawn, in a well-organised surprise attack, the soldiers rushed in from several directions at once only to find the huts were empty. Judging by his other writings, which reveal relative tolerance of Aboriginal people, it's reasonable to assume Watkin Tench would not have been too disappointed to find the camp deserted. He had followed orders, but his heart wasn't in it.

While the British settlements were confined to the coast and occupied small areas of land, violence between black and white was relatively rare. With expansion into the interior, sporadic conflict escalated into open warfare, and the first theatre of the frontier war was along the Hawkesbury River – the closest major waterway to Sydney, marking the outer limits of settlement to the north and west. The river meandered through fertile land with the prospect of becoming the breadbasket of Sydney. That land, which by 1796 had attracted some 400 settlers – mostly families of convicts who had served their time – was also the traditional country of the Dharug.

*

Relations between black and white along the river the Dharug called the Deerubbin had been mutually beneficial at first. The whites traded goods for labour, and the blacks taught the whites bush survival skills. By the mid-1790s, however, farmers upriver were harvesting corn on land cleared from dense forest, and before long there was no room for the Dharug. Settlers, out of sight and out of mind of colonial authorities, granted themselves licence to dispossess and murder Dharug people, and even kidnap Dharug children to work as slaves on their farms. In retaliation, the Dharug began raiding homesteads, setting fire to crops and killing settlers.

The colony's judge advocate, Captain David Collins, recorded early instances of violence on the Hawkesbury, noting that 'a settler there and his servant were nearly murdered in their hut by some natives from the woods, who stole upon them with such secrecy as to wound and overpower them before they could procure assistance. A few days after this circumstance, a body of natives attacked the settlers and carried off their clothes, provisions and whatever else they could lay hands on.'[6]

In reprisal, the settlers shot dead seven or eight of the raiders. 'This mode of treating them had become absolutely necessary from the frequent and evil effects of their visits,' Collins wrote, but added that, in his opinion, 'whatever the settlers at the river suffered was entirely brought on them by their own misconduct. There was not a doubt that many natives had been wantonly fired upon, and when their children, after the fight of their parents, have fallen into the settlers' hands, they have been detained at their huts, notwithstanding the earnest entreaties of their parents to have them restored.

'Some accounts were received from the Hawkesbury which corroborated the opinion that the settlers there merited the attacks which were from time to time made upon them by the natives; it being now said that some of them had seized a native boy, and, after tying him hand and foot, had dragged him several times through a fire until his back was dreadfully burnt, and in that state had thrown him into the river, where they shot at and killed him.'[7]

Settlers granted land on the Hawkesbury were known as 'First Branch' people. That is, they had carved out farms along what Governor Arthur Phillip had named The First Branch of the river. Others settled in remote valleys 'up the branch'. These were illegal settlers, having been granted no title to their property, and included escaped convicts and their offspring.

In 1794, in response to the murder of an Aboriginal boy by settlers 'up the branch', warriors wounded two white men in raids on homesteads. The settlers, in turn, killed eight blacks and captured several children.

The following spring, when the Hawkesbury settlers were harvesting their corn, a Liberty Plains farmer named Thomas Webb was speared by raiders Collins called 'wood natives',[8] and seriously wounded. The same raiding party rained spears on a boatload of soldiers heading upstream.

On a number of occasions, warriors in canoes boarded grain ships headed downstream, overpowering and killing the entire crew in one instance and seizing the vessel and its cargo.

'All these unpleasant circumstances were to be attributed to the ill treatment the natives had received from the settlers,' Collins wrote.[9]

Amid concerns that continued Aboriginal resistance and raids on the harvest could force settlers to abandon their farms and flee to the safety of Sydney, New South Wales Corps troops were sent upriver with orders to kill as many 'wood natives' as they could find and hang the bodies from gibbets. Collins was told that several Aboriginal people were killed but the bodies had somehow been spirited away before the soldiers could hang them.

The troops took a number of prisoners, including one man, five women and some children. One of the women had been shot through the shoulder and the musket ball had also wounded the baby at her breast. The man escaped, the baby died, and another woman, who was pregnant, gave birth to a child – a boy – who immediately died.

Reprisal for reprisal for reprisal – the pattern of endless vengeance had been set, and in this case the price of blood was paid by Richmond Hill settler William Rowe. He and his young son were killed by raiders, while his wife, although badly wounded, somehow managed to escape and hid among reeds in the river, where she was rescued by neighbours some time later.

And so it went on. In retaliation for the murder of two white farmers, a vigilante group of settlers enticed three black teenagers into a barn where their hands were tied and two of them were brutally slain. A third youth escaped, jumped into the river, and, although his hands were bound, managed to swim to the other side. The white men fired at him all the way across but their shots missed and he got clear away.

When the bodies of the two murdered boys were found buried in a garden, their killers were arrested and brought to trial. Yet, curiously, although they were found guilty, all walked free. It seems the court somehow forgot to pass sentence.

A garrison was established on the Hawkesbury to deter further resistance, but reprisal killings by both sides continued, and raids on settlers' crops and farmhouses intensified – so much so that within a year almost all the farming settlements on the lower Hawkesbury had been abandoned.

Officially, between 1794 and 1799, on the Hawkesbury, up to 16 white men and one infant were killed and four wounded. Some 30 black men, women and children were killed, and an unknown number wounded, mostly in night raids on camps by soldiers and settlers. Anecdotally, the casualty count far exceeded the official figures. The military kept no records of its excursions against the blacks, and the government tended to downplay the extent of the trouble. The message to London from Government House in Sydney was that there was no cause for concern; everything was under control.

On separate occasions, two men of the cloth visiting the Hawkesbury were alarmed by the settlers' view of murder as no more than pest control. The Reverend Dunmore Lang was matter-of-factly shown places where Aborigines had been hunted down and shot. And the missionary Lancelot Threlkeld was shocked to hear a settler openly boasting of how many blacks he had killed on his property. The settler saw no need to hide the fact, nor even to be coy about it. After all, the soldiers took no prisoners, so why should he spare powder and shot? And there was nothing to fear from the law. To the contrary, magistrates – who were invariably wealthy landowners – often rode with settlers on killing expeditions. Such hunting parties were called drives or bushwhacks – as much a sport as riding to hounds.

In 1802, outlawed and with a price on his head, dead or alive, Pemulwuy was shot dead – by bounty hunters, according to some accounts, while others claim he was gunned down by First Fleet sailor Henry Hacking, whose reward was 20 gallons of rum.

The colony's governor, Philip Gidley King, sent Pemulwuy's severed head to the famed naturalist Sir Joseph Banks in London, by the whaling ship *Speedy*, along with a keg of pickled insects and other specimens, and a note that read, 'Although a terrible pest to the colony, Pemulwuy was a brave and independent character. Understanding that the possession of a New Hollander's head is among the desiderata, I have put it in spirits and forwarded it to you by the *Speedy*.'[10]

Banks wrote back:

> The manifold packages you have had the goodness to forward to me have always, owing to your friendly care in addressing and invoicing them, come safe and in good condition to my hands. Among the last was the head of one of your subjects, which is said to have caused some comical consequences when opened at the Customs House, but when brought home was very acceptable to our anthropological collectors, and makes a figure in the museum of the late Mr Hunter, now purchased by the public.[11]

Pemulwuy's people would not have found it comical, believing that a person not buried intact was doomed to wander the earth as a restless spirit. To them, decapitation was a sacrilege, an outrage, and, despite the passing of more than two centuries, an enduring sense of outrage has sparked demands for the return of Pemulwuy's head to Australia.

Easier said than done, it seems. The Hunterian Museum houses Britain's oldest collection of anatomical oddities, fossils and pathological specimens, amassed by the eccentric eighteenth-century anatomist and surgeon John Hunter. The museum, at London's Royal College of Surgeons, claims Pemulwuy's head is no longer in its keeping, and its present location remains a mystery.

By 1804, it was clear that the hit-and-run tactics of the Dharug were more than a match for the redcoats and settlers. Faced with the real possibility that continued resistance could prevent the colony expanding beyond the coast, denying the colonists access to the fertile inland, Governor King had no choice but to parley with the Dharug, and promised there would be no more settlements on the lower Hawkesbury.

While there's no reason to doubt that King's offer was sincere, hardly a year had passed before settlers began returning to the lower Hawkesbury – albeit unofficially and in smaller numbers. Clashes became less and less frequent, and by 1816 it was apparent that the first frontier war was over. The following year, Governor Lachlan Macquarie was sufficiently confident to report to the Colonial Secretary in London that 'all hostility on both sides has long since ceased'.[12]

There was peace on the frontier, but it was a fragile peace, and would not last. On the morning of Friday 28 October 1825, two settlers, Forsyth and Allen, stopped by for breakfast at James Greig's sheep run on the river flats of Wollombi Brook – 128 kilometres, or three days' ride, from Sydney. On entering the hut, they found Greig's cousin Robert lying dead on the floor, his skull bashed in. The shepherd's body was found a short distance from the hut, covered by branches, and the hut had been ransacked.

James Greig, who had gone to Sydney on business, had left Robert, newly arrived from Scotland, to manage the farm with the help of a convict shepherd. Robert had apparently been sitting in the hut reading when a group of Aboriginal men approached. He was unaware that James, known for his hatred of blacks, had angered them by refusing to let them cross his property, acquired just 18 months earlier.

The killings at Greig's farm rekindled the fire, as *The Australian* newspaper reported:

Two other stockmen have been speared, and a man of Captain Pike's narrowly escaped being murdered by them, owing to the providential arrival of two men, who found him in the act of struggling with a native for a spear.

The settlers in the neighbourhood are in the greatest state of alarm from the apprehension that a general attack is contemplated by the natives, who for some time have been pilfering everything they possibly could, and who are rambling about the country in formidable parties.

On the receipt of the above melancholy tidings at Newcastle, on Thursday last, a military party, consisting of ten men, accompanied by some bush constables, was instantly despatched by the commandant, Captain Allman, to the protection of the settlers in the distant district of Patrick's Plains [now Singleton, 200 kilometres north-west of Sydney].[13]

The same paper's editorial thundered:

Between the bushrangers and the native blacks, the settlers seem to have a very sorry time. They are constantly called upon to keep a sharp lookout and to repress one or other of these pests. The blacks, some months ago, were the most formidable enemy the up-country people had to encounter. They were, however, got under, and while the bushrangers were committing their out-rages and carrying on their depredations, they remained tolerably quiet, and caused but little uneasiness. It is with considerable anxiety that we have heard of a renewal of the attacks of these sable gentry.

We should be disposed to give as little quarter to this enemy as to the runaways, and, if they be resolved to enter into a mis-chievous warfare, employ the earliest means of convincing them that it can be done only at the hazard of their lives. It is down-right folly to talk of humanity and forbearance; they never can be persuaded into good fellowship; they never can be conciliated; for they never can be divested of their treacherous habits. 'Drop them' here and there, when they show fight – strike terror into them but spare not a single offender. Irrational and beast-like as they are, they have sense enough to know when it is to their interest to remain at peace. And, if not, they must be made to betake themselves to more distant parts of the territory, which will answer equally their habits of life, and save them from the alternative of extermination – a measure even which would be fully justifiable if nothing less could protect the settlers from their cruel and murderous attacks.[14]

Settlement on the Hawkesbury had a drastic impact not only on the Aboriginal population but on the land itself. As a result of the stampede for free land, granted by a generous but careless colo-nial government, native grasses had been destroyed by grazing animals, while unchecked land clearing had eroded riverbanks, silted up the river, and increased the damage done by floods, which stripped the topsoil and spread weeds downriver.

By the 1830s, many Hawkesbury settlers had moved on to fresh pastures in the Hunter Valley and the Liverpool Plains. One such, George Hall, would establish within ten years a string of cattle stations from the Hunter to the Big River (now the Gwydir River) – half a million acres in all. In 1836, Hall was at the centre of early conflict on the plains when, in an attack by Aborigines, one of his stockmen was killed and another wounded. The wounded man was James Oates, who two years later would play his part in the Myall Creek massacre.

In retaliation for the attack on Hall's men, the Mounted Police killed some 80 Aboriginal people.

By 1837, white settlers had taken up land on the Noogera, Slaughterhouse and Myall creeks, all tributaries of the Big River. A little way upstream from Slaughterhouse Creek, a prosperous Hawkesbury farmer named Joseph Fleming set up a new station. Joseph was joined in the venture by his younger brother John Henry, later named as the leader of the Myall Creek killers.

In his 1890 memoir, Hawkesbury settler and member of parliament William Walker recalled that in the 1830s, when the 80th Regiment was garrisoned in the river town of Windsor, 'there were a good many blacks down the Hawkesbury then, and I remember the officers on one occasion getting up a corroboree in Thompson's Square. Of course they plied the darkies well with wine, or something stronger.'[15]

Major Thomas Bunbury was a professional soldier and former commandant of the notorious Norfolk Island penal station, where his claim to fame was halving the hospital queues by announcing that a man too sick to work was too sick to eat. In his memoir, *Reminiscences of a Veteran*, Bunbury makes it clear that he was less than impressed with the quality of the military in New South Wales. He writes:

> The guards with few exceptions are commanded by young officers without experience, and who from the want of other sources of amusement, gladly avail themselves of the society of such of the settlers as casually fall in their way, and insensibly acquire their habits. Intemperance, the bane of the British army in New South Wales, is painfully prevalent. Nor are the officers, I am sorry to say, exempt from this void. The number of promising youths thus prematurely lost to the service and their families would exceed all belief, were these facts not attested by every regiment which has in succession served in that country.[16]

By 1837, the Aboriginal population of the Hawkesbury had shrunk to just one family of four. 'They consisted only of King Jamie and his gin, and two sons, Billy and Bobby,' William Walker wrote. 'Their camping place was a short distance off, up the South Creek. Jamie wore a brass plate suspended by a string from his neck, bearing his name, and which he said had been given him by good Governor Macquarie. The old couple were very harmless, and were objects of charity.

'They have all, however, now passed away, like the Mohicans. First the queen went, then the king, then Bobby who, as well as his brother, was much addicted to rum, foolishly given them by friends in town. Billy had been taught by one of the early clergymen to read, was intelligent, and used to work a little on some of the farms, generally at Mr Freeman's, Cornwallis.

'With them, the Windsor tribe of blacks became extinct. It was a common thing then for mothers to frighten their children into quiescence by telling them that if they didn't be still, Black Bobby would be brought to them, and this, I think, was about the only good use that was ever made of that dark specimen of humanity.'[17]

Some whites seemed positively perplexed as to why blacks simply would not do what was expected of them, even when they were expected to stand still to be easier targets.

In 1834, amid increasing conflict between black and white in the Brisbane Water district – Darkinjung and Kuringgai country on the coast north of Sydney – the local magistrate Jonathan Warner wrote to the governor pleading with him to send a troop of Mounted Police to help him capture black resistance leaders. If not, he wrote, 'I am fearful we shall be obliged to shoot some of them as they will not stand when called to stop even when they are told that they will be shot if they run away.'[18]

Occasionally, voices were raised in protest at the treatment of Aborigines – the most eloquent being that of Saxe Bannister, the first Attorney-General of New South Wales. A barrister, scholar and former British Army officer, Bannister was a maverick among the time-servers and sycophants in the colonial administration. His forthright views on government ineptitude and corruption, his condemnation of the treatment of Aborigines, and his calls for the abolition of convict transportation, made him few friends and many enemies in Sydney, including successive governors and

Robert Wardell, the influential editor of *The Australian* news-paper, who Bannister accused of criminal libel. In order that honour might be satisfied, Bannister and Wardell fought a duel. Both combatants missed.

Appointed Attorney-General in 1824, Saxe Bannister served just two years before resigning, exasperated by continued conflict with Governor Ralph Darling. The last straw was when Darling refused to authorise the execution of three convicts who had murdered an Aboriginal boy – convictions Bannister had success-fully prosecuted.

On returning to England, Bannister pulled no punches in a book entitled *Humane Policy: or Justice to the Aborigines of New Settlements*. He wrote that in New South Wales the Aborigines were the victims of 'frequent and gross injustice'. Their rights, even in matters of life and death, were 'constantly outraged by our neglecting the plainest principles of equity'.[19]

'English rules,' he wrote, 'render it exceedingly difficult to cause the law to be put in force against murderers and other heinous wrong-doers towards the natives. And when a convic-tion has been obtained, the government has sympathised too much with the oppressing class, and too little with the oppressed, to permit justice to have its course'.

He cited cases to support his claim: 'About 1799, several white people committed a murder near Windsor, on the Hawkesbury, and were convicted. The case, however, was referred to England, and the culprits ultimately escaped the punishment due to the crime.'

In 1812, British Parliament noted 'the unequal dispensing of justice between white people and natives', yet nothing had changed by 1826 when 'a black man was shot in cold blood at the stake by the soldiers upon Hunter's River, and other outrages of a like in the same district were necessarily stimulated by the illegal proceedings of the governor of the colony. The administration of the law being then taken out of the proper channel, the natural consequence was the commission of the most cruel barbarities by inferior persons.'

Bannister hoped to convince the British at home and abroad 'that the natives have a keen sense of justice; that if assured of justice being done by us, they will repress their dispositions to do it in their own way; that by activity and firmness justice may be carried into effect; that the partial influence of local white feelings prevents the execution of justice by us'.[20]

He continued to campaign for the abolition of convict transportation, not only to benefit the colonial economy but to protect natives from convicts, prevent the sexual abuse of Aboriginal women, and reduce the endemic violence between white and black.

Bannister did not share the popular view that indigenous peoples were doomed to extinction by their very savagery; that their supposed inability to be civilised would inevitably cause them to disappear. Rather, he believed their survival was threatened by colonial expansion, frontier violence and introduced diseases. The blacks, he argued, were damned whichever way they turned – casually condemned to oblivion by the British refusal to help them adapt to European ways while blaming them for their failure. His critics – and there were many – countered that Bannister's call to treat blacks as rational human beings, capable of engaging with the whites to the advantage of both, while admittedly humane, was nonetheless Utopian and naive, and if put into practice would put the lives of settlers at risk. In short, Saxe Bannister's eloquent voice – the voice of enlightenment – was the voice of one crying in the wilderness.

Chapter 3

A red feather

On the parade ground at Cannanore (now Kannur), the British Army's headquarters on the west coast of India, one of the raw new junior officers carrying the colours was an Irishman from Tralee.

It was September 1826 and Ensign Day was a long way from home. His regiment, the 46th Regiment of Foot, also called the South Devonshires but popularly known as the 'Red Feathers'[1] for the distinctive red tuft on their caps, had manned the garrison at Cannanore for a decade. And although the war with the Burmese Empire for control of north-eastern India had ended in February that same year with a British victory, threats to British interests on the Subcontinent persisted: from rival imperialist powers from without; and from within, growing resentment among Indians of British commercial dominance and social discrimination.

Day had bought his commission in the 46th. The rank of ensign – the lowest officer rank in the infantry – cost about £400, a small fortune in those days, and was most probably paid by his father, courtesy, in some part, of the hated tithe system.

Purchasing a commission had been standard practice since the thirteenth century, and while it ensured that only the wealthy could become officers, the system was generally regarded as fair. True, it meant few soldiers were promoted on merit, but on the other hand it supposedly eliminated favouritism because prices were fixed, and allowed an officer leaving the service to sell his commission – no nonsense and all very civilised. After all, Wellington himself had bought not only his first commission as ensign but the next seven ranks as well. When he reached the rank of colonel, commanding a regiment, he had undergone no military training whatsoever and had seen no action.

Ensigns, invariably young gentlemen from landed families, could buy a lieutenancy after a year or two. The cost was £550, but the £400 already paid for an ensign's commission was deducted. Although that made the next rank more affordable, many ensigns were killed before they could be promoted. It was the ensign's duty to carry the regimental colours into battle, which made him an easy target.

The Red Feathers had fought with distinction in the Seven Years War against the French over disputed territories in North America, in the American Revolutionary War and in the Caribbean. They had also served in New South Wales and Van Diemen's Land (Tasmania) from 1814 to 1817, chasing bushrangers and protecting the white inhabitants from the natives. To the tender ears of young ensigns, the tales these veterans had to tell of service on the Australian frontier were both grim and fascinating.

There was the story of how, in 1815, Sergeant Robert Broadfoot and six privates pursued a notorious gang of bushrangers from

Hobart Town deep into the rugged and unexplored interior of Van Diemen's Land, captured the leaders and brought them back to Hobart for trial and a date with the hangman. For doing their duty, the soldiers received the thanks of the government and a £100 reward to share – the equivalent of more than five years' pay.

The following year, in New South Wales, a troop led by Corporal Justin McCarthy got into a desperate firefight with a bushranger gang led by a deserter from the 73rd Regiment – the regiment the 46th had replaced. The outlaws were well armed, but after exchanging fire for more than an hour, their leader was shot dead and the rest tried to flee. The soldiers hunted down two of the escaping bushrangers, who were tried, convicted and sent to the gallows. A grateful government commended the Red Feathers for their zeal and courage, and awarded them £100 for the deserter and £25 each for the others. Catching bushrangers in the Antipodes, it seems, was not only exciting but lucrative.

The regiment's encounters with Aborigines won even greater praise from Governor Lachlan Macquarie, particularly the exploits in 1816 of Captain W. G. B. Schaw and Lieutenant Charles Dawe, and the man who was now Ensign Day's commanding officer in Cannanore and a fellow Irishman, Captain James Wallis.

Back in 1810, the colony's new governor seemed a beacon of tolerance and enlightenment. In his first week in office, Macquarie proclaimed: 'I need not, I hope, express my wish that the natives of this country, when they come in the way of a peaceable manner, may not be molested in their persons or property by anyone; but that, on the contrary, they may always be treated with kindness and attention, so as to conciliate them as much as possible to our government and manners.'[2]

By 1816, the governor had abandoned conciliation for violent confrontation. His diary entry for Wednesday 10 April reads:

The Aborigines, or native blacks of this country, having for the last three years manifested a strong and sanguinary hostile spirit, in repeated instances of murder, outrages and depredations of all descriptions against the settlers and other white inhabitants residing in the interior and more remote parts of the colony, notwithstanding their having been frequently called upon and admonished to discontinue their hostile incursions and treated on all these occasions with the greatest kindness and forbearance by government; and having nevertheless recently committed several cruel and most barbarous murders on the settlers and their families and servants, killed their cattle, and robbed them of their grain and other property to a considerable amount, it becomes absolutely necessary to put a stop to these outrages and disturbances, and to adopt the strongest and most coercive measures to prevent a recurrence of them, so as to protect the European inhabitants in their persons and properties against these frequent and sudden hostile attacks from the natives. I therefore, though very unwillingly, felt myself compelled, from a paramount sense of public duty, to come to the painful resolution of chastising these hostile tribes, and to inflict terrible and exemplary punishments upon them without further loss of time, as they might construe and further forbearance or lenity, on the part of this government, into fear and cowardice.[3]

The previous day, Macquarie ordered three detachments of the 46th Regiment, under the commands of Captains Schaw and Wallis, and Lieutenant Dawe, to march into the interior 'for the purpose of punishing the hostile natives, by clearing the country of them entirely, and driving them across the mountains; as well as if possible to apprehend the natives who have committed the late murders and outrages, with the view of their being made dreadful and severe examples of, if taken alive.'[4]

In his instructions to the commanders, the governor didn't mince words. Major-General Lachlan Macquarie was sending his troops to war. He ordered: 'All Aborigines from Sydney onwards are to be made prisoners of war and if they resist they are to be shot and their bodies hung from trees in the most conspicuous places where they fall, so as to strike terror into the hearts of surviving natives.'[5]

Schaw's orders were to scour the country on the eastern side of the Blue Mountains for hostile natives, to select 12 'healthy, good-looking children from the whole of the native prisoners of war' and deliver them to the Native Institution at Parramatta, founded by Macquarie for the forced integration of black children into white society.[6]

Dawe's detachment was to take up a central position at the Macarthur farm at the Cow Pastures (Camden, 65 kilometres south-west of Sydney) and intercept and capture any natives driven in that direction by Schaw on the western flank or by Wallis, whose troops were advancing through the Appin district in the south-east. On 12 April, Dawe's party raided a native camp. The soldiers killed two people but all the rest escaped capture except for a small boy, who was taken captive.

On the evening of 16 April, Wallis got word that a group of blacks had made camp on William Broughton's farm at Appin, near the Cataract River. Moving as quietly as possible through thick scrub in bright moonlight, the soldiers caught sight of the camp at about one o'clock the next morning. They could hear dogs barking. The campfires were burning, but when the troops swept in they found the place deserted. Obviously, they had not been quiet enough. The dogs had raised the alarm and the people had fled.

Then someone heard a child cry. It seemed to come from somewhere between the camp and the river. Wallis ordered his men to form line ranks and advance into the bush in the direction of the crying.

There are conflicting versions of what happened next. The official version, as told by Wallis and accepted by Macquarie, was that, regrettably, some blacks were shot by the pursuing soldiers, while others, in blind panic, plunged to their deaths over the gorge of the Cataract River. The unofficial version is that Wallis's men shot at and drove at least 14 men, women and children over the cliff.

Governor Macquarie would praise the Red Feathers for 'having inflicted exemplary punishments on the hostile natives'.[7] So when veterans of Macquarie's dirty little war told this story to their comrades in India, it must have been tempting to present it – suitably embroidered – as a glorious victory against the savages of New Holland. History would remember it otherwise, as the Appin Massacre.

Ensign Day was barely a month at Cannanore when James Wallis, now a major, announced his intention to retire from the army. His superiors praised him mightily; he had served his sovereign well and had a chest full of medals to prove it, although, unsurprisingly, no medal had been struck for the Appin campaign. Wallis, 41, would marry for a second time, settle on the Isle of Man and spend the rest of his days indulging his passion for painting and etching. Denny Day would never meet Wallis again, but, coincidentally, the Australian frontier town where Day's fate would one day find him was founded by and named for the man – Wallis Plains (now Maitland).

In November of 1826, the Red Feathers left Cannanore and marched 900 kilometres to Secunderabad, where they spent the next five years stationed at the military headquarters. Those were relatively uneventful years, during which, in 1831, Ensign Day deposited £150 into His Majesty's kitty and rose to the rank of Lieutenant.

When a regiment was to return to Britain, soldiers were given the opportunity to join another regiment in India. While many British in India found the sweltering heat, relentless monsoonal rains and seething masses of humanity unbearable, even to the point of suicide, a surprising number not only adjusted to the climate and culture but embraced it. In 1832, when the Red Feathers were due to be relieved, 237 officers and men transferred to other regiments. Lieutenant Day was among those who chose to remain in India rather than go home. He would live to regret it.

Chapter 4

Mutiny and misery

In the fort precinct, five men were tied across the muzzles of 12-pounder cannons, each loaded with a double charge. The men's arms were lashed to the wheels and their legs secured to tent pegs driven into the ground. They were about to pay the awful price of mutiny.

Among the redcoats assembled there to witness the execution was a man who had recently exchanged his red-feathered cap for a three-cornered hat with a black cockade. It was Christmas Eve, 1832, and Lieutenant Day was now an officer in a light infantry Wiltshire regiment – the 62nd Regiment of Foot – stationed at Bangalore (now Belgaluru) in southern India.

The 62nd were known as the 'Moonrakers', after a popular tale of Wiltshire smugglers who, when caught red-handed by customs officers while retrieving brandy hidden in a pond, insisted they were innocently trying to rake cheese from the moon's reflection.[1]

For two years, the Moonrakers had manned the fort at Bangalore along with the 13th Light Dragoons, the cavalry unit immortalised in Lord Alfred Tennyson's poem *The Charge of the Light Brigade*. Those had been a peaceful two years, but recently that peace had been shattered. Lieutenant Day could not have arrived at a worse time.

Hoping to drive the British Army from Bangalore, a group of Indian soldiers and civilians hatched a daring plan. At midnight on 28 October, a force of 500 men of the 9th Madras Native Infantry would be let into the fort through the Mysore Gate by a conspirator in the Indian Army, Private Shaik Ismail. The password was 'Tipu Sahib' – the Sultan of Mysore killed by the British in 1799.

Once inside, the mutineers would kill the British commanding officer, Major-General Hawker, and the soldiers guarding the arsenal.

A gun would be fired from the ramparts and a green flag raised as a signal to open fire on the barracks of the 62nd Regiment and 13th Light Dragoons with grapeshot, killing all or most of those within, cut loose the cavalry horses and make off with the cannons. Then, if all went well, a force of Pindari freebooters would be let loose to plunder the town, which was not only a garrison but home to many British and French civilians.

All did not go well, however. When Jemadar Emaun Khan, a Native Infantry officer loyal to the British, heard the whispers of mutiny, the plot was foiled before a shot could be fired. The key conspirators were rounded up, tried by court martial and sentenced to death.

So it was that on Christmas Eve, 1832, before the assembled garrison and a large crowd that included the wives and children of the mutineers, the sentence of death was read aloud. One of the condemned men, defiant to the end, yelled at the officer reading the sentence to hurry and get it over with because he was cold. Another, Seyd Tipu, a tall, handsome man 'with the air of a prince', told the crowd, 'According to law, I have forfeited my life, and I give it freely. They can take my life but they cannot destroy my spirit. This shall revisit the Earth and rouse my fellow soldiers to action.'[2]

The order to fire was given, the cannons roared and the accused men were blown to pieces. As a lesson to all who might be tempted to rebel against British rule, the scattered bodies were left in the dust for the dogs and the flies.

In Bangalore, the New Year brought with it a flu epidemic. To make matters worse, the Moonrakers received orders to relieve the garrison at Masulipatam, 400 miles to the north-east. Masulipatam, on the coast, was reputedly the most disease-ridden post in India, and reaching it meant a two-month march through areas decimated by cholera and famine.

The regimental commander, Lieutenant-Colonel John Reed, requested that his men be allowed to take ship from Madras and complete the second half of the journey by sea. His request was flatly denied, and, on 18 February 1833, the 500 men of the 62nd, many with their families, set out for Masulipatam by way of Kolar, Madras and Chittoor.

It was in Chittoor, a town raging with cholera, that the long march claimed its first victim, the wife of Private Stephen Shipway. A few miles north of Chittoor, at Kolcherry, five men died, along with a child of the regimental surgeon, Dr Radford. All were buried there and the regiment marched on.

Twelve days later, with men falling victim to cholera all the way, they reached Nellore, where they camped for a week by the Pennair River. Much-needed medical supplies arrived from Madras during that week, and when the march resumed it seemed the worst was over. It wasn't. When, on 10 April, the regiment finally reached the fort at Masulipatam, it had lost a quarter of its men, and, of those still standing, only about 100 were fit for duty.

And it wasn't over yet. Within a month, more men had died and only 44 were fit for duty. More deaths followed, due not only to cholera but to a particularly virulent form of dysentery. By August, only two were deemed fit for duty, and a medical committee charged with assessing the situation suggested that the sea air might be just the tonic the men needed. Accordingly, 155 officers and men boarded the 600-ton transport ship *Abberton* for a six-week cruise of the Bay of Bengal. In tropical heat, and with cramped and unsanitary conditions on the small vessel, 11 men died at sea of cholera and dysentery, and, on returning to Masulipatam, many more died of scurvy and heart failure.

The June rains added malaria to the list of miseries, and when the death toll rose to seven a day, the Commander-in-Chief in India, Lord William Bentinck, ordered that the Masulipatam station be abandoned, and that the regiment – or what was left of it – move to Moulmein (now Mawlamyine) the capital of British Burma.

One survivor of the long march had no intention of going to Burma. For Lieutenant Day, the romance with the East was over, as were his soldiering days. He resigned his commission – and most likely sold it, as was the custom – citing poor health. That may have been so, given the gamut of pestilence he had been through, although, in peacetime, illness was a standard and acceptable excuse for British officers wanting to leave the service honourably.

Denny Day, late of the 62nd Regiment of Foot, took ship for New South Wales and a new life.

Chapter 5

First footfall

The tall, burly, dark-eyed Irishman who exchanged the scarlet uniform of a British officer for the plain grey tailcoat of a civilian finds himself in a British colony not yet 50 years old, home to some 15,000 souls, half of whom are convicts or ex-convicts. An imperial outpost of sandstone, wood and canvas, hugging a cove in a deep, wide harbour, the town looks as though it had been flung together in haste.

Sydney is much cooler than he had expected. He presumed the weather would be hot and sticky, as in India, but the morning temperature is only a little above zero and the mountains to the west are capped with snow.

This is a surprise but not unfamiliar. Denny Day was born and raised in an era climate scientists would come to call the Little Ice Age – a period of global cooling that began in medieval times and would last until the 1850s. As a boy in Ireland, he had experienced the worst of it. In 1816, known as The Year Without a Summer, the already frigid conditions were exacerbated by a volcanic winter caused by the eruption of Mount Tambora in Indonesia. The result was famine throughout the Northern Hemisphere and a year-long winter in which some 1800 people froze to death.

The Little Ice Age freezing Europe has affected southern climes too. In the Antarctic, sea ice has increased, and winds off the icecap have caused temperatures across the Australian continent to drop. Those snow-capped mountains he can see are officially named the Blue Mountains but are known by many, appropriately, as the White Mountains.

Like all new arrivals, Day's first footfall is on a makeshift jetty near where the Tank Stream – the town's only source of fresh water – empties into the cove. The port hums with the loading and unloading of freight, merchants' boats bustling back and forth from shore to ships at anchor, and his first sight of men in broad-arrow uniforms – convict work gangs reclaiming mud flats in front of the Customs House for a seawall.

This year has seen the abolition of slavery throughout the British Empire. What, he might wonder, would these men in broad arrows make of that? Do they consider themselves slaves? If he should ask, maybe some would argue that to be a slave a person must be the legal property of another person, which they are not. Others might disagree. Slavery, they might say, is the subjection of a person to another person, especially in being forced to work, and that by that definition they are most certainly slaves. More likely, though, if he should ask, some would merely shrug, some would ignore him completely, and some would tell him to fuck off.

If something seems a little different about the people on the streets of Sydney, it's because Europeans are beginning to adjust to the climate. Gentlemen, except on formal occasions, are abandoning heavy woollen coats, knee-breeches and stockings for more casual attire – cutaway coats, tight trousers, waist-coats, high cravats, riding boots and beaver hats. Male convicts, ex-convicts and poor free settlers wear cotton or woollen smocks with loose-fitting trousers, fustian (heavy cotton) jackets, necker-chiefs, straw hats or kangaroo-skin caps, lace-up boots if they're lucky and bare feet if they're not, perhaps a waistcoat and black hat for Sunday best, and whatever else they can scrounge or afford. For these men it's not about fashion – it's about dressing to suit the work and the weather.

Women of all classes dress much as they do in Europe, with social standing made apparent only by an outfit's state of repair, if you look closely enough. Because the high-waisted, low-cut dresses of lightweight fabrics such as cotton or muslin, now the mode in Europe, are well suited to Australian conditions, women have had little need to adapt. Straw bonnets, wide hats and para-sols shade them from the sun, while shorter hemlines keep skirts from trailing in the dust and the mud.

Watching them promenade à la mode in silk dresses, shawls, and veils, kid gloves, laced boots and glimpses of silk stockings, it's difficult to tell a noble lady from a convict just off the boat. Denny Day will often hear it said that women in New South Wales pay more attention to fashion than women in England, and he'll have to agree.

He notes that blue is the colour of authority. There are gov-ernment officials strutting about importantly in blue coats with gilt buttons, town constables patrolling in blue jackets with red collars, batons in their belts, and, ambling along on splendid horses, soldiers of the Mounted Police in blue dragoon jackets with white facings, blue trousers with white stripes, and peakless caps, armed with carbines, pistols and sabres – an impressive sight.

Dirt tracks wind past stores and commercial buildings of stone and whitewashed brick, and rows of timber cottages fronted by small gardens. Many of the grander buildings have wide eaves and verandahs – an adaptation of the Georgian style to provide shelter from the sun. Dominating the skyline to the east is the rambling two-storey governor's residence – the seat of power in the colony – and to the west the round clock tower of St Phillip's Church. A hodgepodge of styles and materials, it is reputed to be the ugliest church in all Christendom.

Everywhere he looks are reminders that this town, this settlement, is essentially a gaol – an institution of punishment and correction. Most of Sydney's public buildings, unlike those in his native Ireland and British India, are dedicated to the business of penal servitude. It's as if every stone, brick and tile in this place has been stamped with the broad arrow.

By sea, the town is connected to penal stations and small settlements north and south, and by river to the farmlands at Parramatta, just 23 kilometres to the west. Roads are few and the haunt of bushrangers, and, for convicts, lead to perdition. Should any guest of His Majesty be tempted to stray, the law of the lash tallies some 6000 floggings a year, at an average of 45 strokes per flogging. Hangings are frequent, and as popular a public entertainment as cockfighting, dogfights and bare-knuckle boxing.

Sydney in 1834 has 197 licensed inns and an even greater number of illegal grog shops pedalling smuggled rum and rotgut gin. Public drunkenness is common, and to walk the streets at night risks assault, robbery and rape. With four men to every woman, prostitution is flourishing, and in one street alone, 20 houses in a row are brothels.

In its editorial of 28 August 1834, *The Sydney Herald* muses on why so many more Britons chose to emigrate to North America rather than to Australia between 1832 and 1833. 'During these two years, 118,907 persons reached Canada and the United States from Britain,' the *Herald* says. 'One year's influx of such a number, into our scantily peopled wilds, would nearly double our population, free and bond.

'The penal character of our colony, and the dread of our society prevents the emigration of thousands of respectable characters to these shores, whose influence would correct the vicious propensities of numbers who enjoy enviable advantages without benefit to themselves or to the country at large.'[1]

Of the native blacks Day heard so much about from fellow officers who had served in New South Wales, there are few to be seen about the town. And, he is not to know, even fewer who can remember this place as it was before the white sails came. It was called Warrane then, and on its shores, on any given day, warriors prepared to go hunting while women set off to gather fruit and roots in the forests of red gum, bloodwood and peppermint that ran down to the cove. On its waters, families fished from canoes and from the massive sandstone outcrops. These were the people of first contact – coastal nations on a continent of more than 400 nations and a population estimated at from 700,000 to a million before 1788.

In that first year of British settlement, the Aboriginal population of the 1300-square-kilometre Sydney district was about 600. Within a year, at least half of that number had died of smallpox and other introduced diseases. For ships entering port, dead bodies on the beaches, under rock shelters and floating in the harbour were a common sight.

By 1834, some of the Sydney clans have ceased to exist, while countless inland peoples yet to see a white man have fallen victim to the white man's diseases. Wherever the European explorers go, they find that the pox got there ahead of them.

Denny Day, like many before him, has come with high hopes of success in business of some kind, and of eventually becoming a man of property in his own right. Such dreams will have to wait, however. His immediate need is to find a job, which, as an officer and a gentleman, he has no problem finding. The choices are limited, though, and all fall under the tyranny of tedium. As a clerk in the office of the Colonial Secretary, he spends his days pushing a pen in a corner of a dingy government office. The duties of a clerk in the colonial administration include nothing more exciting than arranging meetings, preparing documents, taking the minutes of proceedings and filing records.

Day's boss Alexander Macleay, the Colonial Secretary, is a squat, hard-of-hearing, gouty, grumpy, quarrelsome Scot whose main claim to fame is having the world's largest private collection of beetles. As consummate a bureaucrat as he is a bug catcher, Macleay often works 12 hours a day, six days a week. Although he doesn't expect his staff to emulate his workaholic ways, the role of Colonial Secretary involves spending much of the working day in consultation with the governor, Richard Bourke, and the two do not see eye to eye, to put it mildly.

Bourke is a man in the mould of Judge Day and Saxe Bannister – a champion of humane and progressive reforms in the treatment of convicts, public education, trial by jury, freedom of the press and religious tolerance. On these and other proposed reforms he is opposed and frustrated by his Colonial Secretary. The implacably conservative Macleay hates the very idea of press freedom, and detests emancipated convicts, whom he considers ignorant, drunken and immoral. It is a toxic relationship, growing more poisonous by the day, and for the Colonial Secretary's clerk, who supports and admires the governor, the situation is fast becoming intolerable.

Chapter 6

Some bones and a Manilla hat

Captain Henry Zouch hails from Quebec, Canada, and is the son of the British commandant of that city. Zouch has come to New South Wales to serve as commander of the Mounted Police at Bathurst, in the Central Tablelands west of Sydney. The Bathurst troop is one of three divisions of the Mounted Police, the others being stationed at Sydney, and to the north at Wallis Plains, on Hunter's River.

On the frontier, British soldiers serve as police. The Mounted Police is a cavalry force formed in 1825 from regiments stationed in the colony. Its mission is to hunt bushrangers and keep the peace between settlers and natives, protecting each from the other.

Since 1825, several British Army regiments have served in New South Wales as Mounted Police. Few have served with distinction, however. If there were such a thing as a Mounted Police Dishonour Roll, it would list the names of scores of troopers discharged and sentenced to 150 lashes for drunkenness and disorderly conduct. Others have been declared medically unfit or mentally ill. Some have deserted, some have been jailed for assault, trafficking, robbery, perjury and other crimes, and one trooper, Private Robert Cruden of the 80th Regiment, became a bushranger.

Of about 20 mounted troopers who have died in the service, six committed suicide, two drowned, one perished in a bushfire, and one drank himself to death. The few killed in the line of duty include Private James Hardman of the 17th Regiment, shot dead by an unnamed bushranger, and Private John Muggleton of the 39th Regiment, gunned down by the bushranger Jack Donahoe, immortalised in Australian folklore as the original Wild Colonial Boy.

The roll of dishonour would certainly include Lieutenant Nathanial Lowe, of the 40th Regiment, commander of the Hunter River detachment, based at Wallis Plains, who was tried for the murder of an Aboriginal man in custody. In June 1826, following the killing of two stockmen during a Wonnarua raid at an upriver station, Lowe and a detachment of troopers set out from Wallis Plains to track down the raiders. A man the whites called Jackey was arrested and taken back to Wallis Plains, where Lowe ordered his soldiers to tie him to a tree and execute him. The following month, three more Wonnarua men were shot dead by Lowe's troopers, reportedly while trying to escape.

A year later, Lowe was brought to trial, not for murder but for shooting a prisoner. The evidence against him was damning and the judge advised the jury that a guilty verdict was appropriate, but the jury – all of whom were army officers – took just five minutes to return a verdict of not guilty.

With that, people in the crowded courtroom burst into cheers and applause. It was a result, after all, that pleased the settlers and local magistrates, and also the press, as summed up by *The Australian* newspaper, which declared: 'To strike these with

terror, by the discriminating application of firearms, will ultimately prove a saving of human life, and leave the people in the
quiet enjoyment of their farms.'[1]

This was not a radical attitude. Such a justification for terror
was common throughout the British Empire, and in New South
Wales would be employed to the extreme by Major James Winniett
Nunn, of the 80th Regiment and commander of the Mounted
Police. Nunn would surely be at the top of the dishonour roll
for his involvement in the slaughter of up to 300 Aborigines
at Waterloo Creek, on the Big River (see Chapter 13), and is
destined to cross paths with Denny Day.

In October 1835, Captain Henry Zouch leads his troopers to the
Bogan River country, in central western New South Wales, in
search of Richard Cunningham, the government botanist, who
on 17 April, in the great tradition of Australian explorers, got
himself hopelessly lost. He wandered away from an expedition
while searching for plant specimens, and has been reported
missing.

Cunningham, who is no bushman, had been repeatedly warned
not to venture off alone but his botanical enthusiasm tended to
override common caution. After two weeks of searching, the only
clues to his fate are his tracks, a few of his belongings and his
dead horse.

By September, with still no sign of the missing botanist, *The
Sydney Monitor* presumes he has met a grisly end:

What could have induced a government officer, the chief of
a department, to wander alone from a party of such magnitude

as this, we will not attempt to explain, but such is the fact. He was seen no more. To fancy this good-minded and zealous man after an exhausting peregrination, pierced with the weapons of ferocious savages, beaten down amidst their sanguinary acclamations and perishing in dreadful agony, is a picture which to the feelings of all who knew him must be truly appalling.

Although we heartily wish that Mr C. may have survived, and may yet return to his friends, nevertheless, speaking candidly, and taking all the circumstances into consideration, we do not think that even mentally or bodily he was formed to exist under such toil as he must have gone through. His memory, as a zealous botanist, as an upright man, and open-hearted gentleman, will be ever cherished by many of the inhabitants of this colony, especially as both he and his brother [the explorer Allan Cunningham] were thorough Australian patriots. Both of them have been living, and Richard, we are sorry to say, died to advance its scientific interests.[2]

The *Monitor's* pre-emptive obituary is close to the mark, as Captain Zouch will soon discover. The trail has gone cold but luck is with him; just a week after setting out from Bathurst he meets two Aboriginal men who, through Zouch's black companion and interpreter, known as Sandy, tell of a white man who was murdered on the Bogan. The men offer to guide the troopers to the killers' camp, and on the evening of 6 November the party reaches the shores of Lake Buddah, where, as Zouch later reports, they 'could see the smoke from the fires of the Myall blacks'.[3]

On the lake shore is an encampment of some 40 men, women and children. The troopers gallop in, meeting no resistance, and begin interrogating people about the killing of a white man. 'They acknowledged to one having been killed on the Bogan by four of their tribe, three of whom they delivered up,' Zouch writes. 'The fourth, they stated, was absent on the Big River.'[4]

A search of the camp reveals a knife, glove and part of a cigar case that belonged to Richard Cunningham. All these items, the three accused men – Wongadgery, Boreeboombalie and Bureemal – admit were taken from the murdered white man.

They tell Zouch that they and another man, 'about six moons ago, met a white man on the Bogan, who came up and made signs that he was hungry; that they gave him food, and that he encamped with them that night. The white man repeatedly getting up during the night excited suspicion, and they determined to destroy him the following morning, which they did by Wongadgery going unperceived behind him and striking him on the back of the head with a nulla-nulla. The other three men then rushing upon him with their weapons, speedily effected their purpose.'[5]

Apparently, the odd behaviour of Cunningham, crazed from exposure and dehydration, caused the men to believe he was possessed by evil spirits. In fear and alarm, they killed him.

Zouch, determined to examine the scene of the crime, three days' ride away, sets off with Bureemal as a guide, leaving orders that the other two prisoners be taken to a station near Wellington to await his return.

He writes:

On Tuesday the 10th I arrived at a place called Currindine [now Burdenda Station, on the west bank of the Bogan River] where the black showed me some bones, which he said were those of a white man they had killed, and pointed out a small portion of a coat, and also of a Manilla hat. Being thus convinced of the truth of their statement, and also of the spot where the melancholy event had occurred, I collected all the remains I could discover, and having deposited them in the ground, raised a small mound over them and barked some of the nearest trees as the only means in my power of marking the spot.[6]

On returning to the station where the other two prisoners were held, Zouch is informed that they have escaped. Enraged, he charges the sentry on duty with neglect and rides off in search of the fugitives. Lack of provisions force him to abandon the chase, however, and he sets off back to Bathurst with Bureemal his sole remaining prisoner, who he intended to send on to Sydney for trial.

In his *The Story of the Blacks*, serialised in the *Bathurst Free Press* from 1889, editor and author Charles White writes:

> Zouch took the remaining prisoner to Sydney, where he was doubtless made to learn, by dangling at the end of a hempen chord from one of the many gallows trees at that time among the institutions of the metropolis, that British justice in its comple-tion was not unlike Aboriginal revenge, albeit the method of its administration was somewhat different.[7]

That is pure speculation on White's part, however. There is no record of Bureemal standing trial in Sydney or anywhere else. Given that he was arrested for the murder of a notable and popular identity, the absence of any record suggests that either the charges were dropped because there was insufficient evidence to support them, or that somewhere along the track Bureemal felt the wrath not of British justice but of frontier justice.

Chapter 7

The postmaster's daughter

With a gloved knock at the door of the postmaster's study, a servant announces that a certain young gentleman has arrived for his appointment and is waiting without. The postmaster, James Raymond, knowing the young man's visit relates to an affair of the heart, keeps him twiddling his thumbs for about 20 minutes, as dictated by custom.

In the small world of the colonial upper crust – there are no secrets in Sydney Town – the postmaster knows his caller by reputation: noble lineage, military service, impressive references, excellent prospects. He is 34 years old, arrived in the colony about a year ago, and is a clerk in the office of the Colonial Secretary.

The young gentleman waiting, Edward Denny Day, Esquire, knows the postmaster by reputation: affable enough, but risibly vain and famously stupid.

James Raymond has climbed high in colonial society not in spite of, but because of breathtaking incompetence. Like Day, he is a member of the Anglo-Irish ascendancy, and it so happened that the Days and Raymonds are related, albeit distantly. Both families claim as an ancestor the most famous lavatory attendant in the history of the world – Sir Anthony Denny.

The Raymonds had estates in County Limerick, and previously in County Kerry – thanks to Sir Anthony's talent for nepotism – so the name would have been familiar to the Days and Dennys of Kerry. And the circumstances leading to James Raymond's flight to the Antipodes were common knowledge.

Raymond had been such an irresponsible and unreasonable landlord that his tenants revolted. In 1824, his manor, Hollywood House, in Ballyvara, County Limerick, was sacked and his steward murdered. Raymond and his family barely escaped with their lives, and were left destitute.

Luckily, James Raymond was well connected. His wife Aphrasia was the daughter of a Member of Parliament and the granddaughter of the High Sheriff of Limerick, while an old family friend, Henry Goulburn, happened to be Chancellor of the Exchequer. Goulburn wrote to Earl Bathurst, Secretary of State for the Colonies, requesting free passage to New South Wales for James, Aphrasia and their nine children. Bathurst complied, and in 1826 Raymond arrived in Sydney bearing a request from Bathurst to Governor Ralph Darling to find the exiled aristocrat a suitable appointment in the colonial administration.

Darling, already notable for poor judgement after banning all forms of theatrical entertainment, made Raymond coroner, a decision he soon had cause to regret. Not only did Raymond's performance in the role make it clear he had neither the aptitude nor the intellect to do the job, but he kept nagging the governor for a pay rise. James Raymond apparently considered himself an adornment to the colonial administration, despite all evidence to the contrary, and thus insisted it was the government's duty to support him and his large family in grand style.

For Governor Darling, this was quite a dilemma. Raymond was clearly a fool, but a fool with friends in high places, so sacking him and letting his family starve was not an option. In 1827, Darling made him Surveyor of Customs, at which he proved typically inept. But then, conveniently, the colony's post-master died, allowing Darling to appoint Raymond to the post, which carried a generous salary and a shove up the pecking order.

Before long, it was all too apparent that the new postmaster's interests in horse racing and lavish entertaining took precedence over his official duties. He left the running of the department to his very competent clerk, but then, to the despair of the governor and the detriment of the department, Raymond sacked his clerk in a spiteful act against a potential rival.

Denny Day knows all this gossip. Everyone does. Still, the preposterous postmaster had a beautiful daughter, and that's why Denny has come calling.

In white colonial society, the class divide is a yawning chasm. At one end of the social scale are convict road gangs and assigned servants, ex-convict labourers, soldiers and the poorest of free settlers scratching out a living in trade or farming. At the other end is the colonial elite, small in number but high in status – govern-ment officials, military officers, clergy, rich merchants parading Sydney's streets on fine horses and in handsome carriages, ladies promenading in the latest English fashions.

Sydney's imported gentry have brought with them the sensibili-ties of Georgian England, but Sydney is not London, where young ladies could expect a no-expense-spared 'season' to herald their entry onto the marriage market. In Sydney, where grand coming-out balls are few and far between, private parties are the usual venue for respectable flirtation. And while in the New World, as in the Old, a young gentlewoman's sole purpose in life is to make a good match, the prospects – like the gene pool – are extremely limited.

The rigid rules of courtship make husband hunting more art than science. A lady must never signal her intentions and a gentleman must always be seen to be the one doing the wooing. At a private soiree, a romantic encounter might be no more than a furtive exchange of smiles, hands held a little too long at the end of a dance, as if reluctant to let go, a blush of the cheek or a barely restrained sigh when parting company for the evening with a curtsey and a bow.

James Raymond, who had several marriageable daughters, is renowned for his opulent soirees, and with eligible young men of quality rather thin on the ground, Edward Denny Day, Esquire, late of the Wiltshire Moonrakers, is a suitable match for his 19-year-old daughter Margaret.

The postmaster is pleased to grant the young man permission to court his daughter. In due course Denny proposes, Margaret accepts, her father consents and, after a suitable period of engagement, during which time the betrothed couple meet only in company and on chaperoned walks, the banns are read and, in a private ceremony – Georgian weddings being low-key affairs – vows are exchanged.

For the newly wed clerk, an opportunity arises – a chance to escape the humdrum and poisonous atmosphere of the Colonial

Office. The role of police magistrate had been created in 1833 by a British Act of Parliament to keep the peace, initially in Sydney, then in settlements elsewhere. Unlike the office of Justice of the Peace or Magistrate, which is an honorary position comprised almost entirely of members of the wealthy landowning class – notoriously self-interested, and with no legal knowledge or experience required – police magistrates are paid government officers, appointed by the governor, with sweeping powers.

Under the Act, it is the duty of a police magistrate not only to perform the magisterial offices of a justice of the peace, but to recruit and command the district constabulary, apprehend criminals, oversee the conduct of convicts, and to suppress 'all tumults, riots, affrays or breaches of the peace, all public nuisances, vagrancies and offences against the law'.[1]

An Australian police magistrate of the 1830s does not merely sit on the bench, like a modern-day magistrate. He must also take to the streets or to the bush to track down criminals and bring them to justice. Arguably, the nearest equivalent to the role is that of a United States frontier marshal, with the addition of judicial duties.

The honorary magistrates – the landowning justices of the peace – do not welcome the appearance of police magistrates in their fiefdoms. Until now, they have been laws unto themselves. The honorary office has brought them power, prestige and influence, and the opportunities for corruption and nest-feathering have been almost boundless. Thus had it ever been in the motherland, where the local lord or squire was the undisputed authority, so the arrival of meddling upstarts in New South Wales is an affront to tradition. To the landed elite, Governor Bourke's 1832 Summary Offences Act, which attempted to curtail the honorary magistrates' often excessive and illegal exercise of their powers, was bad enough. This latest government attack on the time-honoured privileges of rank was far worse. It was simply flying in the face of nature.

So far, however, there has been little cause for such connip-tions. Many police magistrates apparently share the landed elite's view of the world, and have proved amenable to financial persua-sion and the temptations of patronage.

It so happens that a position has become available at a newly designated police district below the western escarpment of the Blue Mountains, 130 kilometres from Sydney. Denny Day applies, Governor Bourke accepts, and on 5 January 1836 *The Sydney Gazette* reports, 'His Excellency the Governor has been pleased to appoint Edward Denny Day, Esq., to be Police Magistrate for the district of the Vale of Clywdd.'[2]

The appointment is signed 'Alexander Macleay, Colonial Secretary's Office, Sydney.'[3]

Denny and Margaret Day prepare to leave Sydney, the iras-cible Colonial Secretary and the risible postmaster far behind. They're headed for the gateway to the wilderness, where Denny Day hopes to make his mark as a frontier lawman.

Chapter 8

The gateway

Archie Bell took the credit, but it rightly belonged to a young Booreberongal woman whose name was never recorded for posterity. She was one of six women kidnapped in 1823 by Gandangara raiders when camped on a Hawkesbury farm owned by the Bell family. The Gandangara were mountain people, a clan of the Dharug nation, and in earlier years had fought well against troops sent out on capture-and-kill expeditions by Governor Macquarie. Raiding the camps of other clans for women was a longstanding Gandangara practice, carried off with military precision, so when the six Booreberongal women were taken, neither their own people nor the white settlers expected to ever see them again.

But then, six days later, one returned. The young woman had somehow escaped her captors and made her way back by an ancient path unknown to the whites. Intrigued, 19-year-old Archie Bell convinced two Dharug men to guide him on the track through the wild ranges.

The track, named Bell's Line of Road, ran from the Hawkesbury to the western slopes of the Blue Mountains, opening an alternative route to the original road across the mountains, cut through the dense bush and sandstone ridges. That road, which closely followed the 1813 path of Gregory Blaxland, William Lawson and William Charles Wentworth – the first white explorers to cross the range – was all but impassable. Driving a cart downhill involved dragging a log behind the cart on a rope to slow the descent. To bring a cart uphill, bullock teams driven down the other side of the hill hauled on ropes and pulleys attached to iron rings in the rock walls. It was slow, laborious and terrifying.

Bell's wider route enabled cattle and sheep farmers to push further into the fertile western plains, but was extremely rugged, with many steep grades, and by the 1830s was seldom used. For the colony to expand and flourish beyond the Great Divide, another route had to be found.

In 1827, the government offered a reward of land and cattle for the discovery of a route avoiding, if possible, the mountains and passes that presented 'serious impediment to the communication with the country beyond the Blue Mountains'.[1]

The Surveyor-General, Major Thomas Mitchell, was sure he had the solution. In 1830 he mapped out a new route that would avoid the steepest hills by building a stone causeway bridging a deep ravine between two hills. The main hill in the pass, One Tree Hill, Mitchell renamed Mount Victoria, after the 11-year-old heiress to the British throne, who at that time was touring the English countryside, winning hearts and generating newspaper column inches.

The Victoria Pass, an engineering marvel of the age, took two years to build and cost the lives of at least 16 of the hundreds of convicts who worked on the project, most of them in irons. And when the pass and the new route grandly named the Great Western Road were opened to travellers, townships and inns soon sprung up along the way. One such township, at the base of a hill in the Vale of Clwydd (now in the central western city of Lithgow), was Hartley, at the crossing of the River Lett – so named, according to local lore, by a surveyor who could not spell 'rivulet'. And it's at Hartley where, in the summer of 1836, Denny and Margaret Day arrive to begin their lives anew.

Hartley, as the Days find it, is an important resting point for travellers who have crossed the Victoria Pass. It is also the hub of an area with few free settlers but large numbers of convict labourers, kept there in stockades to maintain the road, and is increasingly plagued by bushrangers and cattle thieves. Thus, the Vale of Clwydd has been declared a police district, with a police magistrate, a clerk of the bench, a chief constable, five constables and a scourger to lay on the lash. Day's salary is £250 a year, less £50 because he is still receiving full army pay as a retired officer.

But while the Vale of Clwydd now has its own police magistrate and constabulary, it does not yet have a courthouse, police station or jail. Denny Day has arrived at a place replete with glowing promises but with nothing to show for them. The district has three inns – The Travellers Inn, The Eagle and Child and Collit's Inn – and several convict stockades, but little else. Day soon finds his sworn aim to keep the peace has been compromised by his obligation to supervise the building of the courthouse, watch house and jail. In the meantime, he has no choice but to use some old huts at Mount Victoria as a temporary courthouse and jail.

With no official residence for the police magistrate, he and Margaret, who is pregnant with their first child – the first of five daughters and six sons – make their home in the run-down but livable officer's cottage of an abandoned military station. The station, coincidentally, had been a post of Day's first regiment, the Red Feathers, the first post west of the Blue Mountains and the site of one of the earliest battles between redcoats and Aborigines.

That summer, while the Days are settling in to life in the vale, a 27-year-old Englishman makes his way across the mountains and down through Victoria Pass. The Englishman, his face leathered from four years at sea, is a naturalist and geologist named Charles Darwin, recently arrived on the HMS *Beagle*.

A week earlier, while still at sea, he wrote to his sister Caroline, 'I am looking forward with more pleasure to seeing Sydney than to any other part of the voyage. Our stay there will be very short, only a fortnight. I hope, however, to be able to take a ride some way into the country.'[2]

With that aim in mind, Darwin hired a man and two horses and set off across the Blue Mountains to Bathurst, 'a village about 120 miles in the interior, and the centre of a great pastoral district'.[3]

Dashing off entries in his journal, he marvels at the soaring sandstone cliffs and waterfalls, muses that platypus and other native animals he sees might have been created by another god, and along the way notes a resemblance to England, except that 'perhaps the alehouses here were more numerous'. The iron gangs of convicts he passes 'appeared the least like England.

They were working in chains, under the charge of sentries with loaded arms.'[4]

On encountering a group of Aboriginal warriors, he writes:

At sunset, a party of a score of the black aborigines passed by, each carrying, in their accustomed many, a bundle of spears and other weapons. By giving a leading young man a shilling, they were easily detained, and threw their spears for my amusement. They were all partly clothed, and several could speak a little English. Their countenances were good-humoured and pleasant, and they appeared far from being such utterly degraded beings as have usually been represented. In their own arts they are admirable. A cap being fixed at 30 yards distant, they transfixed it with a spear, delivered by the throwing-stick with the rapidity of an arrow from the bow of a practised archer. In tracking animals or men they show most wonderful sagacity, and I heard several of their remarks which manifested considerable acuteness. They will not, however, cultivate the ground, or build houses and remain stationary, or even take the trouble of tending a flock of sheep when given to them.

It is very curious thus to see in the midst of a civilised people a set of harmless savages wandering about without knowing where they shall sleep at night, and gaining a livelihood by hunting in the woods.

The number of aborigines is rapidly decreasing. In my whole ride, with the exception of some boys brought up by Englishmen, I saw only one other party. This decrease, no doubt, must be partly owing to the introduction of spirits, to European diseases (even the milder ones of which, such as the measles, prove very destructive), and the gradual extinction of the wild animals.[5]

The latter comment was perhaps based on his disappointment at having joined a kangaroo hunt with settlers, only to return without spotting a single kangaroo.

It's not known whether or not Charles Darwin, while at Hartley, calls on the new police magistrate to pay his respects. Darwin is not yet the famous and controversial author of *The Origin of Species*, just another traveller passing through. And Denny Day is not yet the most feared and respected lawman on the frontier, just another country policeman.

What is known is that Darwin's overall impression of the colony is not favourable. 'On the whole, from what I heard, more than from what I saw, I was disappointed in the state of society,' he writes. 'The whole community is rancorously divided into parties on almost every subject. Among those who, from their station in life, ought to be the best, many live in such open profligacy that respectable people cannot associate with them. There is much jealousy between the children of the rich emancipists and the free settlers, the former being pleased to consider honest men as interlopers. The whole population, poor and rich, are bent on acquiring wealth.

'There are many serious drawbacks to the comforts of a family – the chief of which, perhaps, is being surrounded by convict servants. How thoroughly odious to every feeling to be waited on by a man who the day before, perhaps, was flogged, from your representation, for some trifling misdemeanour. The female servants are of course much worse; hence children learn the vilest expression, and it is fortunate, if not equally vile ideas.'[6]

And his parting words: 'Farewell, Australia! You are a rising child, and doubtless some day will reign a great princess in the South. But you are too great and ambitious for affection, yet not great enough for respect. I leave your shores without sorrow or regret.'[7]

The Days see a future for themselves in the vale, and in August 1836, Denny Day offers to buy 320 acres of government land near Hartley, which includes the former army post. It's prime land overlooking where the River Lett meets Cox's River, but Day's dream of becoming a man of property is frustrated by a certain James Byrn Richards, who glories in the title of Fourth Assistant Surveyor of Lands. Sent out from Sydney to assess the property, Richards recommends that the portion of the land containing the cottage and buildings should not be sold but retained as a government reserve. Richards' superiors do not agree, but the wheels of colonial bureaucracy move at the speed of continental drift. Six months of paper-shuffling later, the land is put up for sale, but in the meantime the Days have given up in disgust and the property is snapped up by an absentee Sydney buyer.

Much of the trouble in the vale comes from the convict stockades. Thanks to corrupt overseers who release men from their leg irons and turn a blind eye, convicts who are compliant road workers by day rampage by night as bushrangers, rustlers and thieves. Bringing them to justice is difficult because overseers are accessories to the crimes, and made even more difficult by the quality of the constabulary, many of whom are dismissed for corruption, drunkenness or incompetence.

In April 1837, after what seems an eternity of dealing with troublesome tenders and prevaricating politicians over the style and location of the proposed Hartley courthouse, 12 men and four horses arrive to quarry stone and cart it to a site by the river. The site suggested by Denny Day had been rejected by the builder and quarrelled over by assorted bureaucrats until eventually approved by Governor Bourke, who supports Day's choice.

Then, just as work is set to begin, word arrives that Day is to be transferred and replaced as police magistrate for the Vale of Clwydd by John Kinchela, eldest son of Judge John Kinchela. The judge is a former disaster of an attorney-general who, much like Denny Day's father-in-law James Raymond, owes his success to his incompetence. He is known for being constantly and desperately in debt, and for handing down death sentences despite being almost stone deaf and thus oblivious to argument from either side.

Governor Bourke, tolerant to a fault, gently removed him as attorney-general and set him on the bench, and now has to regularly review his judgements. In a recent example, Judge Kinchela sentenced to death a young farmhand convicted of 'that detestable crime of buggery, not to be named amongst Christians'.[8]

The prisoner's pleas for mercy fell upon deaf ears, literally, and the judge told the prisoner to 'prepare himself for another world, as it was impossible any mercy could be extended to him in this' and ordered him to be hanged.[9]

Governor Bourke later commuted the man's sentence to penal servitude for the rest of his natural life on Norfolk Island, with solitary confinement at night.

John Kinchela junior had been a clerk in the Crown Solicitor's office in Sydney, and at just 22 is the youngest police magistrate ever appointed, thanks to his father's influence, yet his career is destined to be far from stellar. Because of his lack of experience, other magistrates will refuse to sit with him, and, after publicly horsewhipping a man who had ridiculed his father, he will find himself in the dock rather than on the bench, and fined £50 – one pound for every lash of his whip.

As for Denny Day, he is leaving the vale behind him, most likely without regret, to journey on another road hewn from the living rock by convict hands. The Great North Road, winding 240 kilometres through gorges and razorback ridges to Patrick's Plains on Hunter's River, has replaced the original road north, Comleroy Road, a stock route named after – but not in honour of – the Kamilaroi.

Drovers still use the Comleroy but travellers almost never do. The Great North Road is easier and safer, and there are too many ghosts on the old road. In 1816, in reprisal for the spearing of five white men on the Kurrajong Slopes, on the north side of the Blue Mountains, four black men were hanged in a line from the Grose River, across the slopes to the Comleroy. All were shot as they strangled. About every ten kilometres along the Comleroy are reserves where travellers can camp, but these days the reserves accommodate only snakes and spiders. For too long, blood was the toll on that road, and the Days, like most sensible travellers, are taking the high road, bound for a frontier settlement with a bad reputation. Denny Day has been appointed police magistrate at a place named for his old commander in India – Wallis Plains.

In the wider world, the steamer *St Peter*, a trader out of St Louis, on its way up the Missouri River to Fort Union, docks at Fort Clark, near a village of the Mandan people. As well as a cargo of furs, the *St Peter* is carrying smallpox, and within a few months an estimated 15,000 Native Americans in the Missouri Valley will be dead, with many more yet to die as the epidemic spreads across the Great Plains.

And in England, at six o'clock in the morning, Alexandrina's mother, carrying a lighted candle, enters her daughter's room and gently wakes her. The girl, in her dressing-gown, takes her mother's hand and together they go downstairs to where the Archbishop of Canterbury and Lord Conyngham, the Lord Chamberlain, are waiting.

Later that day, 18-year-old Princess Alexandrina Victoria, known to her family as 'Drina', writes in her diary, 'Lord Conyngham then acquainted me that my poor uncle, the King, was no more, and had expired at 12 minutes past two this morning and consequently that I am Queen.'[10]

It is Tuesday 20 June 1837. The Victorian Age has begun.

Chapter 9

Masters of the plains

They are the very model of the so-called Myall blacks – mercurial, warlike and feared. Kamilaroi territory ranges south from the plains and the Big River to the headwaters of Hunter's River, almost to Wallis Plains, where the neighbouring Geawegal live in dread of Kamilaroi raids into their country. A confederation of groups claiming hunting and religious rights over this vast area, and related by ancestry and a common language, the Kamilaroi are powerful and, as one settler describes them, 'proud, free masters of the land'.[1]

What the white man calls the Liverpool Plains they know as 'Corborn Kamilaroi', meaning the great country of the Kamilaroi, and the upper reaches of Hunter's River they call 'Gummun Kamilaroi', meaning the lesser country of the Kamilaroi nation.[2]

Leaders are not hereditary chiefs but gain authority by bravery, wisdom and force of character, and are responsible to a council of elders. 'They are truly a law-abiding people,' declared the missionary and linguist William Ridley. 'Probably no community in Christendom observes the laws deemed most sacred so exactly as the Australian tribes observe their traditional rulers.'[3]

Ridley, who was fluent in Kamilaroi, and dedicated to saving Indigenous languages from extinction, was impressed by the way the language conveyed 'accuracy of thought, and a force of expression surpassing all that is commonly supposed to be obtainable by a savage race'.[4]

He was equally impressed by the people's songs, poetry and traditions, which made it clear to him that 'they are by no means destitute of some qualities in which civilised men glory, such as the power of inventing tragic and sarcastic fiction, the thirst for religious mystery, stoical contempt of pain, and reverence for departed friends and ancestors'.

It was generally supposed that Aboriginal religion was not monotheistic, but Ridley knew better. Kamilaroi warriors had told him that Baiame, the creator spirit, lived far to the west, and that while they never saw him, they heard his voice in the thunder. They believed in life after death, and that Baiame welcomed the good to a spirit world in the sky.

'British colonisation,' the missionary warned, 'has done much to destroy, and British Christianity has done little to save, the Aborigines of Australia.'[5]

Since white incursions made them fugitives in their own country, their dwellings have been necessarily rude, temporary shelters. But until the 1830s they lived in established villages of circular huts with conical roofs of reeds and flat-roofed porches. The explorer and Surveyor-General Major Thomas Mitchell, who came upon such a village by the Big River in 1831, described the huts as well made, clean and comfortable.

Kamilaroi women wear possum or kangaroo skin skirts and fur cloaks. Men go naked but for a woven belt in the warmer months and wear animal skin cloaks in cooler weather. They keep their hair shoulder length, trim their beards short, and wear a white headband over a red headband.

Disease and dislocation have taken a greater toll than musketry on the Kamilaroi of the upper Hunter, but the people of the plains remain defiant, and their fighting skills are legendary. Settlers' folklore includes the tale of a stockman who survived a Kamilaroi attack on a Liverpool Plains station, in which warriors fought courageously against the settlers' guns for two hours. In his 1841 memoir, Liverpool Plains settler William Telfer claims the stockman – who unfortunately he does not name – later left Australia during the California gold rush, then joined the Texas Rangers and fought the Comanche. On returning to Australia, he declared the Aborigines to be finer and braver than the Indians.[6]

In 1834, the explorer Geoffrey Blaxland reported finding graves in the Hunter Valley that were of casualties from a recent battle between Kamilaroi and Wollombi warriors from the Hunter highlands. That same year, a Kamilaroi war party was seen on the Great North Road, their bodies painted with intricate designs in white – the colour of war and death – on their way to do battle with the Wollombi.

When a party of whites came upon a group of Wollombi, the meeting was cordial but memorable, because one of the warriors, who agreed to give a former naval officer, William Brenton, a lesson in spear throwing in exchange for tobacco, chastised Brenton for his poor attempts at throwing.

*

When the first pioneers crossed the mountains onto the Liverpool Plains, the Kamilaroi challenged them to battle but gave them a fortnight's notice to prepare. On the appointed day, the warriors, painted, armed and strung out for about two kilometres, in traditional fashion, slowly closed ranks and advanced, then charged head-on into a fusillade of 16 muskets from behind a barricade. The Kamilaroi bravely held their ground but in the end were forced to retreat. It's uncertain how many warriors fell that day, but according to some accounts it was as many as 200. According to the bushranger Martin Cash, who heard about the battle firsthand, there were so many dead that it took seven men two days to bury them all.[7]

To the Kamilaroi the lesson was clear. In fighting the white man, the old ways would only bring slaughter and defeat. It was time to change tactics.

In skilled hands, the Land Pattern Musket, better known as the Brown Bess, can fire an 18-millimetre musket ball at a rate of up to four but usually three rounds a minute. By the 1830s, this .75-calibre flintlock musket has been the British Army's standard-issue weapon for more than a century, and has served the empire, for better and for worse, in the American Revolutionary War, the Napoleonic Wars, the War of 1812 and the colonisation of Australia.

The range of the Brown Bess is around 160 metres, but its smooth bore, lack of sights and often undersized ammunition – used to avoid jamming – make it inaccurate at less than half that distance, rendering it more effective fired in volleys than in single combat.

To load and fire the weapon, a shooter first takes a paper cartridge of gunpowder from an ammunition pouch, tears off the tip of the cartridge with his teeth, sets the hammer to half-cock, pours some of the gunpowder into the flash pan and shuts the hammer, then pours the rest of the powder into the barrel. That done, he inserts a musket ball and paper wadding into the barrel and, removing the ramrod from under the barrel, rams the wadding down the barrel, replaces the ramrod, pulls back the hammer to full-cock, shoulders the musket, aims and fires. The misfire rate is five per cent in dry conditions, and significantly higher in humid conditions, when damp gunpowder fails to ignite. In a notable example, when the first governor of New South Wales, Arthur Phillip, was speared through the shoulder by an Eora warrior in September 1790, four marines shot at the assailant, yet all but one of their muskets misfired.

In the hands of a skilled Aboriginal warrior, a four-metre war spear, with a sharp point of shell, stone, bone or fire-hardened wood, is deadly accurate up to 50 metres and reaches its target within two seconds. When thrown using a woomera as an extension of the human arm to boost velocity, it is accurate over greater distances and can reach speeds of up to 160 kilometres an hour. A warrior can hurl spears at a rate of one every four to five seconds, with lethal force.

Although a spear wound to the chest, puncturing the heart and lungs, is invariably fatal, spears can be deflected by heavy clothing. A musket ball, travelling at a much higher velocity than a spear, cannot be deflected, inflicts a much larger wound and is usually lethal. It's worth noting that Governor Phillip survived his shoulder wound but Bangai, the Eora man who speared him and was shot in the shoulder, bled to death because the musket ball had severed an artery.

Still, most shooters are poor shots due to lack of practice. For civilians, musket balls have to be made by hand and are not to be wasted, and, even for British soldiers, target practice for most regiments is limited to only about four shots a year. Shooters also have a habit of shutting their eyes when firing to avoid the flash of the pan, whereas Aboriginal men, trained from boyhood with spears and other weapons, regard deadly accuracy as a point of pride.

A Kamilaroi warrior's weaponry includes pointed and barbed spears, woomeras, clubs, war boomerangs and shields. Some spears, made from the stems of grass trees, are up to four metres long. Others, made from reeds, are about the size of arrows and spin rapidly in flight. There are several types of club, including a light club carried in the belt, a heavier battle club used in hand-to-hand combat, with a head of stone or fire-hardened wood, and a small club meant to be thrown. A war boomerang – not to be confused with the returning boomerang, which is merely a toy – is designed to whirl at high velocity, hit an opponent and spin off at even greater speed. Difficult to dodge, the weapon can inflict serious wounds. A warrior's shield might be a large, light shield designed for fending off spears, or a smaller, narrow shield for defence when fighting with clubs.

Few Aborigines have adopted firearms. They see no need, since their bushcraft and stealth give them the advantage over musketry, and, just as importantly, the spear is integral to the warrior culture.

Before 1788, warfare between rival Aboriginal groups was commonplace. The usual hostilities were raids for women, revenge attacks for murder and religious violations, attempts to assert superiority over neighbouring groups, and formal battles to resolve grievances. Unlike in European, Asian and African societies, conflicts were seldom sparked by disputes over territory or property.

Formal battles were highly ritualised. Battles were preceded by several days of preparation, fought with a time limit agreed by the opposing sides, and often halted after only a few casualties.

Women, too, fought in battles, mostly in revenge attacks, but more often would assemble at the perimeter of a fight, loudly cheering on their men 'over the clashing of spears and the strokes of lances'.[8]

By the 1830s, the frontier conflict between Aborigines and settlers and soldiers has changed. New methods of fighting have evolved as Aborigines replace their traditional, ritualised methods of warfare with hit-and-run, guerrilla tactics.

For Aboriginal warriors, the key to victory is surprise. Although a spear thrown from, say, 50 metres takes just two seconds to reach its target, two seconds is time enough to step aside and avoid the projectile if you see the man throw it at you. Thus, ambush, particularly at night, is the most common mode of attack. A moving target stands a better chance of survival than an unsuspecting enemy standing still.

While few civilians had guns in the early days of the colony, firearms are widely available by the 1830s and include muskets issued to civilians by the colonial government for use against attack by blacks. Settlers, whose survival once depended on soldiers being deployed to the frontier, are now able to defend themselves. And while the law is clear on the difference between justifiable homicide and cold-blooded murder, the law is a long way away.

The white line – the creeping perimeter of European expansion – has been crossed. For centuries, the Kamilaroi have bloodily repulsed black incursions into their territory, and white invaders will be treated no differently.

Chapter 10

A fine place for scoundrels

The explorer John Oxley once advised settlers selecting sites for future towns on Hunter's River, 'It is subject to severe inundations. You must be specially careful to select high land for such purposes.'[1]

It was sound advice, which the settlers of Wallis Plains blissfully ignored and established a township by the tidal reach of the river, on the site of a cedar-getters' camp that the cedar-getters had sensibly abandoned.

When Denny Day arrives in the town in the summer of 1837 it has experienced five major floods in the past six years – one in which seven people drowned.

The town is called Maitland, after an otherwise undistinguished under-secretary for the colonies, Sir George Maitland. It had long been the habit in Whitehall for bureaucrats to take turns at having colonial towns and landmarks named after them, much as would later be the case with municipal functionaries and suburban streets. Apparently, it was George's turn.

For all that, the place has a certain charm. What just a few years ago was little more than a single rambling street of modest houses with a pub every hundred metres, flanked by dense bush and lagoons of backwater, is gradually putting flesh on the bones of what some say will one day be the second biggest town in the colony. Being close to the head of navigation at Morpeth, with steamers and sailing packets in the river port and warehouses on the dock, and with the ocean just three days' journey downriver at Newcastle, its prospects for prosperity seem good.

Too good to be true, as Day soon discovers. Even a slight scratch beneath the surface reveals a town unable and unwilling to shake off its lawless frontier origins. There are decent, hardworking people here who are determined to make this place a home; not only free settlers but convict farmers along the river and Wallis Creek, as well as town merchants and others, but they don't dare walk the streets at night. Much of the population is transient – teamsters, watermen, hawkers, whores, drifters, drunken brawlers, rogues, rebels, runaways, robbers and worse. There is blood on the streets, unsupervised convicts on the rampage, outlaws on the high road and desperation in the air. It is Denny Day's mission to tame this town, and it will not go down without a fight.

On Wallis Plains as Denny Day finds it in 1837, the walls of older farmhouses have gun slits in case of attack by blacks or bushrangers, but trouble of that kind has since moved on – across the Great Divide to the Liverpool Plains.

Conflict between black and white on Hunter's River – Wonnarua country – was more often stand-off than skirmish until the 1820s, when convicts from the penal station at Newcastle, at the mouth of the river, were sent upriver to Wallis Plains to fell cedar trees and raft the logs downstream.

Newcastle, 60 miles by sea north of Sydney, was a hellhole; a place of secondary punishment where the intractable and the unforgiven laboured under the lash, worked to death in choking coalmines or burning oyster shells to make lime, searing the flesh from their bones. For men already brutalised, this was a breeding ground for the pitiless.

Working parties of up to 30 convicts, under military guard to keep order and protect them from blacks, journeyed upriver to the furthest outpost of settlement – the river flats above Wallis Plains – to harvest a hundred logs a month. The logs were lashed into rafts, and huts built on the rafts as shelter for the men. Floating the rafts downriver to Newcastle took eight days. There was an overland track from Newcastle to Wallis Plains, but although the track was only 30 kilometres long it wound through swamps and was cut by creeks. The river, which mean-dered 120 kilometres between Wallis Plains and Newcastle, was the only practical mode of transport.

So, for weeks at a time, gangs of men embittered by tyranny, banished from what passed for civilisation on the far side of the world, spent their days sending giant red cedars – some up to 30 feet in girth and among the largest ever found in Australia – crashing to the ground, sawing, heaving and rolling logs. Their nights were spent huddled together in rough thatched huts that kept out neither wind nor rain nor mosquitoes.

There in the bush, in the middle of nowhere, escape seemed only a few easy paces away. A side step into the scrub was all it would take, and some took it. Few believed the tall tales of convicts who, like Marco Polo, found a path through the wilds that led all the way to China, but all had heard the more credible whispers of a secret track from Hunter's River to the Hawkesbury settlement in the south, not that anyone had ever returned to confirm the rumour. It was known that runaway convicts had survived for months in the bush, living on kangaroo meat and robbing isolated settlers, but that most had been recaptured or shot dead by soldiers.

And it would be a rare convict who hadn't heard the cautionary tale of James Field. In the winter of 1804, *The Sydney Gazette* reported:

When the *Resource* last made the Coal Harbour [Newcastle], on Tuesday the 29th ultimo, the vessel was faintly hailed from the north side of the river, in consequence of which Mr Craft got into the boat with one of the hands, and proceeded towards the shore, where, to his utter astonishment he beheld a human being in a condition too deplorable to be described or imagined. The unhappy author of their astonishment was unclothed, wore a beard that swept his breast, had received a spear in the right shoulder by which it was pierced through, and had his right hand barbarously crushed.

He endured additional torture, if humanity could be susceptible of more than the wounds already recounted were capable of inflicting, from three ghastly wounds on the head. The air was cold and penetrating, and the unhappy sufferer endeavoured to alleviate the misery of his condition by shielding his mutilated head from the wind with a scrap of withered bark.

Eyeing with heartfelt gratitude the good Samaritans sent by Heaven to his relief in this last stage of human wretchedness, the transport of his soul rose superior to his accumulated afflictions, and he sunk to all appearance lifeless, when the hope of preserving him vanished. It was the will of Heaven, however, again to restore him, and he was conveyed with care and tenderness to the settlement, where such marks of attention were shown him as reflect honour to the feelings of the gentleman in command, as well as of the resident assistant surgeon, Mr Mileham.

But when the *Resource* sailed, the prospect of his surviving was by no means promising. As the hardships he had undergone, added to the dreadful wounds he had received, precluded the possibility of recognising him, who or what he was could only be ascertained upon probable conjecture until he was sufficiently revived concisely to gratify the interested curiosity that prevailed. He proved to be James Field, who in company with William Johnston and James Broadbent some months since, made off with a boat belonging to Sergeant Day, in hopes of being taken on board an American vessel about to leave the port, but, disappointed and rejected, were driven to the northward of Port Stephen, about 30 miles beyond Hunter's River, where, after a series of unspeakable hardships they were assaulted by a body of natives who showered spears upon them with a barbarity only to be conceived by those that have witnessed the brutal ferocity of these unfeeling savages.

Johnston, he believed, was the first who fell a victim to their fury, but very soon sinking beneath the wounds he had himself received, only recollected that when Providence had restored him to life, both his companions lay breathless by his side. The boat was slaved [captured], and death in a new shape again presented itself. Famine and extreme anguish were now to complete a destiny which the cruelty of the savages had only half accomplished.

Unconscious of the situation of the place, he left the mass-acred associates of his imprudence, and wandered hopeless along the extensive sand beach that separates Point Stephens from the entrance of Hunter's River, and after a three days' fatiguing travel, arrived at the spot of his deliverance.

And the moral of the story?

A thousand times did he rebuke his destiny for having reserved him alone for still protracted sufferings, and as often did he envy the peaceful condition of his unfortunate companions. Good heavens, how strange and paradoxical must be the texture of the human mind, that can consent to renounce the certain benefits attendant upon industry acquired without hazard, for a chimerical desire of emigrating from a spot to which nature has been so truly bountiful, and where those very unfortunate people had, notwithstanding the sentence under which they laboured, enjoyed a comfortable maintenance.

All attempts that have been made of this kind have proved uniformly ruinous and abortive, and if example can deter, surely none will leap headlong into the destructive vortex through the want of unhappy instances to warn them of the certain danger.[2]

The official line was that the few who got away either starved to death or were killed by blacks, and that their bleached bones litter the bush, but with no evidence to support that claim, men with nothing to lose continued to take their chances. No one knew if any runaways had ever made it to freedom, and so in convict hearts a deep resentment took root towards those they had come to believe stood in the way of escape – the blacks.

It was a resentment fuelled by the fact that Aborigines had often helped soldiers track down and capture runaway convicts.

The first issue of Australia's first newspaper, *The Sydney Gazette*, of 5 March 1803, reported the capture of a group of runaway convicts from the penal settlement at Castle Hill 'after having committed many acts of violence and atrocity' including the rape of a settler's wife and the brutal wounding of a farm labourer, shot in the face.[3] After a week's rampage, 11 of the 15 fugitives were recaptured by redcoats at a bush hide-out somewhere between the Hawkesbury River and the mountains after 'information had been given of their haunt by a body of natives'.[4]

An 1822 report on the state of the colony noted:

The native blacks that inhabit the neighbourhood of Port Hunter and Port Stephens have become very active in retaking the fugitive convicts. They accompany the soldiers who are sent in pursuit, and by the extraordinary strength of sight that they possess, improved by their daily exercise of it in pursuit of kangaroos and opossums, they can trace to a distance, with wonderful accuracy, the impressions of the human foot. Nor are they afraid of meeting the fugitive convicts in the woods when sent in their pursuit without the soldiers. By their skill in throwing their long and pointed darts they wound and disable them, strip them of their clothes, and bring them back as prisoners, by unknown roads and paths, to the Coal River [Hunter's River].

They are rewarded for these enterprises by presents of maize and blankets, and notwithstanding the apprehensions of revenge from the convicts whom they bring back, they continue to live in Newcastle and its neighbourhood.[5]

To the white felon far from home, the dark man lurking out there in the wilderness was a bogey; a nemesis. To those sent upriver to fell and haul timber at Wallis Plains, the only advantage was a longer leash, and if that brought opportunities to take revenge on their nemesis – for murder and rape – who was to know or care? Their self-appointed betters apparently saw no harm in it; some even encouraged it.

Even if the convict cedar gangs had left the Wonnarua unmolested their presence would have been resented. The whites were in blackfellow country hunting game, disturbing the natural balance of the forest and, most offensively, felling large numbers of trees, some of them of totemic significance. But as if that wasn't reason enough to hate the intruders, the whites committed atrocities that the blacks found intolerable.

One such incident, reported by the missionary Lancelot Threlkeld, involved 'the ripping open of the bellies of the blacks alive, roasting them in that state in triangularly made log fires, together with many other atrocious acts of cruelty, which are but the sports of monsters'.[6]

In 1825, Threlkeld reported hearing at night the screams of girls of only eight or nine years old taken by force by the cedar gangs. 'One man came to me with his head broken by the butt of a musket because he would not give up his wife,' he wrote.[7]

Little wonder, said the missionary, that the blacks took delight in tracking down escaped convicts, and showed them no mercy.

Now, in 1837, black faces are seldom seen at Wallis Plains. Displacement and despair drove off most of the Wonnarua, and influenza and poisoned flour took care of the rest. Trouble now, when it comes, and it seems to come often, is whitefella trouble. Day sets about cleaning up the town, cracking down on alcohol-fuelled violence in public houses and sly grog shops, unruly convicts and riotous assemblies in the streets, making full use of the powers of summary justice afforded a police magistrate. Taking to the roads, he soon makes it clear to bushrangers and would-be outlaws that plying their trade around Wallis Plains is a sure ticket to Stockade Hill and the noose.

He gets occasional assistance from civilians who volunteer for a posse, but little or no help from the local constabulary. Under the 1830 Bushranging Act, it is legal for anyone suspecting a person of being unlawfully at large to apprehend them without warrant and take them before a magistrate or justice of the peace. Constables can even supplement their meagre incomes by claiming rewards for bringing in outlaws and runaway convicts. Regardless, Maitland's police, recruited from the ranks of paroled convicts, are more likely to be found carousing and running rackets in the inns and grog shops than chasing bushrangers or keeping the street safe for decent folk. For Day, who has dismissed some of his constables for drunkenness and corruption, and regards the rest as a clutch of cowardly layabouts, keeping the peace is basically a one-man job. Yet he does it so well that Maitlanders will thereafter remember him as a hard man for hard times who 'in his administration of the law made it a terror to evildoers'.[8]

In fact, he pacifies Maitland so effectively that after just nine months, once again he is replaced – this time by Patrick Grant, the brother-in-law of the Colonial Secretary, Lord Glenelg. Day is to be transferred to the district of Invermein (now Scone), further inland, with a £100 drop in salary. He protests to Governor

Bourke, but the governor's hands are tied. His Lordship in London has made up his mind.

Patrick Grant, Esquire, a young gentleman fresh out from England, and experienced at little more than playing whist and shooting grouse, finds Denny Day a hard act to follow. And when Grant, who favours the social democratic ideals of the Chartist movement, announces his preference for a more moderate, conciliatory approach to crime and punishment, the law-abiding locals are less than impressed. In a letter to the editor of *The Sydney Herald*, a Wallis Plains settler styling himself 'Scrutator' offers a scathing review of the new police magistrate's performance:

As Mr Grant (like many other local governors) has commenced by a comparison between his own intentions and the conduct of his predecessors, permit me to make a few remarks thereon.

It is certainly true that one of them found this district in a truly disorganised state. But what, I ask, was the cause? Temporising and tampering with a horde of villains; and the result was as anticipated by the thinking class of our community. Search the annals of the police offices and the jails – the answer is recorded in letters of blood. A mistaken leniency, and the protection of a kind-hearted though erring magistrate, had engendered a feeling of insolence and insubordination in the district, which at last rose to such a pitch as to cause the removal of the then Police Magistrate, and a man fully qualified for the task [Denny Day] stepped in to supply his place.

The result was almost instantaneous. Just severity, and no hope of escaping condign punishment for their misdeeds, operated as it was sure to do. Insolence was checked, laziness and destruction punished, and to complete the work, the hydra, insubordination, was crushed and annihilated.[9]

Wallis Plains, which under Day's firm but fair hand has gone from bad to good, is now predicted to go from good to bad to worse. And so it does, according to an open letter to Grant in *The Sydney Herald* barely a month later, from 'A Settler' of Maitland.

I sometime since observed your address to the free and prison population of the district over which you have been appointed to act in a magisterial capacity. The policy of such a measure seemed at the best but questionable; it remained to be proved how such an unusual course would operate. All seemed to give you credit for the philanthropy which dictated its promulgation, but none could regard other than a weakness the adoption of a style of conciliation to the offender, and of masked threatenings to the unfortunate emigrant, whose fate it has been to be surrounded by the offscourings of society to whom you so prematurely proffer advice and support – who, for the most part, are as incapable of estimating your motives as of understanding or appreciating the conciliatory measures you suggest.

Would it not have been better, before promulgating your views, to have made yourself acquainted with the peculiar structure of society in this colony, or at least to have learnt the conventional phraseology which has been introduced into this happy country by the fortunate race to whom you promise your protection? No better proof of the latter can exist than the ludicrous mistake one of your expressions has occasioned.

You state that you have been 'unfortunate' yourself. The emigrant population, no doubt, sympathise with you, but the prison population know of no other misfortune than being convicted of crime, and condemned to suffer its consequences. The phrase was, therefore, an unhappy one when used by a new magistrate in such a state of society as this.

It is said, I do not know how truly, that you are in the habit of questioning convicts, when at the triangles [for flogging], with regard to the conduct of their masters and mistresses. Do you indeed seek information from such polluted sources? Do the courts at home ask of culprits the characters of their prosecutors? If you wish for correct information, why not enquire of those of the prison population who are never brought before you – and I am happy to say from long experience that there are many deserving men among them? Why not ascertain the character of their employers from the well-conducted or deserving, instead of from the idle and dissolute culprits on whom, in spite of your false philanthropy, you have been obliged to inflict punishment, and that too whilst they are smarting under the lash which they have made for their own backs by their dishonesty to their masters? Be assured, sir, there are some who never speak the truth; make the experiment on a few ascertained facts and then question them on points relating to those facts, and you will find that they cannot speak the truth even if it should be for their own benefit.

Not content with painting Grant as a soft-touch, a dupe and a laughing stock, the anonymous correspondent injects a hint of scandal.

'As a proof, I need only instance the barefaced and unprincipled assertion of one of the women whom you a short time since dismissed from the lock-up without trial. Do, sir, enquire, what the report is to which the woman has given circulation.'

The letter concludes:

No-one can suppose but that your motives are good; yet, sir, a moment's reflection will convince you of the evil attendant on such a course. The inference these people will draw is that they are to receive protection and support in the practice of their evil propensities, or at least that the lock-up, with plenty of good food, is better than labour on their masters' farms. The result has already been that the prison population are in a complete state of insubordination, and we can now only hope that the false impression instilled into this class by their misapprehension of your intentions may not lead to more important results.[10]

It is the beginnings of low-key but persistent lobbying by the law-abiding people of Wallis Plains for the removal of Patrick Grant as police magistrate and the return of Denny Day.

Chapter 11

The greater glory

The colonial government has ruled that no one can occupy crown land beyond the limits of settlement without first obtaining a licence. The prohibition is the result of lobbying by pioneer landowners who are already established on the frontier but increasingly under threat of attack by lawless bands of men – mostly runaway convicts and parolees but in some cases free men who have turned to crime.

The interior of the colony, the settlers say, is infested with cattle thieves and marauding outlaw gangs, many of whom have in a short time acquired large herds of cattle – all of them stolen.

The licensing scheme is doomed to failure. It is clear from the outset that it will only keep poor but honest folk from venturing beyond the pale. And nothing will keep the missionaries out, not even the fear of God.

William Watson and Johan Handt are on a mission from God. Or so it seemed back when they and their wives arrived at a God-forsaken place far beyond the pale. As clergymen of the Church Missionary Society, an evangelical Protestant organisation dedicated to civilising and Christianising the heathen savages of Africa, the East and New Holland, they had come to Wiradjuri country to establish a mission in the Wellington Valley, near the village of Montefiores (now Wellington), 360 kilometres north-west of Sydney, to bring the good word to the Aborigines. They had been granted 10,000 acres by the colonial government, and £500 a year to run the mission.

The missionaries, Watson and Handt, have spent four frustrating years failing to convince the blacks that the Christian God outranks their own supreme being, Baiame, the Sky Father. Even when provided with food, tobacco and other incentives, and told that the Queen of England herself sent the missionaries to bring them into the fold, the Wiradjuri stubbornly refuse to see the light; to accept that their religion, ancient long before Jesus was born, is mere superstition and should be discarded for a greater truth.

In the annual report of the Wellington Valley Mission to the governor, Watson and Handt lay the blame for their poor tally of saved souls on stockmen from nearby frontier stations. The stockmen, they claim, have been telling Wiradjuri people that if they go to the mission they will be captured and yoked like bullocks, and that their children will be taken from them and thrown into prison in Sydney. The whites give the women food and other goods in exchange for sexual favours, and 'are ready to use threats, or even violence, when they find opposition to their vicious inclinations'.[1]

The missionaries report that 'the cruelty of some of these stockmen to the natives of both sexes, it is to be greatly feared, will ultimately lead to revenge on the part of the natives, and the result may be the murder of any or of every white man they meet with'.

Watson and Handt find it frustrating that the Aborigines remain suspicious that the missionaries have evil intentions towards them. They lament, 'It is rather surprising that they will believe what the stockmen say, rather than be convinced of the purity of the intentions of the missionaries, when they have received so many acts of kindness from the latter.'

They are happy to report that despite the drought they have managed to sow about ten acres of corn, and hope to raise enough grain and stock to supply another mission station they plan to establish further west 'amongst the wild black natives, where they have not been corrupted by intercourse with Europeans'.[2]

On the night before he is to be hanged for rape, a man known to the whites as Mickey sits in a condemned cell in Sydney Gaol. With him is Reverend Lancelot Threlkeld from the Ebenezer Aboriginal Mission at Lake Macquarie, south of Newcastle. Threlkeld has come to visit Mickey in the hope of saving his soul, but he's not getting through to him.

Mickey, who protests his innocence, responds to the missionary's attempts to convert him to Christianity by assuring him, in a threatening tone, that if the white men hang him, all the blacks of his tribe and the inland tribes will descend on Sydney and burn it to the ground.

When Threlkeld persists in proselytising, Mickey declares that the Supreme Being of the blacks is much more powerful than that of the whites, and, if he is executed, will put out the eyes of all the whites, blinding them.

On the morning of his execution, as Mickey's leg irons are removed, and during the long walk to the gallows, the missionary is by his side, reciting Bible passages to him. Mickey climbs the scaffold, heaves a deep sigh and is launched into an eternity he perhaps hopes is mercifully free of nagging Christian clergy.

'Hitherto, the blacks under confinement had not been permitted to be present at the executions, in consequence of a general order respecting all prisoners in the gaol to that effect,' Threlkeld writes in his annual report for 1835, 'but, at my suggestion, the Aborigines under confinement were allowed to behold the sentence carried into effect. Their pale visages, their trembling muscles, indicated the nervous excitement under which they laboured at the melancholy sight. Some, who were about to be brought to trial, urged me to speak for them to the judge, and all requested that I would ask the jailer not to hang them during my absence. Previously to this, it was a matter of joke amongst the blacks, their being sent to any jail.'[3]

On deaths from natural causes, he writes: 'During the present year the measles have been very prevalent amongst the Aborigines, and have carried off many of the natives, from whom Mrs Threlkeld and our nine children caught the complaint, and were laid up at one time. Providentially, the disease has now subsided.'[4]

Threlkeld reports that the previous August he had ministered to a man the whites called Charley, sentenced to be hanged for the murder of an Englishman in the Hunter Valley village of Upper William (now Dungog), in Wonnarua country.

Charley had admitted his guilt but pleaded justification on cultural grounds. He told the court that 'a talisman, named mura-mai, was taken from him by the Englishman, who with others were keeping a black woman amongst them, was pulled to pieces by him, and shown to the black woman, which, according to their superstitious notions, subjects all the parties to the punishment of death; and further, that he was deputed with others, by his tribe, to enforce the penalty, which he too faithfully performed.

'From him no murmur arose, no threat of vengeance escaped his lips, but only an expression of sorrow that he had listened to his tribe, and of lamentation that he knew no better, his tribe had deceived him. When urged to believe in, and pray to the Lord Jesus Christ, he asked how was he to address Him. On being taught what we deemed suitable prayers, in his own tongue, he repeated them; and subsequently, when asked, if he had prayed in the night, his reply was that he had asked Jesus to cast away all his evil deeds, and to receive his spirit when the whites kill his body.'[5]

On the morning of his execution, Charley asked Threlkeld, 'When I am dead, shall I make good houses and be like the whites in the other world?'[6]

Threlkeld's reply is unknown. It's not in his report.

Chapter 12

Courage and caprice

It is often necessary when arriving at a frontier settlement to ask the name of the place. There will seldom be a signpost, and even if there is, the name on the sign might not be what the locals actually call the place. Such is the case when Denny Day, after crossing the Liverpool Range by the Great North Road, arrives at where he is to take up his new posting as police magistrate for the Invermein, Merton and Muscle Brook district, 270 kilometres north of Sydney, on the borders of Wonnarua and Kamilaroi lands.

Henry Dangar had surveyed the area back in 1824 but did not name it. Under attack by Wonnarua warriors, he was too busily involved in beating a hasty retreat.

A year later, the first settler granted land in the district named his property Invermein, after which the district was named. At about the same time, a settlement sprung up nearby, then another and another. So now, depending on who you ask, you've just arrived at Invermein, Kindon Ponds, Redbank or St Aubins.

And to compound the confusion, the settlement has recently been gazetted as Scone, after the ancient seat of the Scottish kings, but the new name is slow to catch on.

Invermein, while officially the head town of the district, is little more than a few houses, an inn and a store. Muscle Brook, 26 kilometres to the south, is a more suitable base – centrally located with an existing courthouse and plans for a Mounted Police barracks. It's here the Days hope to make their home, but there is no suitable accommodation, so for the next 12 months Denny Day will occupy a hut at Muscle Brook while his family remains almost 100 kilometres away at Maitland.

And it's here at Muscle Brook that Day himself plays the frontier name game. The township, near where the Goulburn River meets Hunter's River, was so named after the discovery of shellfish in a local stream. But its name is altered forever when Denny Day, in an official letter, changes the spelling from Muscle Brook to Muswell Brook, later contracted to Muswellbrook.

The reasons are unclear, but it's known that Amelia, the wife of Sir Francis Forbes, a local landholder and recently retired chief justice, was born in Muswell Hill, London. Forbes, celebrated for his integrity and humanity on the bench, has become a close friend and confidante of Denny Day, and it's possible that one night, over port and cigars, they hatched the idea as a private joke.

Merton, a 6000-acre estate of lush river flats and forest, is the home of William Ogilvie, a wealthy settler and justice of the peace who, unlike most of his ilk, earns Day's respect. Ogilvie, a former Royal Navy officer, is known for his close relations with the Wonnarua. He deals with them fairly, speaks their language and has won their trust and affection.

William's wife Mary is one of two women of the district who have become living legends – one for her courage, the other for her eccentricity.

In his book *Two Years in New South Wales*, Peter Cunningham, a former navy surgeon who served with William Ogilvie, and later a neighbour of the Ogilvies, describes an incident at Merton in 1826, during a period of violent clashes between blacks and settlers on Hunter's River. Cunningham writes:

The natives around Merton, the residence of Lieutenant Ogilvie, R. N., had remained all along on the most friendly terms with his establishment, but during his absence were provoked into hostility by a party of soldiers and constables who had wantonly maltreated them.

Mrs Ogilvie was at home, surrounded by her young family and domestic servants, when the loud and threatening yells of a body of savages, who had surrounded her dwelling, suddenly aroused her attention, and made her summon all her energies to meet the impending catastrophe. They had seized on two constables within a few yards of the door, whom they were shaking by the collars, and reproaching in the most bitter terms their slight knowledge of English would admit of, preparatory to beating their brains out with their waddies, when Mrs Ogilvie, rushing fearlessly in among the brandished clubs and poised spears, by the firmness and persuasiveness of her manner, awed and soothed them into sentiments of mercy, and in half an hour they parted with all the members of the establishment upon the most cordial terms.[1]

The other Invermein woman to win a place in folklore is the mysterious Madame Ramus, the mistress of settler Thomas Potter Macqueen, whose 20,000-acre 'Segenhoe' estate was the largest and grandest in the territory.

Macqueen, a former British army colonel with more money than sense, had a vision of transforming his land grant into a reasonable facsimile of an English country manor, with parkland, manicured gardens, stores and even a hospital, and with himself as the benevolent squire, lording it over a compliant peasantry. To this end, he sponsored the immigration of the families of 160 convicts, intended to be his servants, artisans, stockmen, shepherds and tenant farmers on Segenhoe, along with shiploads of sheep, horses, stud and dairy cattle, and farm machinery. And to defend his fiefdom against bushrangers and blacks he hired a private army, equipped with the latest armaments and kitted out in flashy uniforms.

Macqueen was no radical. He shared the prevailing view among the colonial elite that the status quo of the old world must be maintained in the new. As *The Sydney Herald* put it:

> Any man, whether an emancipated convict or free migrant, who drinks, smokes and eats with his convict servants, will at last also rob with them. Therefore, from all such persons' convict servants should be immediately withdrawn, for it is impossible to preserve discipline, even the distinction between vice and virtue, master and servant, free man and convict, where such familiarity exists.[2]

In his book *Australia As She Is and As She May Be*, Macqueen opined that convicts should only be assigned to settlers with enough land and wealth to remain 'wholly above the society of such convicts'.[3]

The squire of Segenhoe's Antipodean Versailles couldn't last, and it didn't. Although Thomas Macqueen was careless to a fault with money, his extravagant habits were frugal when compared with those of his mistress. Keeping the fragrant Madame Ramus in the manner in which she was determined to become accustomed meant a townhouse in Sydney, an endless supply of the latest fashions from London and Paris, and, each day at Segenhoe, a massive Italian marble bathtub filled with warm milk for her morning bath.

To meet Madame Ramus's demand for milk baths, convict farmhands would rise before dawn each day to milk specially selected cows, heat the milk and fill the bathtub. Afterwards, courtesy of Madame's munificence, the milk would be distributed among the estate's convict workers. It might have had a peculiar flavour, but at least it was pasteurised.

By the time Denny Day arrives at Invermein, Macqueen's grand dream, like his mistress' milk, has gone sour. Mired in debt, he is reduced to selling stock and equipment, and will soon be forced to sell Segenhoe itself. Day doesn't get to meet the madcap Madame Ramus. When Macqueen's fortunes began to fade she ran off to Sydney with the surgeon at Segenhoe's hospital, Dr Thomas Hollingsworth Fowler. It seems that Madame and the doctor knew each other back in Van Diemen's Land, when she was plain Mary Ann Maria Ramus, the widow of Lieutenant Henry Ramus of the 30th Regiment of Foot, who died in the Azores during the Portuguese Civil War.

Thomas Fowler and Mary Ann marry in Sydney in December 1837 and return to Van Diemen's Land, where they buy a large farm near Hobart. Five years later, they are forced to sell the farm, apparently unable to pay the mortgage. It can only be guessed as to whether or not Mary Ann's wasteful ways contributed to their ruin.

Denny Day, in spite of his reputation for rectitude, could be intolerant and even cruel when the mood took him, as illustrated in this letter to the editor of *The Australian* from an anonymous settler:

'The inhabitants of Patrick's Plains had last week the benefit of Mr Day's assistance on the bench. A servant of a gentleman, one of those out and out dreadnought youngsters who had allowed his hair to grow over his countenance, as if he had intended passing himself off as one of the other sex. Mr Day suggested to his brother magistrate on the bench that such a fancy was unbecoming the man's situation, and he was ordered down and underwent the necessary hairdressing by the flogger before the case was gotten into.

'The same man very properly received a sentence of 50 lashes for giving an improper answer to the court. Such is as it should be, but such will never be in some of our police courts.'[4]

Chapter 13

The other Waterloo

In his 1837 report on 'Outrages by Aborigines on the Namoi, Gwydir and Big Rivers' Alexander Paterson, Commissioner of Crown Lands for the Liverpool Plains, writes:

> On my route I heard of many outrages committed by the natives on stock at a number of the stations, and also of their having murdered five men, and I made it my business to make every inquiry to find out the cause of this increasing evil.
>
> On the Namoi River, the stations are more or less subject to their depredations, and at Loder's [station] the blacks are so numerous and daring that the men have all quitted the station from fear. The whole of this country is of the richest description. If it were better watered, it would be the finest grazing land in the world. The black boy who traced them says there are three white men with them painted like the blacks.[1]

It is December 1837, and the commandant of the Mounted Police, Major James Nunn, has been called to Government House in

Sydney on urgent business. The colonial authorities have received word from the north-west that at least a thousand Kamilaroi are gathered on the Liverpool Plains, preparing to wage war on the settlers. The camp fires of the warriors are so numerous they light the hills at night, with more than 250 fires counted in one camp alone. White men have been killed on the Namoi River and the Big River, and a bloodbath seems imminent.

The colony is between governors at the time – Sir Richard Bourke's term had ended and Sir George Gipps has not yet arrived – so Nunn is briefed by the acting governor and former Mounted Police commander, Colonel Kenneth Snodgrass.

Snodgrass, a 53-year-old Scotsman with kind eyes set in a well-fed face, is, like Denny Day, the son of a clergyman, with aristocracy on his mother's side. Unlike Day, he is a war hero honoured by Wellington himself, with a string of medals across his chest – one of which, along with a golden sword, was awarded to him for leading the siege of San Sebastian, Spain, in 1813. Snodgrass, in storming the heights of the fortress, lost a third of his 600 troops in hand-to-hand fighting with the French, but took the citadel. Twice wounded in action, he is greatly admired by military men such as Major Nunn, but among civilians his reputation since coming to Australia has been mired by allegations of corruption. It's rumoured that he has enriched himself by dipping too deeply and too often into the government coffers – a rumour later proved to be true. And he is said to be obstinate and erratic – the latter trait attributed to a severe head wound sustained during the siege of San Sebastian. Snodgrass is also a landowner, with a sizeable estate on Hunter's River.

Brevet Major James Winniett Nunn, of the 80th Regiment of Foot, is a striking figure in his dress uniform of dark blue with gold epaulets, red and gold sash and high collar, with a tall shako topped by an even taller plume of green feathers above a thin, pointy face with a neat moustache and sideburns. Nunn, a 47-year-old Englishman, has been in Australia barely three months. Like Snodgrass, he is a veteran of the Napoleonic Wars, having served in the failed campaign to capture Alexandria, in Egypt, from Bonaparte's Turkish allies, and the successful capture of Genoa from the French in 1814.

Colonel Snodgrass orders Nunn to set out for the north-west territory with all the troopers he can muster. According to what Nunn later tells Denny Day in a sworn deposition, the colonel's orders are: 'You must lose no time in proceeding. You are to act according to your own judgement, and use your utmost exertion to suppress these outrages. There are a thousand blacks there, and, if they are not stopped, we may have them presently within the boundaries.'[2]

Nunn will also claim he was told only swords could be used to capture the blacks, and that he ordered his men not to use fire-arms unless in self-defence.

A few days before Christmas, Nunn's force of 23 Mounted Police set out from Jerry's Plains, in the Hunter River valley, to take the fight to the Kamilaroi. A month later, at about noon on Friday 26 January 1838, the troopers are riding through thick scrub near Waterloo Creek (now Mille Creek, 50 kilometres south-west of the town of Moree), a branch of the Big River, when they spot smoke from the fires of a Kamilaroi camp. Corporal Patrick Hannan and Sergeant John Lee are scouting ahead of the troop when a warrior appears from nowhere and spears Hannan in the leg. The warrior is preparing to hurl another spear when he is shot down by Sergeant John Lee. As more and more warriors spring forward to confront the riders, Hannan, breaking the spear and pulling the shaft from his leg, spurs his horse to the rear of the troop, yelling that they are under attack.

Nunn, who is riding at the rear, orders his men to charge the ranks of warriors. It is guns, not swords, versus spears and boomerangs, as the troopers blaze away. Later, some will justify it as self-defence, others will blame the fog of war. Their commander will assert that in the rugged terrain it was impossible to maintain discipline. The riders scatter among the trees as fighting spreads over a wide area, and, when the smoke clears the blacks have retreated and a number of them lie dead.

The size of that number depends on who is asked. Nunn claims it was no more than five. Some among the troopers reckon it to be seven or eight. Sergeant Lee estimates it to be between 40 and 50, while others put the number of Kamilaroi dead at from 100 to 300.

What history will call Major Nunn's Campaign or the Waterloo Creek Massacre is the cause of much disquiet among the colony's overlords in London. In April, hoping to put the affair to bed, the new governor, Sir George Gipps, writes to the British Colonial Secretary, Lord Glenelg, assuring him that 'the measures which I have thought it right to adopt, in consequence of the late unfortunate collision between a party of Mounted Police and a party of the native blacks' would include giving the authorities 'beyond the boundaries of location' (that is, outside the legal limits of settlement) responsibility for the protection of Aborigines.

'Your Lordship must be, I am sure, aware that these matters are calculated to produce a considerable sensation in the colony, and that therefore much management is required in the treatment of them,' he writes. 'In the Executive Council, an apprehension arose of the mischief that might ensue if any offence were given to the officers and men of the Mounted Police.

'Major Nunn has stated to me that he thinks the natives he fell in with must have consisted of not far short of 1,000 persons, including women and children; that they consisted of tribes but little accustomed to intercourse with white men; and that they are particularly dextrous with their spears as well as a peculiar instrument called a boomering [sic] which they hurl with great effect. Your Lordship will observe that Major Nunn does not state in his report the number of men that were killed, but I should think they were less than ten or 12, beside a number wounded. I lament to say that we have since heard of some outrages, which have the appearance of being retaliatory on the part of the blacks.'[3]

The new governor, Sir George Gipps, another vicar's son, born in Kent and formerly a major in the Royal Engineers, is a veteran of the Peninsula Wars. After joining the Colonial Service in 1824 he served in the West Indies and Canada before being appointed governor of New South Wales.

Tall, clean shaven, with fierce, bushy eyebrows cantilevered over dark eyes, some consider him haughty, but beneath a defensive veneer of arrogance is a rather shy man, quietly determined to make his mark but not at the cost of his integrity. Denny Day will come to like him. The frontier settlers will not.

That same month, a party of 18 drovers working for Hunter Valley settlers William and George Faithfull are pushing sheep and cattle south in search of new grazing grounds in what is now north-eastern Victoria, when they are set upon by Aboriginal warriors. In what will be known as the Battle of Broken River, or the FaithfullMassacre, the ensuing fight leaves between seven and 13 of the white men dead. Only one black man dies in the battle.

While details of the battle are sketchy, some accounts claim the whites, although well armed, were hopelessly outnumbered by up to 200 warriors intent on raiding their stock. Others claim the blacks numbered no more than 20 and that the attack was in revenge for murders of blacks by whites or was sparked by the Faithfulls' men shooting at the blacks. What is known is that the white men were overtaken and speared as they fled and that the bodies were scattered for several miles.

Settlers' reprisals are swift and bloody, and cost an estimated 100 Aboriginal lives. As well as leading punitive raids on Aboriginal camps, some settlers take hostages, as George Faithfull later boasts in an 1853 letter to Victoria's governor Charles La Trobe:

'At last, it so happened that I was the means of putting an end to this warfare. Riding with two of my stockmen one day quietly along the banks of the river, we were all at once met by some hundreds of painted warriors with the most dreadful yells I had ever heard. Had they sprung from the regions below we could have hardly been more taken by surprise.

'Our first impulse was to retreat, but we found the narrow way blocked up by the natives two and three deep, and we were at once saluted with a shower of spears. My horse bounded and fell into an immense hole. A spear just then passed over the pommel of my saddle. This was the signal for a general onset. The natives rushed on us like furies, with shouts and savage yells. It was no time for delay. I ordered my men to take deliberate aim and to fire only with certainty of destruction to the individual aimed at.

'Unfortunately, the first shot from one of my men's carbines did not take effect. In a moment we were surrounded on all sides by the savages boldly coming up to us. It was my time to repel them. I fired my double-barrel right and left, and two of the most forward fell. This stopped the impetuosity of their career. I had time to reload, and the war thus begun continued from about 10 o'clock in the morning until four in the afternoon. We were slow to fire, which prolonged the battle, and 60 rounds were fired, and I trust and believe that many of the bravest of the savage warriors bit the dust.

'It was remarkable that the children, and many of the women likewise, had so little fear that they boldly ran forward, even under our horses' legs, picked up the spears and carried them back to the warrior men.

'The fight I have described gave them a notion of what sort of stuff the white man was made, and my name was a terror to them ever after,' Faithfull writes. 'I picked up a boy from under a log, took him home and tamed him, and he became very useful to me, and I think was the means of deterring his tribe from committing further wanton depredations upon my property. My neighbours, however, suffered much long after this.'[4]

Faithfull concludes his letter with an assertion that official policy has backfired.

'The government during all this time gave no help, no assistance of any kind, and at last threatened to hang anyone who dared to shoot a black, even in protection of his property,' he writes. 'This, instead of doing good, did much evil. People formed themselves into bands of alliance and allegiance to each other, and then it was the destruction of the natives really did take place.'[5]

Governor Gipps is clearly shaken by the attack on the Faithfull brothers' men at Broken River. In response, he more than doubles the numbers of Mounted Police patrolling the territory, ordered military posts to be established along the road to Port Phillip, and for infantry to advance into the interior if needed.

He is also able to report to Whitehall that he has ordered an investigation into the incident at Waterloo Creek, and that the man he has trusted to get to the truth of the matter is the police magistrate at Invermein, Denny Day.

But Day's investigation of Nunn's campaign will have to wait. Governor Gipps writes to Lord Glenelg, explaining why the promised inquiry has been indefinitely postponed. 'I lament now to have to state to your Lordship that, in consequence of similar outrages, the calls for the services of the mounted police have been so constant that I have not been able to spare the men who would have been required as witnesses in the proposed investigation at Invermein; also that, under the advice of the Executive Council, I have refrained from issuing the proposed notice, on account of the degree to which the public mind continues to be exasperated against the blacks.'[6]

A new allegation of mass murder demands Day's urgent attention. It happened not far from Waterloo Creek, on another branch of the Big River, at Myall Creek.

Chapter 14

The bare bones

It is the morning of Sunday 10 June 1838, and there's a chill in the air. The people camped at Myall Creek station – Wirrayaraay people of the Kamilaroi nation – were invited there about three weeks earlier by convict stockman Charlie Kilmeister, and in that time they have been getting along exceptionally well with the whites at the station. Hutkeeper George Anderson, in particular, seems very fond of the children. Unlike the station overseer William Hobbs, who treats the territory's old custodians with respect and understanding, the stockmen under his charge use the women as servants and sex slaves.

A rider approaches. It's Tom Foster, the superintendent at nearby Newton's station, come to ask if any of the Wirrayaraay men are interested in a day's work cutting bark at Newton's. Ten men accept the offer and leave with Foster.

For those remaining at Myall Creek, mostly elderly people, women and children, the rest of the day is uneventful and, apart from the shouts and laughter of children playing, is quieter than usual. The overseer, William Hobbs, and stockman Andrew Burrowes are away with cattle, leaving Kilmeister and Anderson the only hands at the station. Consequently, little or no work has been done today.

Then, about four o'clock in the afternoon, in misty rain, the thunder of hoofs shatters the peace and 11 horsemen gallop up to the station huts. They are bearing muskets and pistols, and brandishing swords.

At once, there is a menacing air to add to the chill, but the Wirrayaraay, gathered around cooking fires, do not anticipate trouble. They have not been involved in any conflict with the whites, and many of them have struck up friendships with settlers on the Big River. So only the most agile – including two boys of about eight or nine – manage to escape into the bush when the riders surround them and train their guns on them.

John Henry Fleming's men are not hardened criminals brutalised by the lash and the iron gang. Only men convicted of minor crimes and reported to be of good behaviour are trusted to work on frontier stations as mounted and armed stockmen, with only token supervision and little or no contact with their masters.

And yet, this is what they do:

Herding the people like cattle, they drive them into a hut, where one of the riders, John Russell, tethers them in a line with a long rope while others bind their hands. That done, as old men yell in defiance and weeping mothers try to calm their terrified children, they are led by the rope towards a stockade some 800 metres away. Kilmeister doesn't wait to be asked – he joins in enthusiastically.

George Anderson has worked at the station for only about five months, and the others do not know him well enough to trust him to keep his mouth shut. As the people are led off, he is told to stay behind and mind his own business. Fifteen minutes later, he hears a shot, then another, coming from the direction of the stockyard.

At the stockyard, the leader of the horsemen, John Henry Fleming, fired the first shot, unleashing an orgy of shooting, slashing and hacking that leaves at least 28 defenceless men, women and children lying dead. The youngest is a boy aged about three. It will be his tiny rib bone, gathered as forensic evidence by Denny Day, that will change history.

While the butchery continues, the moon rises. All the victims are beheaded, some while standing frozen with fear or running in frantic circles, others where they fall, and one, an elderly man known as 'Daddy' (his actual name is unknown), is singled out for special treatment.

The white-haired old patriarch is distinctive for his size – he is said to be the biggest man, black or white, thereabouts – and is much admired for his gentle nature. With age taking its toll, he seldom joins the hunt these days, and is with the women and children camped near the station huts. Daddy is thrown onto the fire and burnt alive.

Only one is spared, a woman John Blake has selected for carnal comforts. Over the next day or so – until he tires of her or she manages to escape – she will be raped repeatedly by Blake and by others.

That evening, after the killers have gone, the ten men working at Newton's return to Myall Creek to find a scene of horror awaiting them. George Anderson, who managed to hide a boy in his hut, saving him from certain death, warns the men that the riders are likely to return. Taking with them two women and three boys who managed to evade capture, the men hurry off to get as far away from Myall Creek station as possible.

As Anderson predicted, the riders return on Monday and spend the night in his hut, drinking and boasting of the previous day's deeds like warriors recounting tales of valour.

When Anderson tells Kilmeister he intends to report the matter, Kilmeister begs him not to. Anderson does not reply.

The next morning, leaving Edward Foley to keep an eye on Anderson and guard the weapons, the killers return to the stock-yard where they build a large fire, gather the butchered remains of their victims, which they throw in a heap onto the fire, then, using tree branches, brush over the murder site to cover the blood in the dirt. Watching from the hut, Anderson sees smoke rise from the basalt ridge above the stockyard.

Satisfied that their hurried and half-hearted attempt to destroy the evidence is good enough, since no one is likely to investigate anyway, or to care, they saddle up and ride off to Newton's run, hoping to track down the blacks who had gone there with Tom Foster on Sunday to work. Foster tells them the men have long gone, and that he has no idea where they were headed. When he asks the riders why they want to find the men, Kilmeister tells him they had stampeded cattle. Foster knows that is a lie but holds his peace.

On Friday, the same day the murderers disperse, station over-seer William Hobbs returns to Myall Creek where Anderson tells him of the atrocity, and Kilmeister swears he took no part in it. Hobbs is inclined to believe Kilmeister's lies, but will later change his mind.

When Hobbs is led to the massacre site by Davey, a young Aboriginal station hand who witnessed the slaughter, he finds the remains only partially destroyed and being mauled by dogs. The stench makes him physically ill.

Horrified after inspecting the massacre site, Hobbs decides the crime must be reported to the authorities and to his employer, Henry Dangar. When Hobbs insists, for unspecified reasons, that he cannot leave the station at present, the task of reporting the incident falls to a neighbouring cattleman, Fred Foote.

Equally appalled by the scene of slaughter, Foote volunteers to deliver letters from Hobbs to Henry Dangar and to the police magistrate at Invermein, Denny Day.

An unsubstantiated version of events leading up to the massacre claims that John Henry's vigilantes, having vowed to get rid of the blacks once and for all, began their rampage about eight days earlier, by driving every Aborigine they could find into a dry creek bed beneath a sheer cliff. What happened there gave the water-course its name – Slaughterhouse Creek.

The gang then set off in pursuit of some warriors who had managed to escape, but after chasing them to the Big River, through the ranges and onto the plains, lost their quarry and gave up, frustrated and angry. It was then, while calling in at stations in the district, urging stockmen to join them in their campaign of extermination, they learned that a group of peaceful blacks were camped in their traditional country on Myall Creek station.

This version of events contradicts the generally held belief that if further atrocities were committed by the gang, they occurred after the massacre rather than before. It's worth noting, too, that

Slaughterhouse Creek was so named long before the Myall Creek massacre, most likely because it was once the site of an abattoir.

Those are the bare bones of what happened on Dangar's run. Much more will be revealed by Denny Day's investigation – to the extreme discomfort of the colony, and to the dismay of the wider world.

Chapter 15

The unlikely event

The bearer of bad news, Fred Foote spurs his horse through the gates of Neotsfield, Henry Dangar's grand Regency homestead at Patrick's Plains. Foote, who has a cattle run not far from Dangar's Myall Creek station, is carrying a letter to Dangar from William Hobbs, the overseer at Dangar's run.

Dangar, a 42-year-old Cornishman, arrived in the colony 17 years earlier and made his name and his fortune as a surveyor and explorer. He was the first European to explore and map the country north of the Hawkesbury, sparking a frantic land grab which greatly benefited Dangar himself and led to his being sacked as government surveyor for misappropriation of land.

Disgraced but not disheartened, Dangar turned his energies to increasing his herds of cattle and flocks of sheep, and land on which to run them. His first attempt to find grazing land on the Liverpool Plains failed. While crossing the ranges in 1824, his party was attacked by blacks and forced to retreat. Since then, however, Dangar has acquired a string of grazing leases along the

Big River, including a run at Pond Creek and further upriver at Myall Creek.

William Hobbs, a 26-year-old freeman from Somerset, has been employed by Dangar at various runs for about two years, and Dangar has apparently judged him sufficiently trustworthy to oversee his new cattle station at Myall Creek. Working under Hobbs' supervision at Myall Creek are four of Henry Dangar's assigned convicts, all men in their twenties, hand-picked by Hobbs. They are hutkeeper George Anderson, a 24-year-old Londoner, serving a life sentence for robbing his master, and stockmen Charlie Kilmeister, 23, from Bristol, also serving a life sentence, for burglary, and Andrew Burrowes, a 25-year-old Irishman from Sligo, transported for life for highway robbery. Also working on the station is stockman Charles Reid, a 'ticket-of-leave' (paroled) convict serving seven years, and two Aboriginal brothers, Yintayintin, 18, and Kwimunga, 14, known to the whites as Davey and Billy.

Hobbs and his men have built three huts on the run – one for Hobbs himself, one for the men and another for a store – a stock-yard and a fenced paddock, and have dug a well.

To prevent overgrazing, stock is regularly moved between the Myall Creek and Pond Creek stations. At such times, Hobbs' men are on their honour. It's essential that while he, Burrowes and Reid are away with cattle, Kilmeister and Anderson can be trusted to tend the remaining stock and take care of the property and stores. Apparently, his trust was misplaced.

The contents of Hobbs' letter to Dangar are not known. It can only be assumed it provides a broad outline of events; that the overseer returned to Myall Creek after a cattle drive to learn that in his absence a band of men rode in and killed a number of Aboriginal men, women and children.

However, Hobbs also wrote to the police magistrate at Invermein, Denny Day, and that letter has survived. It reads:

I beg to acquaint you that about a month since I had occasion to leave Mr Dangar's station on the Big River for a few days. On my return I saw near the hut the remains of about thirty blacks, principally women and children. I recognised them as part of a tribe that had been at the station for some time and who had since they first came conducted themselves in a quiet and proper manner. On making enquiry I was informed that a party of white men had come to the station who after securing them had taken them a short distance from my hut and destroyed nearly the whole of them. I should have given information earlier but circumstances having prevented my sooner coming down the country.[1]

Fred Foote tells Henry Dangar he intends to report the matter to Denny Day, and rides off for Invermein. But when he arrives there to find Day away on business, he takes it upon himself to ride to Sydney and report the matter in person to the governor.

Still, there is no reason for Dangar to suppose anything will come of it. After all, Dangar might well reason that such things have happened before and will probably continue to happen until the problem of the blacks has been settled once and for all. There will be the usual tut-tutting from Government House and Whitehall, no doubt, but any investigation – in the unlikely event that there will be an investigation – will, as always, turn up nothing. Ranks will close and lips will be sealed.

For a while, that assumption seems correct. But then, word reaches Neotsfield that Governor Gipps has ordered an investigation, and that the Invermein police magistrate, with a troop of

Mounted Police, has trekked 300 kilometres to the scene of the crime and is gathering evidence.

Two days before the massacre, on Friday 8 June 1838, a group of colonial notables, led by prominent landowners and parliamentarians Sir John Jamison and John Blaxland, met in Sydney to draft a petition to Governor Gipps. Signed by no less than 82 'Colonists, Landholders and Proprietors of Stock', including celebrated explorers Hamilton Hume and William Hovel, and Philip Gidley King, grandson of the former governor of that name, the 'Memorial' expressed grave concerns for the survival of the new settlement at Port Phillip in the southern part of the colony. There, the 'hostility of the aborigines' had forced many settlers to 'abandon their stations, leaving, in some cases, their flocks and herds at the mercy of the hostile tribes'.

Alarmed by news of the Battle of Broken River, a battle the blacks won, the petitioners claimed to be unaware of 'any aggression on the part of Her Majesty's white subjects which could have excited the blacks to commit the excesses and barbarities, of fresh instances of which almost every post brings the account, but believe that the natives, unrestrained by moral principles, and placing little or no value on human life, have been stimulated by their natural cupidity and ferocity in perpetrating the outrages of which they have lately been guilty'.

The time had come, said the petitioners, for 'coercive measures' against the 'outrages' of the blacks. 'It is only when they have become experimentally acquainted with our power and determination to punish their aggressions that they have become orderly, peaceable, and brought within the reach of civilisation.'

If the government would not take action to protect the settlers, they warned, 'the settlers will undoubtedly take measures to protect themselves, as it is not to be supposed they will remain quietly looking on whilst their property is being destroyed and their servants murdered, and your memorialists need hardly observe that such a mode of proceeding would inevitably be attended with consequences of the most painful nature'.[2]

A deputation of these self-described 'pioneers of civilisation' presented their petition to the governor. Two of the signatories, Robert Lethbridge and William Sims Bell, were the masters of convict stockmen William Hawkins and George Palliser, who were involved in the atrocity at Myall Creek.

In a letter of reply to the first signatory of the petition, Philip Gidley King, Sydney Colonial Office official Edward Deas Thomson, on behalf of the governor, assured the petitioners that His Excellence shared their concerns, and was determined to take immediate steps to 'repress and prevent such aggressions on the part of the Aborigines'.

Thomson added, 'I am, however, directed to acquaint you that there is nothing in the Governor's instructions to prevent his protecting to the utmost of his power the property of settlers in every part of this territory, and that this His Excellency is determined to do. Sir George Gipps, moreover, readily allows that after having taken entire possession of the country without any reference to the rights of the Aborigines, it is now too late for the Government to refuse protection to persons, who have come hither, and brought with them their flocks and herds on its own invitation, though it must be evident that every wanderer in search of pasturage cannot be attended by a military force.'[3]

Thomson's letter is dated 23 June, ten days before the governor received Fred Foote's report and subsequently informed the

Colonial Secretary that 'in consequence of a horse having been speared at Mr H. Dangar's station, a party of white men had assembled for the purpose of attacking the blacks; that they had taken 22 of them, including many women and children, and put them all to death. No official account has as yet been received of this atrocious deed, but a magistrate with a party of mounted police has been despatched in pursuit of the perpetrators of it. The scene of this atrocity is supposed to be not less than 200 miles to the north of Sydney.'[4]

The press is yet to take more than a passing interest in gruesome events on the Big River, distracted as it is by gala events in London. It is only a few sleeps now until the new Queen's coronation, and the British world is as giddy as a baby on a swing.

'The coronation of Queen Victoria may be expected to be one of the most brilliant events that has taken place in Europe for the last century,' gushes *The Hobart Town Courier*, before dishing the royal dirt.

'Reports have long been in circulation of a very delicate and interesting nature respecting an attachment formed by the most exalted lady in the realm for a nobleman of northern descent who, having been appointed to a distant colonial government, was recalled from his banishment by one of the first acts of the present reign.

'As the announced recall of Lord Elphinstone from Madras has occasioned, even in quarters which ought to be informed, a renewal of an absurd rumour which was industriously circulated at the time of the accession of our present Sovereign, we think it right to notice what otherwise we should have thought too contemptible to call for observation. It was hinted then, as it is now, that the Queen had required the recall of Lord Elphinstone from his distant government not on public grounds but for reasons connected with her own personal happiness. That a maiden Queen, just 18 years of age, should in the first days of her accession overstep at once the limits of female delicacy for which she was known to be remarkable, was so contrary to all reason and probability that we disdain to refute the ridiculous rumour.'[5] Rumours that John, Lord Elphinstone, had been Victoria's lover before her marriage to Prince Albert would persist into the twenty-first century.

Chapter 16

Cometh the man

Two riders rein in by the banks of Myall Creek. Despite recent rains, after a year of drought it is almost dry. Even the Big River itself is barely a trickle linking a string of ponds.

The riders are Denny Day and Lieutenant George Pack of the Mounted Police. It's late afternoon, they're bone weary, and Pack's blue jacket and scarlet sash are as dusty brown as Day's coat and hessian boots.

A month earlier, acting on information from Fred Foote, Day made preliminary inquiries on his own initiative, since the station was out of his police district, in territory effectively beyond the reach of the law. He could easily have done nothing, which is exactly what many in his place would have done. On 3 July, he reported his findings to Governor Gipps, and set off for the Big River with Lieutenant Pack and eight troopers, under orders to 'institute a strict inquiry into the circumstances and all parties concerned in it or suspected of being so'.[1]

As the posse rode out from Invermein, past the Burning Mountain (then thought to be a volcano but in fact the world's oldest burning coal seam), and on to the Liverpool Plains, they followed a stock route mapped a decade earlier by the explorer Allan Cunningham, who set out from Invermein with six companions and 11 packhorses to find an overland route to what is now Queensland. On the way, he crossed the Big River at Myall Creek before continuing north.

This was challenging country, a landscape not just of wide, grassy plains but of rolling hills, plateaus, mountain ranges, rivers and creeks, escarpments and steep uplands that rise suddenly from the plains. In such country, a man was only as good as his horse, and Denny Day could be confident that his mount and those of his posse – Australian-bred horses called Walers – could make it to Myall Creek in five days at the most.

It was as an infantry officer in India that Day first made the acquaintance of the Waler, so called because they were originally bred in New South Wales from Arab, Cape, Clydesdale and thoroughbred horses and Timor ponies. Highly favoured by the British army in India for their stamina, speed, courage, intelligence and temperament, Walers imported from Australia were the perfect mount for extremes of climate and rugged conditions.

The mount of a cavalryman or infantry officer in India needed to be 15 to 16 hands (152 to 163 centimetres) high, and be able to carry a rider and equipment with a combined weight of up to 110 kilograms with little effort, for days at a time. Walers could make a steady ten to 12 kilometres an hour from dawn to dusk, shod or unshod, at a fast walk or a canter, with little food or water, and even in the harshest conditions could travel 60 kilometres a day for hundreds of kilometres.

In Australia, they were prized by the military, explorers, stock-men and bushrangers. And for a lawman in pursuit of criminals on the Australian frontier, there was no horse better suited for the purpose.

Although the posse carried adequate provisions, Day planned for the men to stay overnight at stations along the way rather than make camp. It being mid-winter, temperatures on the plains dropped to below freezing at night, and unlike, say, the Vale of Clwydd or Wallis Plains, there were no inns along the road offering warmth and comfort to weary wayfarers.

On reaching the Big River, the posse called in at Fred Foote's outstation, 'Piedmont'. From Foote's, they rode on to Newton's station, some 23 kilometres from Dangar's Myall Creek run, arriving there on Saturday 28 July.

Newton's, owned by former army surgeon Doctor William Newton, being the largest and best-equipped station in the district, was ideally suited for a base of operations. There, Day immediately set to work, interrogating Newton's overseer, Tom Foster, and two station hands, Bates and Murphy. Fred Foote had told Day that Foster was ready to talk, and Foote was right. The overseer didn't hold back.

That afternoon, Day and Pack rode to Dangar's Myall Creek station, where the stench of death still lingered.

It's hard to believe the devil stalked these pretty hills. Birds are chattering in the branches overhanging the creek bed, rehearsing their evening calls as if all is as it should be. And indeed, as the riders glance about, all does seem as it should be. That is, until they dismount and walk across to the stockyard.

There, moving about steadily and methodically, Denny Day and George Pack find grisly evidence of hasty attempts to burn and scatter butchered human bodies. Spread about are more than 20 charred human heads, teeth and fragments of bone, and, almost hidden in the yellow grass just outside the yard, the rib of a child. Day picks it up, carefully wraps it in cloth and stows it in his saddlebag. One day, it will prove invaluable.

Returning to Newton's, Day continues his investigation, sending troopers out to round up suspects from the stations thereabouts, and often riding with them, a notebook and pencil in his pocket and a brace of pistols in his belt.

Tom Foster and others have provided able evidence for him to arrest Charlie Kilmeister, Dangar's stockman, who is the first occupant of a makeshift jail in a station shed. Witness statements are taken from Dangar's overseer William Hobbs, and from his hutkeeper George Anderson.

In a scour of the countryside on Tuesday 31 July, stockmen William Hawkins, from Andrew Blake's 'Mosquito Creek' station, and John Johnston, assigned to George Bowman, are tracked down at 'Bingara' station and brought in for questioning. Johnston, an Afro-Caribbean man nicknamed 'Black' Johnston, is serving seven years for robbery. In the 1830s, skin colour is not of itself a basis for discrimination. Johnston, because he lives within white society, is by the standards of the day 'white'.

Also brought in is Charles Toulouse, a convict stockman at Glennie's station. All three join Kilmeister in the lock-up.

Over the following four days, Day and his posse crisscross the Big River to question potential witnesses and arrest suspects at Smith's, Cobb's and Fleming's stations. Taken into custody at John Cobb's Gravesend station is Cobb's convict superintendent James Lamb, known as 'Jem', an Englishman who reputedly rode with Major Nunn at Waterloo Creek.

Throughout the district, Day's inquiries are met with sullen silence or open hostility. Witnesses have brazenly lied, played dumb or attempted to abscond; a herd of cattle has been stampeded towards the posse; shots have been fired in their direction. 'I have had to encounter every obstacle that unwilling witnesses could possibly throw in my way,' Day writes.[2] Some of those interviewed seem to find the whole thing rather amusing, as if incredulous that Day has bothered to show up; that he is going to such trouble over such a trifling matter. Even those he charges and commits for trial clearly cannot imagine themselves dancing at the end of a rope for killing blacks.

Day has a way of wiping the smirks off smug faces, however. His persistent, dispassionate manner of questioning is unnerving, and even men innocent of the crime find themselves feeling guilty under his steely gaze. One such blameless stockman, Andrew Burrowes, will later recall, 'I was afraid because Mr Day was making such inquiries that I might have been brought in to the business.'[3]

By Wednesday 8 August, the posse has netted James Oates, known as 'Hall's Jemmy', a stockman assigned to George Hall at 'Bingara', James Parry, hutkeeper at Daniel Eaton's 'Biniguy' station, and George Palliser, head stockman at Archie Bell's 'Bengaria' station – the same Archie Bell who gave his name to Bell's Line of Road. Palliser, a 27-year-old Yorkshireman, is serving seven years for stealing a coat.

At Joseph Fleming's 'Mundowie' run, Day arrests stockman Edward Foley, a 30-year-old farmhand from Queens County (now County Laois), in the Irish midlands. Foley is serving life for rebel activity as a member of the Whiteboys, a secret organisation dedicated to violent opposition to oppressive rents, tithe collections and the closing off of common grazing land by landlords. Denny Day would certainly have heard of them in his youth, particularly during the Tithe Wars, and might have even spied them some night through a window of his father's vicarage, wafting through the parish in the white sheets that gave them their name, on their way to knock down the landlord's fences.

It's at Mundowie, after grilling Edward Foley and several witnesses, where Day discovers the leader of the Myall Creek butchers, and the only freeman among them, Joseph Fleming's younger brother John Henry. And John Henry Fleming – the 22-year-old scion of a prominent Hawkesbury family – is nowhere to be found. No one at the station has the faintest idea where he might be, or so they do solemnly swear. It seems John Henry has simply disappeared.

By Saturday 18 August, ten suspects are under lock and key at Newton's and committed for trial, including the Irish overseer at Bengaria, John Russell, 33, a Tipperary domestic servant serving seven years for theft. With all those he believes were involved in the slaughter now in custody, apart from the fugitive John Henry Fleming, Day takes the opportunity to investigate two unrelated incidents. The first, at Fitzgerald's run, two days' ride down the Big River, is the murder by blacks of the overseer, George Watters. The second, at Crawford's station, is the shooting of a black by the superintendent, Charles Eyles. After spending two days at Crawford's, he returns to Newton's to find that the Mounted Police had arrested another suspect, John Blake, a stockman at James Glennie's 'Gunerai' station. Blake, a 27-year-old butcher from County Meath, Ireland, and the only married man among the prisoners, was serving life for sheep-stealing.

On Thursday 30 August, Day's posse mounts up to return to Invermein with 11 prisoners and a key witness for the prosecution, hutkeeper George Anderson. There will be no cause for complacency on the journey home. Anderson is convinced his life is in danger from friends and supporters of the accused men. He has been under close guard at Newton's and will need continued protection. In a letter to the Attorney-General, John Plunkett, Denny Day makes it plain that he believes Anderson's fears are well founded. 'Any evil disposed person,' he writes, 'might feel inclined to put his testimony beyond reach.'[4]

There is also the risk of ambush by supporters attempting to free the prisoners, and at least one settler has warned Day to expect trouble along the way. Day might well be mindful, too, that some among the Mounted Police could share the supporters' sympathies, particularly those troopers who were with Nunn at Waterloo Creek. In general, relations between Mounted Police and police magistrates had always been tense, at best. Many troopers, and their officers, resented being subject to civilian control, so in a volatile situation such as this, mutiny was a genuine possibility.

Luckily, though, the troopers' commander is a man Day has come to trust and respect. They have much in common: Lieutenant George Denis Pack, late of the 80th Regiment of Foot, is from an Anglo-Irish family of soldiers and clergymen, and a cousin of General Sir Denis Pack, who fought at Waterloo. Another cousin was killed in the battle. The Packs have estates in Kilkenny but George is not from the landed side of the family. He came to New South Wales about a year ago, enlisted in the Mounted Police and, confounding the unit's reputation, has served with distinction. Denny Day considers him a man of honour and innate decency.

It is because of his faith in Pack that, after just a day into the journey, he leaves the prisoners in Pack's care and rides on alone, hoping to pick up the trail of John Henry Fleming before it goes cold.

On Saturday 8 September, Lieutenant Pack, true to Day's expectations, arrives with the prisoners, safe and sound. Here comes the tricky business of bringing them to justice.

By now, news has reached Henry Dangar at Neotsfield that Denny Day has arrested 11 men for murder at Myall Creek, including his stockman Charlie Kilmeister, and that his hutkeeper, George Anderson, will be the main witness for the prosecution. Dangar once had Anderson flogged for neglecting his duties, an accusation the man hotly denied. With the scars from a hundred lashes still raw, what might Anderson tell the court? It's clear to Henry Dangar that something has to be done about this turn of events, and quickly.

Right on cue, *The Sydney Herald* weighs in:

From various parts of the colony we receive accounts of the continued depredations by the blacks. The settlers are, certainly, placed in a most unenviable position, for while the vengeance of the law is denounced against them for the consequences (often inevitable) of any collision with the blacks, the latter, under the present state of things, are placed in a far more favourable position than the whites.[5]

The colony's empire-building elite have come to both hate and fear Denny Day. He is openly scathing of their lax supervision of assigned convicts, who are often left alone for months on end in remote and lawless places, armed and restless, and warns that he intends to report the landholders to the government for failure to exercise proper control over their convicts. He has told them the men they choose as overseers and superintendents are too often corrupt and irresponsible, and that he is well aware they turn a blind eye to their stockmen's shameful abuse of black women. Should that continue unchecked, he warns, the Kamilaroi, who have thus far been remarkably tolerant, will fall upon them with fury.

Day is now convinced that a war of extermination is being waged along the Big River by bands of armed and mounted stockmen, and that great numbers of Aborigines have been killed. He is equally convinced that as far as the settlers are concerned, the atrocity at Myall Creek was just one among many and no cause for fuss and bother.

Chapter 17

Count Bobby

The chairman calls the meeting to order. It is the inaugural meeting of the Hunter's River Black Association, October 1838, and the cream of settler society from near and far, including magistrates, have gathered at Patrick's Plains to lend their support to what all agree is a worthy cause. For the defence of the 11 benighted men accused of the killings at Myall Creek, they are asked to dig deep. The top attorneys in the land do not come cheap.

The handsome, flame-haired chairman, 39-year-old Robert Scott, is Hunter River royalty, known about the district, and in Sydney, where he has many business interests, as 'Count Bobby'. Born in Bombay, India, he and his Scottish father, Dr Helenus Scott, and his younger brother Helenus, sailed from England for New South Wales in 1821. Dr Scott, having retired after 20 years' service as a physician for the East India Company, was en route to southern climes for his health's sake – and to take up a land grant on Hunter's River – but died at sea off the Cape of Good Hope.

The Scott brothers, on arrival, were granted 2000 acres each at Patrick's Plains, combined their properties, bought up adjacent land to establish a 10,000-acre estate they named 'Glendon', and began breeding thoroughbred horses. By 1832 their stud boasted more than 300 blood horses, including some of the best Arabian and colonial-bred stallions in the colony.

Both brothers, having the essential credentials of elite public schooling, connections to London society, land, wealth and Protestant religion, were naturally appointed magistrates. Helenus, a rather reserved but fair-minded man, devoted himself to administering the law, and would go on to make a career of it, with distinction. Robert, on the other hand, preferred to shoot first and ask questions later, as he did in 1833 when a member of a posse in pursuit of convicts who, rebelling against brutal treatment, had absconded from the estate of his neighbour across the river, the notoriously cruel Major James Mudie. When the runaways were cornered in a deep ravine, and one of their number, James Henderson, refused to surrender, Scott shot him dead.

Of the many convicts assigned to Glendon, one is remarkable not only for the circumstances that brought him there but for his incendiary effect on Robert Scott, who singled him out for special treatment. James Brine was one of six English farm labourers history would call the Tolpuddle Martyrs.

On 24 February 1834, in the Dorsetshire village of Tolpuddle, Brine, George Loveless and his brother James, James Hammett, Thomas Standfield and his son John were arrested and charged with taking an illegal oath.

It was a trumped-up charge. The six labourers' actual crime, in the eyes of Britain's landed class, was forming a union to protest against starvation wages. Because the union members had sworn an oath of secrecy, they were convicted under an obscure law on taking 'unlawful oaths'[1] and each sentenced to transportation to New South Wales for seven years.

In his account of his days as a convict assigned to Robert Scott, Brine writes that he arrived at Glendon exhausted, starving, barefoot and with only the clothes on his back, having been robbed by bushrangers on the long walk from the river port to the Scott brothers' estate. Robert Scott did not believe he had been robbed, swore he was a liar and said he would give him 'a damned good flogging' in the morning. 'You are one of the Dorsetshire machine-breakers,' Scott said, 'but you are caught at last.'

'He gave me nothing to eat until the following day,' Brine writes. 'In the morning I was employed to dig post-holes, and during the day he came and asked how I was getting on. I told him I was doing as well as I could, but was unable to do much through weakness, and that, having walked so far without shoes, my feet were so cut and sore that I could not put them to the spade.'

His master showed no sympathy. 'If you utter another word of complaint I will put you in the lock-up,' Scott told him. 'And if you ask me for an article for six months to come, or if you do not your work like another man, or do not attend to the over-seer's orders, whatever they may be, I will send you up to Major Mudie, where no mercy shall be shown you.'

For the next few months, Brine worked without shoes, a change of clothing or bedding, and slept on the ground at night.

'Shortly afterwards I was sent to the pool to wash sheep, and for 17 days was working up to my breast in water. I thus caught a severe cold, and having told my master that I was very ill, asked him if he would be so good as to give me something to cover me at night, if it were only a piece of horsecloth.'

'No, I will give you nothing until you are due for it,' Scott said. 'What would your masters in England have had to cover them if you had not been sent here? I understand it was your intention to have murdered, burnt and destroyed everything before you. If you ask me for anything before the six months is expired I will flog you as often as I like.'

When Brine tried to explain that the unions had no intention of murdering, burning or destroying, Scott exploded in rage. 'You damned convict!' he shouted. 'If you persist in this obstinacy and insolence I will severely punish you! Don't you know that even the hair on your head is not your own? Go to your hut or I will kick you!'[2]

In 1837, after an 800,000-name petition to parliament and a mass demonstration in London, calling for the men to be pardoned, the Tolpuddle Martyrs were freed and returned to England, hailed as working-class heroes. James Brine returned home later than the others – it seems his master was in no hurry to tell him the good news – but once back in England, he married Thomas Standfield's sister Elizabeth, moved to Ontario, Canada, fathered 11 children and lived to the ripe old age of 90.

Scott's views on the native population are revealed in his evidence to an 1838 parliamentary inquiry into 'the Aborigines Question'. Scott declares that in his experience Aborigines are treacherous by nature, particularly those who have been in regular close contact with whites. 'And what is more lamentable,' he tells the committee, 'these very persons have almost invariably been the instigators of, and leaders in, the aggressions committed upon Europeans.'[3]

News of the Myall Creek defence fund was bound to get out, and it's not long before the press gets wind of it. *The Australian*, with a liberal dose of sarcasm, reports on 17 November:

A new association has been got up at Hunter's River, bearing
the title of the Hunter's River Black Association. We understand
that several magistrates of that district who are the projectors
of this humane and moral company have renounced some of
their former habits, and never intend again to sound the alarm
of 'insubordination' and 'convict discipline.'[4]

The same newspaper, three days later, adopts a more serious tone:

It is with deep feeling of shame and regret that we hear of such
a thing as an association of gentlemen, the virtual object of which
is to protect the stock-keepers and shepherds in the extermination of the blacks! Surely no man, or set of men, in a civilised and
Christian land, can be found to unite in countenancing and abetting a moral warfare on the blacks and their defenceless women
and children! We are not ignorant of the danger and depreda-
tion to which life and property are exposed at the stations in the
interior from the aggressions of the blacks, but, while we recommend a prompt and decisive resistance to any actual or attempted
aggression from the blacks, we denounce, in our highest keynote,
that resistance when it emanated from a spirit of retaliation and
revenge.[5]

At the founding meeting of the Hunter's River Black Association,
at Patrick's Plains, Robert Scott's like-minded peers, inspired by
his leadership, donate £300 for the legal defence of the accused
men. One of the subscribers is Henry Dangar.

Chapter 18

Tracks of naked feet

John Hubert Plunkett, an Irishman from County Roscommon, is a Catholic, and thus by definition, in the eyes of many among the colonial elite, a person not to be trusted. His family had estates, thanks to connections with the old Irish aristocracy, which afforded him the chance to study law at Dublin's Trinity College, but it was his talent that earned him respect among the legal profession and the admiration of the legendary champion of Catholic emancipation, Daniel O'Connell.

In 1832, Plunkett was appointed Solicitor-General of New South Wales – the first Catholic appointed to high office in the colony – and soon established a reputation as a reformer, extending the right to trial by jury to emancipists, then to convicts and assigned servants. As Attorney-General, such reforms, along with his vocal support for civil and religious liberties, have won him many more enemies than friends among the colonial gentry. And now, as attorney for the prosecution in the Myall Creek massacre trial, he's about to risk losing the few friends he has.

John Plunkett clears his throat, ready to make his opening address to the jury. It is Thursday 15 November 1838, the gallery of the Supreme Court in Sydney is packed to capacity, and he is acutely aware of the significance of the case he is about to prosecute. He is not a commanding orator, so his words will need to be well chosen.

On the bench above him, regal in red gown and wig, is Sir James Dowling, Chief Justice of New South Wales. Looking every inch the patrician, complete with aquiline nose, he is popular with the legal fraternity, being consistently fair, and, above all, a good listener.

Across from Plunkett sit the counsels for the defence, three of the top silks in the land: William Foster, peering over the spectacles perched on the tip of his nose, his expression, as ever, unreadable; the gimlet-eyed, sepulchral William a'Beckett – in the colony barely a year but already a rising star of the Sydney bar; and Richard Windeyer, eloquent, tenacious, and, since February, a landowner on Hunter's River, his open, boyish face belying a mastery of the art of seducing juries.

At the bar, looking somewhat overawed but, curiously, unafraid, are the 11 accused men – Charles Kilmeister, William Hawkins, John Blake, John Johnston, Charles Toulouse, James Lamb, Edward Foley, James Oates, James Parry, George Palliser and John Russell.

The indictment is read aloud by the clerk of the court. There are nine counts in the indictment, charging the prisoners at the bar, in different forms, with the wilful murder of an Aboriginal man known as Daddy. The judge then orders the police magistrate, Denny Day, to leave the court until called to give his evidence.

Plunkett glances at the gallery, where many among the crowd have the smug look of men at a cockfight who know the challenger has been nobbled, then turns his attention to the jury, where some among these 12 men and true share that same smug expression.

'The case, gentlemen, which you are called upon to try is one of no ordinary importance to this colony,' he begins. 'I am sure the case will receive all the attention which it demands. When 11 men are placed at the bar for a capital crime, it is itself sufficient evidence of the importance of the case. Before going into this case, I must entreat you, gentlemen, to dismiss from your minds all impressions which may have been produced by what you may have heard or read on the present subject.'[1]

Explaining why there are nine counts in the indictment, he says, 'When you hear the evidence you will know the reason why we were obliged to have so many counts. The last count, gentlemen, charges the whole of the prisoners with casting the deceased Daddy into the fire and thereby causing his death.

'Gentlemen, murder is regarded as the greatest crime in all nations, but here is a case which shows that there are graduations even in murder. The information only shows at the utmost the death of two men, whereas, in fact, on the same day and in the same hour the lives of 28 individuals – men, women and children – were sacrificed without any probable cause or provocation to palliate the atrocious crime in the sight of any laws human or divine.'[2]

He then outlines the case for the prosecution, beginning with how the accused men, all armed and mounted, scoured the country in pursuit of blacks, riding from station to station until arriving at Henry Dangar's run at Myall Creek.

After recounting the horrific details of the crime, he has something to say regarding his learned friends opposite. 'I am sincerely glad to see prisoners defended by counsel. I am glad to see the present prisoners in that situation, but a rumour has gone abroad that this defence is made at the instance of an association illegally formed for the purpose of defending all who may be charged with crimes resulting from any collision with the natives. I say that if such an association exists, that if there be men who have joined together for the purpose of defending men such as these, the object of that society is to encourage bloodshed and crime of every description.'[3]

Then, taking aim at the press: 'Gentlemen, I have too high an opinion of you, and of the discrimination of the public at large, to think for a moment that any bloody article appearing in any paper or papers will at all influence you in the verdict which you are to give this day.

'Gentlemen, it has been promulgated from the bench, by the judges of the land, that the black is as amenable for his evil acts as the white man, and therefore as much entitled to protection by the laws. These crimes were committed in cold blood and arose from no dispute. It was malicious and not caused by momentary irritation and excitement. I have endeavoured to do part of my duty, and I will now conclude by calling the witnesses.'[4]

First to take the witness stand is the superintendent at Newton's station, Thomas Foster. He tells the court that at Myall Creek he saw George Anderson the hutkeeper and 'about 30 or 40 blacks; there were men, women and children'. Ten of the men returned with him to Newton's to work, but upon hearing that armed men were hunting blacks in the district he sent them back to what he believed to be a safe haven at Dangar's station.

'I never saw them again,' Foster says. 'I saw them about half a mile off going to Mr Dangar's. It was about four in the afternoon when I sent the blacks away.'

The next morning, shortly after sunrise, a party of mounted men rode into Newton's station, armed with pistols.

'What's the matter?' Foster asked James Oates. Oates asked him where the blacks had gone.

'God knows where they are now,' Foster replied, then asked Charles Kilmeister, 'Are you after the blacks?'

'They rushed my cattle yesterday,' Kilmeister said, but Foster didn't believe him. He tells the court, 'I had been over to Mr Dangar's the day before, but I did not hear anything about the cattle.'

After about a quarter of an hour the men rode off, headed back to Dangar's.

Two days later, Foster rode to Myall Creek where the overseer, William Hobbs, took him to the stockyard where he saw 'the body of a black man with the head on; the limbs had apparently been burned off'.

'I saw another head without any body, and several other skulls so destroyed by fire as to render it impossible to say whether they were men or women. There appeared to have been a large fire recently. There were two men's heads that were not burned, and I am positive they were black men's heads. I did not examine whether there were any wounds on the body or not. I did not see any arms of a body. I did not see any smaller limbs. I tracked some horses from Mr Dangar's to that place. I cannot say how many, but there must have been several.

'I only stopped ten minutes at the furthest. I was overcome by the smell.'[5]

Under cross-examination by William a'Beckett, Foster says he could only swear to two of the men being armed with pistols, and that it's customary to carry pistols in the bush as protection against attack by blacks.

He tells the court he recognised Daddy's body because he had known him in life, but, when pressed, admits he could not swear as to whether the body was that of a man or a woman.

Called to the stand, William Hobbs supports Foster's version of events, adding greater detail.

'I left my station on the 7th of June for the Big River,' he recalls. 'It was Thursday. I had a station 60 or 70 miles lower down. I left Kilmeister and Anderson in charge.'

Hobbs says there were up to 50 blacks at the station when he left, that they were peaceable and had been there ten or 12 days. When he returned to find them gone, and having been told during his journey home of a massacre in the district, he asked Kilmeister what had become of them.

'He said he did not know. I told him I knew they were murdered and all about it.' When Kilmeister continued to insist he knew nothing of any murders, Hobbs revealed that he knew that he and a band of armed men had been to Newton's and to other stations, but Kilmeister assured him they were only looking for cattle.

The young Aboriginal servant, Davey, led Hobbs to the stockyard, about a kilometre west of the station huts. 'There had been a shower of rain and the tracks of horse and of naked feet were quite discernible. It was a regular track, there were children's footprints, the horse tracks were on either side and the tracks of the naked feet were in the middle. They were in the same direction as the horse tracks.

'I arrived at a spot where there were a great number of dead bodies, but the stench was so great that I was not able to be accurate in counting them. I endeavoured to count them and made more of them sometimes than others – the most I made was 28. The skulls which had been burnt were easily discernible – the last number I counted was 20. I will undertake to swear that there were the remains of above 20. I saw some of the bodies; they were much disfigured; I cannot say how many.

'I did know Daddy. He was an old man. He was the largest man ever I saw, either white or black. I saw a large body there, but the head was gone – from the size of the body I think it was his.

'I saw the children's heads distinctly – there were ten or 12 small heads, also some children's bodies.'

Hobbs returned to the massacre site with Tom Foster the next morning. This time, he noticed blood stains on the gravel all around the site, that dingoes had mauled parts of the remains during the night, and that eagle hawks and other birds of prey were now doing the same.

Again, he confronted Kilmeister. 'I told him I thought it a very cruel thing to sanction the murder of these people as they were on such friendly terms, and also it was altogether through him that the blacks were permitted to be on the station at all. I said I considered it my duty to report it. He said he hoped I would not – not that he had anything to do with it – but that the blacks having been with us for some time it would cause his removal. He appeared excessively uneasy and begged me not to report it.'

After Hobbs had written his letter to Henry Dangar he read it to Anderson and Kilmeister.

'Kilmeister was very much agitated. He entreated me not to report the matter; he said the blacks had been spearing his cattle while I was away, he did not tell me that when I first told him of the murder. I requested him to show me the cattle which he said had been speared. I was on the run four or five days, but I saw no signs that the cattle had been disturbed.'

Hobbs was now convinced that Kilmeister was lying. 'I asked Kilmeister how the blacks were taken away, and he told me the men took them. He did not say that he was present, but I understood that he was.'

A few days later, at Eaton's station, Hobbs came across James 'Hall's Jemmy' Oates. 'Jemmy, this is a bad job, and I am very sorry you are one of the number.' Oates replied, 'It is, sir, but I hope there will be nothing more about it.'

Hobbs had reported the matter to Denny Day, and was at the station when Day arrived. He showed Day where the fire had been, and told him that most of the bodies and heads had been removed – he did not know by whom.

Cross-examined by William Foster, Hobbs admits that Kilmeister had always been a good servant. 'I very much doubt whether there is in New South Wales a better servant than Kilmeister,' he says. 'I should not have thought he would wantonly attack another.'[6] He also admits the possibility that the bodies could have been dragged away by dingoes.

William Hobbs is excused and the clerk calls the next witness – the police magistrate at Muswellbrook. Word is sent outside, and Denny Day re-enters the courtroom.

Chapter 19

Sword and pistol, rope and fire

The man in the witness stand has no truck with flowery phrases. From his mouth, words are tools carefully chosen to make clear what happened, how it happened, by whom and to whom it happened, without embroidery of any kind.

'I received information at the latter end of June, which induced me to report the circumstances to the Colonial Secretary,' Day tells the court. 'Some time after, I was directed to proceed with a party of police to that part of Dangar's. On the evening I arrived, Mr Hobbs and one of the officers of the Mounted Police accompanied me to the spot.

'There appeared to have been a fire about 15 yards in circumference. There were a great quantity of fragments of bones. The place had the appearance of having been swept, and all large portions had been removed. I found a bone which I supposed to be the rib of a young child, the jaw bone of a human being, and a few teeth.

'I examined into the case and committed the prisoners. The prisoner Parry, I was informed, had expressed great regret for having been concerned in the affair. I accordingly had a communication with him, thinking perhaps that he had some communication to make. I found much difficulty in obtaining information on the subject.'[1]

And that's it. Short and sharp. No further questions. The witness may step down.

Now it's the turn of the prosecution's star witness – hutkeeper George Anderson, and everyone in the courtroom knows that this is the man who can name names and point the finger.

'On Saturday, about ten men came on horseback, armed with muskets, swords and pistols,' he begins. 'I was at home when they came. I was sitting in the hut with Kilmeister, the stockman. They came up galloping, with guns and pistols pointed towards the hut; they were talking to Kilmeister.

'They all came up together, Russell, Toulouse, Foley, "Black" Johnston, Hawkins, Palliser, Lamb and Oates were there. Blake and Parry I cannot swear to. There were about ten on horseback. I will not say Parry was not there, but I cannot say I saw him.'

'They were spread out in a line about to surround the blacks. The blacks were all camped, ready for the night.

'The blacks, on seeing them, ran into the hut. The men then got off their horses, the prisoner Russell took a rope from his horse's neck and commenced undoing it.

'While he was preparing his rope, I asked what they were going to do with the blacks. He answered me that they were going to take them to the back of the range and frighten them.

'Russell went into the hut, and the blacks were brought out tied. I heard the blacks crying out for assistance. The mothers and children were crying, and the little ones that could not walk. Russell brought out the end of the rope that they were tied with, and gave it to one of the men on horseback. They then started, taking the blacks with them.

'One black was handcuffed. Their hands were all tied, with palms to each other – the rope was a very long one.'

Anderson testifies that all the people in the camp were led away, except for two boys who jumped into the creek and escaped into the bush, an attractive woman left in the hut for his use, another left for Davey, and a little girl who was at the back of the hut while the others were being tied. 'Instead of allowing her to go with the party, I pulled her into the hut and kept her there,' Anderson says. 'The oldest of the lot was called Old Daddy. He was a very old, big, tall man.

'Kilmeister got his horse while they were tying the blacks. He went with them, and took a pistol with him.

'Oates was armed. He had a brace of pistols. They had a great many among them. I saw Foley standing at the door with a pistol in his hand. I did not notice his sword – I saw the swords in the distance.

'I did not keep them in sight more than a minute or two. About a quarter of an hour afterwards I heard the reports of two pieces, one after the other, in the same direction as they had gone – the sound was quite plain. I did not notice more than two.' He heard nothing more.

The following night, the horsemen returned and spent the night in Anderson's hut. Recalling the events of the next day, Anderson mentions John Henry Fleming for the first time, and it's apparent that Fleming was the leader.

'After breakfast, Russell, Kilmeister and Fleming took out fire sticks, and when they were going, Fleming told Kilmeister to bring the leg rope. They all went off in the same direction as the night before, excepting Foley, who remained with me. Foley and I were in the hut, and during the time they were away I asked Foley if all the blacks had made their escape. He said none that he saw; they were all killed but one.

'A short time before the party came home, Foley drew a sword belonging to one of the party – it was covered with blood.

'In about an hour they came home. I saw the smoke a short time after. They got up their horses, and Fleming told Kilmeister to go up by and by and put the logs together, and to be sure that all was consumed.' Kilmeister went off in that direction and was away most of the day, but it seems he did not do as he was told.

On his return, Kilmeister said to Anderson, 'For God's sake mind what you say! Do not say I went with them!'

'But he did go with them,' Anderson tells the court, 'and at the same time the women who were left with me I sent away with the ten blacks who had left our station with Mr Foster. It was a moonlit night – I turned them away the same night because I did not want them to be killed by those men who I knew to be out after the blacks.'

If George Anderson has polished a halo for himself, defence counsel Richard Windeyer is just the man to knock the shine off it. Under withering cross-examination, Anderson concedes that he wasn't sure when the ten men returned from Newton's, that he had asked for one of the women to be untied and given to him, and that he let her go with the ten men because she was not the woman he wanted. 'I wanted a gin that I had had before,' he admits, 'not the one they left me.' He admits, too, that in his second interrogation by Denny Day he contradicted some of his statements in the first deposition. However, he will not be shaken from his testimony that he recognised John Henry Fleming, and then, standing in that witness box, moved to tears, he proceeds to pour out his heart.

'I have been in the colony about five years,' he says. 'I am here for life. I never said that my evidence would get me liberty; I would take anything I could get. I only ask for protection. I do not know what made my evidence more against them the second time – I do not know! The magistrate said he would commit me for perjury. He said I might be committed for not thinking. It was after this that I began to recollect everything that was said and done.

'I have been punished twice – once for neglect of duty and being absent from the station. I do not think I deserved that punishment. It was eight days coming. I had a hundred lashes.

'I came here for robbing my master,' he says. 'I was ignorant and misled by others.

'I have been frightened by the blacks. I saw a black fellow one night run away directly he saw me, and I was very much frightened.' Still, he had grown fond of those he came to know at Myall Creek. 'I knew Old Joey,' he says. 'He was at the station with the others. King Sandy, his wife and little Charley were also taken away. The gin I wanted was Heppita – she, Sandy and Joey were taken away, and another black fellow named Tommy. I could name nearly the whole if they were before me. I did not know all their names. Sandy, his wife, Charley and the others I have mentioned were tied and taken away.'[2]

After Anderson steps down, a procession of prosecution witnesses fills in gaps in his story. John Bates, the hutkeeper at Dight's station, about 25 kilometres from Dangar's run, recalls that when the horsemen came to Dight's, James Parry said they had 'settled the blacks', and that none of the others denied this.

Andrew Burrowes, the Myall Creek stockman who was away droving with William Hobbs and Charles Reid, swears that on the way to Dangar's lower station on the Big River he stopped for the night at a station where he shared a hut with the horsemen.

'They asked me if the blacks were at our station. I said yes, that they had been there four or five weeks. They then said those could not have been the blacks who committed the depredations down the river. I saw some firearms and one man was putting a leather strap to his sword. They said they were going to look after some blacks. One man was making a leather pouch – it might be used for ammunition.'

A short distance from the hut, Burrowes came upon a man bearing a musket. He did not recognise the man, but was told it was John Henry Fleming.

Warren Mace, a paroled station hand at Dight's, tells the court that the horsemen, who stopped for breakfast, brought with them a black woman who they left at the station. 'There was one person desired her to be taken care of,' he says.

To Mace's narrative, Charles Reid adds: 'I stopped at the lower station. I met Fleming – he was alone.'

Plunkett's last witness is a dentist named Foss, who has examined the remains. 'I have seen a jaw bone; there are two teeth in it,' he reports. 'This is part of a human jaw, and there are human teeth in it. They appear to have been burnt.'[3] Thus ends the case for the prosecution.

William a'Beckett fixes his gimlet eyes on the jury. 'The evidence is perfectly circumstantial,' he says, suggesting that the trial is a shameful waste of everyone's time. 'Mr Hobbs is the only one who speaks to the identity of Daddy, and he could not swear whether the mass of putridity which he saw was a man or a woman. There is simply no proof,' says a'Beckett, 'that Daddy was not alive, or that a dead male black has been found.'

Henry Dangar, called as a witness for the defence, swears that while Charles Kilmeister has been a good and obedient servant, George Anderson is a liar and a troublemaker.

'I would not believe him on his oath,' Dangar says.

Under cross-examination, Dangar says, 'I have had to punish him more than once. At a very recent occasion, at the last sheep shearing, he left his station to the mercy of chance for two or three days.' Again, he says, 'I would not believe him on his oath.'

Dangar swears he has not dismissed Anderson as a result of this case, insisting, 'he is about to leave my service – his term is up'. He admits to contributing to the defence fund for the accused men, declaring, 'I have a servant amongst them – I believe an honest one and perfectly innocent.' Asked how much he has contributed to the cause, he declines to answer.

Henry Dangar is followed by neighbouring Big River cattlemen who testify to the honesty and integrity of their servants.

John Cobb swears that during the two years in his employ, Charles Lamb 'has conducted himself with every propriety. I always thought him a quiet, peaceable man'.

Thomas Simpson Hall states that in the three years James Oates has been in his service he has found him to be 'a steady, correct man'. No mention is made of unsubstantiated reports that in 1835, Oates was wounded when Mounted Police and stockmen killed up to 80 Kamilaroi in retaliation for the spearing of one of Hall's men.

George Bowman describes John Johnston as a good man who has 'always behaved well'.

The Bell brothers' superintendent, Charles Joliffe, says, 'Palliser and Russell have been under my charge two years. Russell has been a very active man, a good servant, and a quiet, well-disposed man. Palliser was the same. I always found them at home and quiet, attentive servants.'[4]

And with that, the defence rests.

Turning to the jury box, Judge Dowling says, 'We have now been engaged many hours in one of the most important cases which has ever come under our notice since there has been a Supreme Court in New South Wales. The case has excited considerable interest, and you were warned at the outset to throw aside any impression which might have been made by hearing or reading descriptions of this affair.

'I hope you will not be offended when I recall to your minds that each of you when entering that box invoked God to witness that he would be determined by the evidence, and return a verdict according to the substance of that evidence. If that were not so, if it were possible that a jury could be biased by outdoor impressions and return a verdict not according to the evidence, our dearest rights were at stake and public justice was a farce.

'It was clear that a most grievous offence has been committed; that the lives of near 30 of our fellow creatures have been sacrificed, and that in order for me to fulfil my duty I must tell you that the life of a black is as precious and valuable in the eye of the law as the highest noble in the land.'[5]

The judge agrees with the defence counsel that a man cannot be committed for murder or manslaughter before a body is found, and directs the jury to determine whether the man killed was Daddy or another, unknown man. He goes on to sum up the evidence at great length before directing the gentlemen of the jury to retire and consider their verdict.

The seats in the jury box are still warm when, after just 15 minutes, the jury returns to deliver its verdict. Not guilty.

The courtroom explodes with cheers and applause, but the celebrations are short-lived. The Attorney-General, dissatisfied with the verdict, remands them all on other charges, to be tried the following week. There will be no walk to freedom today.

Chapter 20

I knew a little boy named Charley

The Attorney-General is not feeling confident – far from it.

For one thing, the press campaign to free the prisoners has been relentless.

'The depredations of the blacks are committed with absolute impunity,' *The Sydney Herald* thunders. 'They come in tribes to spear cattle, and to plunder the lonely settlers; and themselves throughout the wilds, beyond the possibility of capture. In reply to any complaint, the settlers are told that the blacks are British subjects, and can only be dealt with "according to law". We admire the principles of abstract justice as much as the most zealous advocate of the blacks – but we equally admire the principle of even-handed justice. But this justice the settler, at present, knows not. It is easy to seize upon him, and bring him to trial for the (so called) murder of one or more black natives; but where are we to find the savage aggressors? Where is the police magistrate's warrant that can reach them? Far be it from us to assert that the aboriginal natives should be slaughtered with impunity, but we demand adequate protection for the whites.

'The government, it is evident, will not, or cannot, protect the whites from the aggressions of the blacks. It behoves the former, therefore, to protect themselves; and this they can most effectively do in the jury box, by determining not to convict persons on charges originating in collisions with the blacks, except upon the most conclusive evidence of wanton cruelty. Let there be equal laws and equal justice.'[1]

For another, the dough-faced judge on the bench above, Sir William Westbrooke Burton is a firm believer that 'masters of convicts were not sufficiently attentive to the morals of the men',[2] which might be to the prosecution's advantage, and is known to disapprove of the dubious ways some of the colony's landed elite have acquired their wealth, which might also favour the prosecution. He is also known to have a sincere concern for Aboriginal welfare.

That aside, however, Judge Burton is also a puritanical, fire-breathing anti-Catholic, and the Attorney-General, John Plunkett, is Catholic.

It is Thursday 29 November 1838, and here in the Supreme Court of New South Wales, in Sydney, seven of the men accused of the Myall Creek massacre are about to stand trial for a second time. Plunkett knows the defence team of a'Beckett, Foster and Windeyer will have the support of a climate of racial hatred whipped up by the press. He can only hope it will not have sectarian hatred on its side as well.

So, after three days of convoluted legal argument over the indictment, which did nothing to allay Plunkett's worst fears about the judge, it's on with the motley.

Of 48 men called up for jury duty, only 28 have turned up, and the absentees are fined for non-attendance. After challenges, 12 jurors are sworn in and file into the box. They include four publicans, two landholders, a tailor, a blacksmith and a soap boiler.

The seven prisoners – Kilmeister, Oates, Foley, Russell, Johnston, Hawkins and Parry – are brought into court and charged with 20 counts concerning the wilful murder of a child, name and sex unknown, and of a man named Charley, by pistol, sword and casting into a fire. They all plead not guilty.

John Plunkett addresses the jury, beginning by pointing out that although the prisoners had already been tried for murder, it was for a totally different offence. He expresses the hope – a vain hope, probably – that although the first trial had been widely commented on in the press 'according to their different opinions of the case', the jury would not be influenced or biased but would 'strictly obey the oaths they had taken, and conscientiously perform that duty which the stern justice of this country, and the sacred obligation of their oaths demanded at their hands.'[3]

After a précis of the evidence, Plunkett takes the unusual step in an address to the jury of commending the one person whose diligence had brought the case to judgement. 'I could not avoid declaring,' he says, 'that the thanks of the country are due to Mr Day, the police magistrate, for the vigilance he has exercised in tracing this barbarous murder, and they were doubly due to him, as he had every obstacle thrown in his way by those who ought to have assisted him, and was strenuously opposed in the performance of his duty.

'But not withstanding the unworthy opposition he received, he had fearlessly performed that duty, and had, although not without great difficulty, collected proofs which I thought placed the matter beyond doubt.

'As he before observed, there was no doubt but that great prejudice existed in the public mind on this matter, but he trusted that the jury would cast all from their minds, and return a verdict on the evidence which be laid before them, to satisfy their consciences and the justice of the country.'[4]

It can only be imagined what Denny Day, standing at the back of the courtroom, makes of that gracious and inspiring speech. But if, having become the villain of the piece in the eyes of many, he feels vindicated in his uncompromising pursuit of justice, he must surely also share John Plunkett's fear that once again it might all come to naught.

Tom Foster, Newton's superintendent, is called to the stand and reprises his evidence of the first trial. William Hobbs does likewise, adding, 'I knew a little boy named Charley whose father was called Sandy, and they both were with the party of blacks I left at Myall Creek when I proceeded to the Big River. He [Charley] was a big boy for his age. I know his mother, who was called Martha, and they were all at my station when I left.

'I saw the foot marks of persons who appeared to have been engaged in rolling logs to the fire, they were not cut logs but dry timber. I found a basket such as is used by the blacks, on the road between my station and the fire. It contained various articles such as are carried by the blacks; it contained a piece of opossum skin, some pipe clay, which they use for painting, some belts and some small crystal stones which the blacks set great value on. I have been told they worship these stones and consider they possess a charm to cure them when they are sick.'

He reports finding several other baskets and similar articles at the Wirrayaraay camp, including precious items they would not have left behind of their own accord, and a cap belonging to an old man known as Joey. 'When they were at my place I used to give what food I could spare,' he says. 'They went out every morning hunting, and returned at night with opossums and other food enough to keep them. I found no food at the camp.'

Curiously, under cross-examination, Hobbs says he was previously unaware that the term 'Myall' meant 'a savage, ferocious black'. He thought it was a type of wood.

Denny Day then steps up to repeat his testimony from the first trial. He adds: 'I took Anderson under my protection, in consequence of the important information he had given me, and his being in an unprotected state. In the course of the examination, or rather at the close of the examination, and just as Kilmeister was leaving the room, I said that I was more surprised at Kilmeister than at any of the others on account of his great intimacy with them, when he turned round and said, "If you knew what they threatened to me, you would not be surprised."'[5]

George Anderson, despite a blistering cross-examination, does not waiver from the evidence he gave at the first trial.

The physical evidence – bones and teeth gathered at the scene by Denny Day – are brought into court, and the Colonial Surgeon, Dr Thomas Robertson, testifies that he examined the bones and determined that they were the rib bones of a boy six or seven years old. The teeth were human, he reports, but cannot swear that the bones were those of black or white people.

A convict stockman at Newton's run, Robert Sexton, who had not been called as a witness at the first trial, corroborates Tom Foster's evidence that the horsemen had visited Newton's looking for the blacks; that Foster had brought Wirrayaraay men from Myall Creek to work at Newton's; and that Foster, convinced that the horsemen meant to do them harm, told the men to leave.

Sexton continues: 'On the Monday morning following, the same party, with two others, came to the station. They gave me a black gin and said I was to take care of her until someone called for her. The overseer [Foster] would not let me keep her, and they took her away and went over to Mr Dight's station. Hawkins asked if the blacks were there, and when told no, said it was a bad job they were not, and that they were driven away in order that they should not be caught.'[6]

Stockman Charles Reid, adding to his previous evidence, tells the court, 'I saw the place where the murder was alleged to have been committed, and saw bodies and heads lying about, but I walked away as quickly as I could. Kilmeister appeared very angry when I spoke to him about it. The blacks are generally treacherous, but this tribe was particularly peaceable, and had been about Mr Wiseman's and Mr McIntyre's stations for some time.'

Tom Foster, recalled to the stand, testifies that it had rained at about the time of the murders, and William Hobbs, when recalled, is asked to clarify his previous statement that the horsemen were aware that he was absent from Myall Creek station. He answers, 'It must have been known that I was going to the Big River ten or 12 days before I started, because I was collecting cattle for that purpose, and I said that as soon as I could get one herd in I should go.'

That concludes the case for the prosecution, the cue for William a'Beckett to claim, as in the first trial, that there is no evidence of murder. Indeed, Charley, like Daddy, might still be alive and well somewhere, or perhaps the blacks had been attacked by another group of blacks.

Indicating the prisoners, he asks, 'And were these men, merely because they happened to be in their company some time before, to be put on trial for murder?'[7]

This case is a case dependent on vague circumstantial evidence, a'Beckett tells the jury. 'It must altogether fail.'[8]

After argument along the same lines by William Foster and Richard Windeyer, the defence calls Henry Dangar.

Sparks are about to fly.

Henry Dangar is more at ease than at the first trial, and his well-rehearsed testimony is essentially the same – that Charles Kilmeister is as honest as the day is long, while George Anderson is an inveterate liar; a man he would not believe even if he swore on the Bible. But now it's the Attorney-General's turn to question him, and John Plunkett has been keeping his powder dry.

The questions come at a measured pace, and are answered with calm confidence. No, he had never actually seen George Anderson take an oath, but would not believe him anyway because of his bad character. Yes, he had charged Anderson with being absent without permission and neglect of his duties, and the punishment was 50 lashes for each offence. No, he did not believe Anderson's story of a massacre, and yes, he doubted that there were as many bodies as William Hobbs had claimed.

So far, no surprises, but then Plunkett asks Dangar if he had ever been dismissed from a public office.

Dangar, taken aback, replies, 'I was suspended from a public office, and I heard no more about it.'

'Were you not dismissed from your situation?' Plunkett asks.

'I was suspended.'

'Were you not dismissed, I say, sir? You know what I mean.'

Dangar snaps back, 'I was suspended!'

'Answer me without equivocation, sir! Were you not dismissed, and not suspended, as you want us to believe?'

Flustered, Dangar asks the judge if he is bound to answer that question. The judge says yes he is, and Plunkett can take heart in realising he was wrong about Mister Justice 'No Popery' Burton.

'I was a surveyor. I did not ask to be reinstated,' Dangar responds, evasively. 'Perhaps the Secretary of State might have given orders that I was not to be reinstated; perhaps I received a public intimation. It is ten or 12 years ago, and I don't recollect the contents of a letter of so remote a date. I was suspended.'

The judge is not convinced. 'Mr Dangar, if you were not dismissed you can have no hesitation in stating so without equivocation.'

'A suspension is tantamount to a dismissal,' Dangar concedes. 'The Governor ordered my suspension, and perhaps the Secretary of State might have ordered that I was not to be reinstated.' Desperate to change the subject, he blurts, 'I would dismiss one of my servants for shooting a black man – on my oath I would.' Then, 'Mr Hobbs is not to remain in my service. His time is expired.'

The judge, doing Plunkett's job for him, warns Dangar: 'When an answer is given to a question it is to be fully given without reservation. Was that the only reason of his leaving your service?'

'No, your Honour, and I was going to add, he has not given me satisfaction in the case of my property; that is the only cause. I never did express any dissatisfaction at Mr Hobbs' conduct in this case.' Blathering now, under siege from Plunkett and the judge, Dangar says he had made up his mind six months ago to give Hobbs his notice but did not tell him until after the murders. Yes, he told Denny Day that Hobbs was a respectable young man, but no, he did not tell Day that Hobbs was a truthful man. He denies having known there were insufficient jurors or that he advised anyone to attend court to join the jury. He swears he did not say to someone, 'Why did you not sit on the jury, and why did you refuse?' He denies paying the expenses of the defendants but admits subscribing £5 in July or August for the defence of Charles Kilmeister. 'I won't swear that I would not have subscribed if he had not been my servant,' he says. 'I subscribed before I heard the particulars of this matter.'

Then comes the following admission: 'I was suspended for purchasing a piece of ground from a grantee, sooner than the government regulations admitted. It was a common practice at the time – my Surveyor-General [John Oxley] did the same. There was another reason assigned for my suspension, which was the misappropriation of land. That was not true, and was set right by the Surveyor-General at the time. That is the great moral offence I committed! The reason why I would not believe Anderson on his oath is his general habit of lying.'[9]

The nub of the matter, which Dangar is skirting around, is that in 1825 he was commissioned to select properties on Hunter's River for applicants for land grants. In that role, he accompanied Thomas Potter Macqueen's superintendent, Peter McIntyre, to the district to select land for Macqueen and for Peter McIntyre and his brother John. When, on his return to Sydney, Dangar claimed the land for himself and his brother William, McIntyre protested, insisting he had prior claim. Dangar suggested a compromise, which McIntyre considered a bribe and complained to Governor Ralph Darling, who set up an inquiry. In 1827, Dangar was found to have used his public position for private gain and was fired.

Three years later, John McIntyre, known to be rather too fond of the lash, was murdered in his bed. Four of McIntyre's convict station hands were tried and convicted of his murder, on the evidence of a fellow convict attracted by the offer of a free pardon, a ticket to England and a cash reward. On the day of execution, the four men cheated the gallows when another convict, Charles James, confessed to the crime.

Plunkett tells the judge he has no more questions for this witness, and Henry Dangar leaves the stand, his integrity in doubt and his reputation in tatters.

William Hobbs, recalled to the stand, contradicts his former employer. He swears that George Anderson is 'as good a servant as ever I met', and that he would certainly believe him under oath. With that, the case is closed.

Summing up, Judge Burton cautions the jury on the dangers of what later ages will call trial by media. Harking back to Plunkett's opening address, he reminds them they had been advised 'that opinions had been formed and inferences drawn from what had appeared in print, but the jury were, in the solemn situation in which they were then placed, between God, their country and the prisoners, separated from the community.' He tells them that they, like himself, are responsible to God and to their country, not to public opinion.

'I know how pleasant it is to have the good will of friends, and of the public,' Burton says, 'but in the conscientious discharge of the duty now imposed on you by the solemn oath you have taken to administer justice, you must discard all private feelings, and guard against the semblance of being biased by any consideration. There might have been persons who had endeavoured to influence the public mind on either side of the case. You are not, however, to be moved by the opinions of either party, but to do your duty to God and your country, as you were sworn to do so.'

After reading the jury lengthy extracts from the evidence, the judge takes a parting shot at Henry Dangar.

'With respect to the evidence of the man Anderson, it had been impeached strongly by Mr Dangar, who, from some frivolous cause, has stated that he would not believe him on his oath. But if it were allowed that men charged with some trifling disobedience of orders or neglect were to be incapacitated from giving evidence, I am fearful that many crimes and murders amongst the number would go unpunished.

'However, you have heard Mr Hobbs' character of Anderson, and you have also heard Mr Dangar's reason for impeaching the credit of Anderson. You have heard circumstances relative to the misappropriation of land, and you have seen the manner in which Mr Dangar conducted himself in the box.

'It is not for you to judge whether Anderson's testimony has been impeached, or whether Mr Dangar's testimony has not rather been impeached by himself. At all events, Mr Dangar has shown the bias of his mind. He has shown that his opinion had already been formed, and that he came before the court prejudiced.'

In conclusion, calling down the wrath of Heaven itself, his honour intones: 'If the pecuniary interests of gentlemen require that their servants should go armed, it ought to be impressed upon them that nothing but extreme necessity would warrant their using those arms against their fellow creatures. And if the community ever became so depraved that the lives of their fellow creatures are of so little value that it is to be supposed that the blacks might be indiscriminately killed, wherever they are seen, then it will be no wonder that the colony should be visited by the displeasure and heavy visitations of God.'[10]

Outside the court, a frontier settler is overheard explaining to a Sydney man that where he comes from they don't have any trouble with the blacks because they give them food laced with arsenic. No one ever investigates deaths by illness among blacks, the man says. Arsenic is cheap, just tuppence for half a pound, and readily available as rat poison, no questions asked. Even a child can buy it.

The symptoms of arsenic poisoning begin with headache and confusion, diarrhoea and drowsiness, followed by vomiting, blood in the urine, muscle cramps and stomach pain as the poison affects the lungs, kidneys and liver, then convulsions, coma and death. Arsenic poisoning often goes undetected because the symptoms are similar to those of cholera, and, even if detected, doctors have no idea how to treat it.

At a quarter past one in the afternoon, the jurors retire to consider their verdict. At two o'clock, they're back. Before a hushed courtroom, the clerk calls out the name of each of the accused men in turn, and the foreman of the jury delivers the verdict on each in turn. For all seven, the verdict is, 'Not guilty.'

But with hardly time for an orgy of back-slapping or even a collective intake of breath, one of the jurors points out that the foreman has made a mistake; that the jury found the defendants guilty on five of the 20 counts. In other words, they had been acquitted of the murder of Charley but convicted of the murder of an unnamed child. Accordingly, the court is adjourned until noon on Friday.

It's not over yet.

Chapter 21

Seduced by the devil

'All rise!' The judges of the full bench of the Supreme Court take their seats. The faces of the seven prisoners shuffling into court before Justices Burton, Dowling and Wills are downcast. There are no jaunty grins this time, no affected yawns or knowing winks.

After the inevitable thrust and parry on points of law between John Plunkett and William a'Beckett, Judge Burton, clearly of the view that the defence has exhausted its argument, puts on the black cap and addresses the defendants.

He tells them they have been found guilty of murder, and quotes the Bible at them: 'Whoso sheddeth man's blood, by man shall his blood be shed.'[1]

'This was not a case where any provocation had been given, which might have been pleaded in excuse for the deed,' says the judge. 'This was not a case where property or lives of individuals had been attacked, and force had been resorted to, to repel the attack. The murder was not confined to one man but extended to many, including men, women, children and babies hanging at their mothers' breasts, in number not less than 30 human souls, slaughtered in cold blood.

'I cannot conceive that you could have so far forgotten Christian feeling, if you had flattered yourselves that there were many who would exert themselves to conceal your crime, and that you would be protected by them – if you had not flattered yourselves that none would be found to bring it to light. But for the sake of those who stood round, I wish to clearly explain what the law of the country is, and what the judges will do when called on to perform their duty.'

That duty, he says, now forces him to sentence them to death.

Asked to show cause why the convicted men should not be sentenced to death, William a'Beckett argues for a reprieve on the grounds that the prisoners were tried for separate murders on the same indictment. His argument, previously made and rejected, is rejected again.

Judge Burton calls for silence in the court. 'Prisoners at the bar, you have been found guilty of the crime of murder by a jury of your countrymen.'

After describing their crime in gruesome detail, he tells the condemned men, 'These remarks are not made to add to the pain which you must now experience. They are made for the benefit of standers-by. I sincerely hope that the grace of God may reach and penetrate the hardened hearts that surround a funeral pyre lighted by themselves, and gloat on the tortures and sufferings of so many of their fellow beings.

'You know the English laws, and there must have been some moving cause, some hidden hope that your crime would be concealed by parties interested that urged you on. You have flattered yourselves vainly, and I hope that if there be any parties who were interested in its concealment, they will be discovered, for the law holds the life of the black as dear as that of the white.

'In doing my duty as a judge, I have my feelings as a man, and I do, in sincerely commiserating your unfortunate state, hope that no other motive than that set forth in the information has induced you to the crime. I do trust that it was the "being seduced by the devil, and not having the fear of God before your eyes" alone that urged you on, and that you have not been induced by the persuasion of others.'

There is not a murmur in the courtroom as the judge, his voice strained with emotion and with tears welling in his eyes, tells the prisoners, 'Whatever private feelings may exist, I must not allow them to interfere with the stern duty imposed upon me by law, and that is to award the sentence due to your crime, which is that each and every one of you be taken from this place to whence you came, and from there to a place of public execution to be hanged by the neck until you are dead, and may God have mercy on your souls.'

At neither trial did the court hear from black voices. Before Myall Creek, only three white people had been convicted of murdering Aborigines, and none of the three had been executed. In the wake of Myall Creek, John Plunkett, George Gipps and others will push for legislation allowing Aborigines to give evidence in criminal cases, but all such attempts will fail until 1876.

The full depth of the horrors in the stockyard on Dangar's run didn't make the papers or the court records, but the oral history of the Wirrayaraay includes these words from a person whose mother escaped the massacre:

'My mother would sit and cry and tell me this – they buried our babies in the ground with only their heads above the ground. All in a row they were. Then they had tests to see who could kick the babies' heads off the furthest. One man clubbed a baby's head off from horseback. They then spent the rest of the day raping the women, most of whom were then tortured to death by sticking sharp things like spears up their vaginas till they died. They tied the men's hands behind their backs, then cut off their penis and testicles and watched them run around screaming until they died. They killed in other bad ways too.'[2]

So perhaps the judge, when he donned the black cap, should have told the killers, 'It is the sentence of this court that each and every one of you be taken from this place to whence you came, and from there to a place of public execution to be hanged by the neck until you are dead, but do not expect God to have mercy on your souls. You killed God at Myall Creek.'

Chapter 22

Poisoned pens

Nailing its bias to the masthead, *The Sydney Herald* hisses, 'The whole gang of black animals are not worth the money the colonists will have to pay for printing the silly court documents on which we have already wasted too much time.'[1]

On 8 December 1838, *The Australian* publishes a letter from 'An English Juryman':

As the late unparalleled slaughter of the Aborigines has created great excitement in the colony, so when the news shall have reached England, a like excitement will be felt there among the moral and religious classes of every denomination. The question will naturally be asked there – what are the feelings of the people of New South Wales on the subject?

In order that the feelings of some portion of the inhabitants may be known and duly appreciated, perhaps you will favour me with the insertion of the following sentiments expressed by one of the jury who tried and acquitted the men on the first trial.

'I look on the blacks' (said this enlightened and philanthropic juror) 'as a set of monkeys, and the earlier they are exterminated from the face of the earth the better. I would never consent to hang a white man for a black one. I knew well they were guilty of the murder, but I, for one, would never see a white man suffer for shooting a black.'

I leave you, sir, and the community to determine on the fitness of the white savage to perform the office of a juryman under any circumstances (much less such a one as that to which I have referred) or to discharge the moral and social duties in a Christian and civilised way.[2]

'The men found guilty of the alleged murder of certain aboriginal natives have received sentences of death,' *The Sydney Herald* reports.

Pointedly, even after the men had been convicted, the newspaper still refers to the murders as 'alleged', then asks: 'Are we to have equal laws? Are the white settlers and their servants to be protected against the outrages of the blacks? Are blacks to be hanged for murder as well as whites? And if so, what steps have been taken to apprehend and hang the scores of black murderers who have shed the blood of white British suspects?'[3]

The *Herald* cited a recent parliamentary report listing incidents of 'Europeans killed by aboriginal natives'. The incidents included:

In 1832, on the Big River, two men in the party of Surveyor-General Major Thomas Mitchell were speared to death.

Late in 1835, in the Namoi River district, a servant of the pastoralist and magistrate Sir John Jamison was killed.

In April 1836, on the Hall brothers' Bingara run, not far from Myall Creek station, two convict stockmen were attacked while splitting timber. One was killed, and the other escaped with a spear in his leg. The blacks then attacked the storekeepers' hut, and Thomas Hall was speared in the shoulder.

In September 1837, two storekeepers were killed during an attack on the hut at George Bowman's station on the Namoi.

In November that year, at Cobb's run on the Big River, two shepherds were killed.

In January 1838, two shepherds working on the Allman brothers' New England station were slain, and the flock taken.

In March, in the New England district, two convicts assigned to surveyor Heneage Finch were killed during a raid on the stores, and a shepherd on the Cruikshank run was killed and some 70 sheep taken.

In April, on the Big River, an attack on Fitzgerald's run left the hutkeeper dead, another man speared through the leg, and another who escaped unharmed when a spear pierced only the sleeve of his jacket.

The report concluded, 'The sacrifice of property has been immense, and the attacks upon the persons of Europeans innumerable, but none are mentioned except where loss of life occurred. And it is to be remarked that not one of the perpetrators of these 15 murders has been brought to justice, although they have been going on since 1832.'[4]

Claiming the report detailed less than 'one fiftieth part of the numbers of murders committed by blacks', the *Herald* demands: 'Is all this blood to be unavenged, and yet white men to be hanged for slaying blacks, perhaps in self-defence, perhaps in retaliation for injuries previously sustained?

'The law is unequal, and while it is so – while the murder of so many whites has been unavenged, it is nothing short of legal murder to take the lives of white men for the alleged slaying of blacks.'[5]

The Sydney Gazette takes a contrary view:

As to the guilt of the prisoners convicted of having committed this wholesale murder, no reasonable man could have any doubt after hearing or perusing the evidence produced on the first trial. Far be it from us to impute improper motives to the jury by whom the prisoners were pronounced not guilty; but we can only account for their returning a verdict so opposed to the evidence before them by supposing them to have been under the influence of one of those hallucinations to which New South Wales juries are sometimes subject.

The newspaper condemns the conduct of those gentlemen who, 'in throwing obstacles in the way' of Denny Day's investigation into the slaughter, impeded rather than aided the course of justice.

In the *Gazette*'s opinion, Day deserves public acclaim for 'bringing this barbarous murder to light', but that 'judging from the exhibitions some of his neighbours have made of themselves in the matter, we should be disposed to imagine that his firmness in the discharge of his duty in this particular has not increased his popularity at Hunter's River.'[6]

And on comparing the first and second trials:

When the murderers of the Aborigines were first tried at the bar of the Supreme Court, not all the respect we could wish to entertain for the sacred nature of the duties of a jury could prevent us from feeling that a verdict so diametrically opposed to evidence, to which it was impossible for a jury to refuse their belief, could not have been conscientiously arrived at – for we hold it impossible for any man who had listened attentively to the evidence brought forward on that occasion to have left the court unconvinced of the guilt of the parties accused. No doubt whatever exists with us, nor we apprehend with anyone else, that the actuating motive for returning such a verdict was a previously formed determination never to bring a white man to the gallows for the murder of an Aboriginal black.

The same editorial refers to the appearance in court the previous day of two Sydney publicans who had been charged with contempt of court for abusing the foreman of the jury of the second trial, which returned a verdict of guilty – 'both of them stating, in addition to much abusive ribaldry on the subject, that they would have sat for a month before they would have found a white man guilty of killing a parcel of cannibals like the Aborigines'.[7]

In the case referred to, publicans Thomas Douglas and Edward Bolton were brought before the bench of the Supreme Court accused of harassing and threatening George Sewell, who was the foreman of the jury in the second Myall Creek massacre trial.

Sewell told the court that since the trial he had been subjected to insults from people who violently disapproved of the verdict;

that Douglas had called him a rogue; and that Bolton had said that another of the jurors, William Knight, deserved to have his brains bashed out.

Thomas Douglas's defence was that he might well have made such remarks but was only joking, and had parted with Sewell on friendly terms. Bolton swore that he was present during the conversation and that Sewell did not seem to take offence. Moreover, he and Sewell met later for a friendly drink. Two other men present at the time also supported Douglas's version of events, as did Douglas's wife, Elizabeth.

After much convoluted legal argument over whether or not insulting a former juror, even in jest, was an indictable offence, the case was thrown out of court.

The Colonist observes that 'the murders committed from time to time by the whites on the blacks, and by the blacks on the whites, are, to a serious extent, chargeable upon us as a nation. We have not done our duty as a civilised and a Christian people. We have invaded the territory of the New Hollanders – have taken forcible possession of their rightful property – have amassed immense wealth by the tillage and pasturage of their soil.

'Was it not perfectly natural that the native should feel himself an injured man, and that he should appeal to the only authority from which he could expect redress – his spear?

'But the seizure of his property was not the only grievance inflicted on him by the whites. His morals were corrupted by the poisonous seductions of ardent spirits – his person was contaminated by the diseases of British vice – his wife and his daughters were made the victims of the white man's lust – and his friends slain by the Englishman's axe or musket. The only wonder is that, under the provocation of these accumulated injuries and insults, the Aborigines have not slaughtered every European they have encountered in the solitude of their forests.'[8]

In a letter to the editor of *The Sydney Herald*, under the pen-name 'Anti-Hypocrite', a settler describes Aborigines as 'the most degenerate, despicable, and brutal race of beings in existence'. The tirade continues:

> They stand unprecedented in the annals of the most ancient and barbarous histories, as a nation notorious for the anti-civilising propensities they put forth in opposition to every attempt made to reclaim them from their present wandering, abject, and brutal mode of life. Any attempt to civilise the Aboriginals of New Holland is futile and vain.
>
> Everyone who has had the most trifling intercourse amongst the natives must at once perceive (if he has common observation) that their manners, habits, and customs, (laws they have not) are all opposed, and diametrically inimical to civilisation.
>
> *Naturam expellas furca, tamenusque recurret*: 'Nature though expelled by violence, will return', and what it has pleased the Almighty in his wise decrees to ordain they should be, they will remain, in despite of every effort of civilised man, aided, however powerfully, by Christian principles and example. Before they are made Christians you must make them men – they can only be classed in the order of creation as the first great link, which connects, in its chain, man with the brute.

It is stated as a reason for their decrease that the convict population in the interior, do by fraud and bribery, owing to the scarcity of women, seduce the wives of the aborigines from their proper mates, and by illicit connetions introduce amongst the women disease and death. It is not so. Disease almost invariably follows, and death I have known, as the consequence of sexual gratifications with the aboriginal women – but it is the European who suffers, not the native.

Delicacy in a public journal forbids it, or I could lay before you facts of this nature sufficient to harrow up the soul. The frequent and often fatal connetion between the male prisoners and these females I deny not, as I know it to exist to a dreadful extent, but I deny that the Europeans originally contaminated the aborigines – suffice it therefore. Now with respect to fraud being used to seduce men's wives from them, is there a man of any experience who will not tell you it is quite unnecessary – the women are meretricious to a shocking extent – the husband makes a property of his wife. One of their invariable and revolting customs is an exchange of wives!

I am intimately acquainted with their general habits, having studied them a good deal and made very minute enquiries among them, being a grazier on the Murrumbidgee. I am, of course, more cognisant of the habits and better acquainted with the natives of the southern districts than any other, but I believe their manners differ as little as their language, and one tribe is a specimen of all. Cannibals of the most revolting characters they are all – they make no secret of it; their wives and children as often become a prey to cannibalism in the tribe to which they belong as to another; gratitude they have none; to bind them to a home is impossible; they treat their females only as beasts of burden, and have less affection

Privy to the royal rear and the royal ear. Sir Anthony Denny, King Henry VIII's Groom of the Stool.
(THE PRINT COLLECTOR/ GETTY IMAGES)

A swashbuckling pirate at rest. The tomb of Sir Edward Denny and his wife, Margaret. Waltham Abbey, Essex, 1599.

Romancing the postmaster's daughter. 'The courtship of Edward Denny Day and Margaret Raymond'. (UNKNOWN ARTIST, NEWCASTLE REGION LIBRARY)

Denny Day in old age. The only known photograph of the legendary lawman, published with his obituary, 27 May 1876. (UNIVERSITY OF NEWCASTLE, CULTURAL COLLECTIONS)

Integrity before ambition. Governor George Gipps. Painting by Eden Upton Eddis, 1860. (STATE LIBRARY OF VICTORIA)

Son of the Enlightenment. Governor Richard Bourke. (STATE LIBRARY OF NEW SOUTH WALES)

Unrepentant and unpunished. Major James Winniett Nunn, commander at the Waterloo Creek Massacre. (UNKNOWN ARTIST, C.1840, NATIONAL LIBRARY OF AUSTRALIA)

Frontier warfare. A desperate battle between Aboriginal warriors and mounted stockmen. (UNKNOWN ARTIST)

'Mr Dangar has shown the bias of his mind.' Prominent settler and surveyor Henry Dangar. (Turner Collection, University of Newcastle, Cultural Collections)

'A spirit of retaliation and revenge.' Robert Scott, leader of the Myall Creek killers' defence fund. (Attributed to Miss Sharpe, 1820, watercolour on ivory miniature, State Library of New South Wales)

Master of the art of seducing juries. Richard Windeyer, defence attorney for the Myall Creek killers. (Unknown artist, c.1840, National Portrait Gallery)

Losing the few friends he has. The fearless prosecutor at the Myall Creek Massacre trials, Attorney-General John Plunkett. (State Library of New South Wales)

*Monument to a murderer.
The vault of John Henry
Fleming, Wilberforce,
New South Wales.*
(Photo by author)

*No act of contrition. Stained-
glass window donated
by John Henry Fleming,
St John's Church, Wilberforce,
New South Wales.*
(Photo by author)

Forgotten hero. The author at the grave of Denny and Margaret Day in the Old Glebe Burial Ground, East Maitland, New South Wales.
(PHOTO BY DANIEL SMYTH)

The Days' neglected grave. The headstone has collapsed and lies facedown.
(PHOTO BY DANIEL SMYTH)

LEFT, CENTRE: *Stained-glass window in St Peter's Church, Maitland, the right panel dedicated to Denny Day, 1887.* (PHOTO BY DANIEL SMYTH)

BOTTOM: *In the cause of reconciliation. Myall Creek Massacre memorial, Bingara, New South Wales.* (PHOTO BY AUTHOR)

for their children than has a sow for its offspring; friendship they know not of, and the tie of kindred is acknowledged only so far as the fact admits it – it is never admitted by an interchange of affection. As a tribe or tribes they are cowardly, treacherous, and base – revenge, indiscriminate revenge, is their sole guide as law. They know no God, and admit only in the most absurd and ridiculous manner the existence of an invisible agent which is believed to be of a bloody-minded character – and they are thus, as I said before, the most abject beings on earth.[9]

Amid the fear and loathing stirred by the second trial, the above hate-filled rant is not unusual, but rather typical of comment published in *The Sydney Herald* under the editorship of Alfred Ward Stephens.

Stephens, founder, owner and editor of the *Herald*, is also a landowner, with several large runs on the frontier territories, and is a close friend of Robert Scott. Since 1831, when the *Herald* joined its older rivals, *The Sydney Gazette* and *The Colonist*, on the scene, it has come to dominate the market by tapping into the popular prejudices of a growing middle class and working class, free and felon alike, while at the same time promoting the interests of the elite minority – the wealthy landowners.

In the imaginary world Stephens' *Herald* has skilfully created for its readers, the settlers, especially the rich ones, are the embodiment of the pioneering spirit – noble, stoic, courageous, Protestant and, of course, white. Pitted against these bold pathfinders are the natural enemies of civilisation, the blacks – ruthless savages determined to block the path of progress, aided and abetted by missionaries and other misguided do-gooders, and an arrogant and ineffectual government.

When the *Herald* maintains that the second Myall Creek trial should not have gone ahead, and that the convicted men should not hang, its main rival *The Colonist*, founded by larger-than-life politician, writer and Presbyterian minister John Dunmore Lang, takes an opposing stance, and the rivals wage an ink war over the issue. The liberal-leaning *Sydney Gazette* joins the battle, allied with *The Colonist*, and the vitriol flies fast and furious. While the *Herald*, pushing the populist white-is-right barrow, grows increasingly strident, its rivals assume a measured but mocking tone, referring to the 'infamous language' and 'intemperate ravings' of the *Herald*,[10] and condemning the *Herald*'s defence of the 'inhuman monsters' who committed the crime.[11]

As for the likes of Robert Scott, Henry Dangar and other contributors to the killers' defence fund, *The Colonist* doesn't hold back, describing them as 'men calling themselves gentlemen and Christians but whose conduct in this bloody transaction has been disgraceful to their rank, to their religion, and to their species'.[12]

Stephens meets his Waterloo after throwing out a challenge to his nemesis, Presbyterian minister and Aboriginal welfare activist John Saunders, to prove that he (Stephens) 'or any of the respectable settlers throughout the colony, have expressed or entertained the opinion that the Aborigines should be ill-treated, far less murdered'.[13]

In *The Colonist* Saunders fires Stephens' own published words back at him, notably those Stephens emphasised in capitals. In his editorial of 14 November 1838, the day before the first Myall Creek trial, Stephens wrote:

We say, protect the whites as well as the blacks. Protect the white settler, his wife, and children, in remote places, from the filthy, brutal cannibals of New Holland. We say to the colonists, since the Government makes no adequate exertion to protect you, protect yourselves; and if the ferocious savages endeavour to plunder or destroy your property, or to murder yourselves, your families, or your servants, do to them as you would do to any white robbers or murderers – SHOOT THEM DEAD, if you can.[14]

The Sydney Gazette, after the second trial, slams the Hunter's River Black Association and praised Denny Day.

Up to the close of the first trial we looked upon the conduct of the gentlemen who had associated themselves together for the defence of the prisoners as praiseworthy because we considered the association to have been formed under the impression that the accused were guiltless of the crime with which they were charged, or if guilty, that they had been hurried on to commit the excess in defence of their masters' property.

When, however, we found that protection continued even after it had become apparent to the whole community that so large a number of defenceless human beings had been slaughtered by the inhuman wretches in cold blood, our opinion became changed, and we look upon the continuance of that protection in no other light than as, if not arguing a previous knowledge of the foul deed, of at least betokening on the part of the members an approbation and encouragement of a crime so atrocious that the mere mention of it is sufficient to produce a shudder.

Coupling this with the fact sworn to on the trial by Mr Day, the Police Magistrate, that such obstacles were thrown in the way of an investigation into the slaughter as to cause it to occupy the very lengthened period of 47 days, we cannot but express our extreme disapprobation of the conduct of gentlemen whose station in society is such as to have led us to expect that they would have aided, rather than impeded the course of justice, and we cannot but express our fear also, lest their conduct should leave a stain on the reputation of the community, which ages may not remove.

It has been argued that the outcome of the Myall Creek trials did not stop the murder of Aboriginal people, but only served to make the killers more careful. And while there were indeed further massacres after 1838, it would be drawing a long bow to suggest that Aborigines would have been better off if Denny Day had stayed home; if Anderson and Hobbs had kept their mouths shut; if George Gipps had turned a blind eye; if John Plunkett had merely gone through the motions.

What Myall Creek did do was to raise the level of debate over Aboriginal rights, with the result that laws were passed shortly afterwards to better protect blacks against whites, such as the establishment of a Border Police force to regulate white incursions into Aboriginal land, and prohibitions against the forcible detention of Aboriginal women in frontier districts.

And while, after the immediate response, it was one step forward, two steps back, and many supposedly protectionist policies were discriminatory, at least issues such as equal pay for blacks were on the table. Even the previously unmentionable matter of whites and blacks cohabiting raised its head in public. In an instance that made plain the nonsensical rules applied to mixed-race relationships, Bishop Broughton, despite his supposedly enlightened attitude towards blacks, strongly disapproved of mixed marriages on the ground that Aborigines were heathens. When Reverend William Cowper – the same reverend gentleman who will one day snatch a girl named Mary Ann Bugg and her brother from their mixed-parents (see Chapter 36) – asked the bishop's permission to marry a white man to a black woman and baptise their children, Broughton allowed the baptisms but forbade the marriage. In other words, he was letting the kids into heaven while kicking mum and dad downstairs.

Englishman Thomas Bartlett, after visiting Australia in the 1840s, noted in his book, *New Holland*, that there were 'two opinions, diametrically opposed to each other, respecting the character of the Aboriginal population' which influenced the way Aboriginal people were treated. Some settlers considered they were 'not entitled to be looked upon as fellow creatures' and treated them accordingly.

Other settlers, horrified by 'the inroads made into the possessions of the natives', considered it their duty to treat their 'ignorant but innocent' black brethren humanely.[15]

Chapter 23

A fall from grace

At dawn on Saturday 26 January 1788, when able seaman Owen Cavanough became the first European to step ashore at Sydney Cove – to secure the longboat carrying Governor Arthur Phillip – he brought with him the common law of England. And with English law came the so-called Bloody Code, a list of more than 220 crimes punishable by death. Capital crimes included cutting down trees, shoplifting, poaching, stealing hares, theft of goods valued at 12 pence, and being in the company of Gypsies for a month.

While in Britain capital offences were often commuted, leaving only about 25 for which execution was mandatory, New South Wales was particularly fond of the noose, and slow to introduce reform laws passed in the mother country.

Between 1832 and 1838, Britain had removed the death penalty for shoplifting, theft of sheep, cattle and horses, sacrilege, burglary, theft from a dwelling house, letter stealing, forgery, returning from transportation, shooting at, and cutting and maiming.

James Pratt and John Smith, hanged at Newgate in 1835, were the last Britons to be executed for sodomy.

Lawrence Curtis and Patrick and Edward Donnelly, hanged at Shrewsbury in August 1836, were the last executed for robbery.

That same year, Daniel Case was the last to be hanged for arson.

Britain has repealed The Murder Act of 1751, which decreed that 'in no case whatsoever shall the body of any murderer be suffered to be buried'.[1]

Denied burial, the bodies of murderers were publicly dissected or left hanging in chains on a gibbet. Most often used for murderers, traitors, highwaymen, pirates and sheep thieves, this posthumous punishment, employed under The Murder Act as a means of 'better preventing the horrid crime of murder'[2] involved placing the corpse in an iron cage hoisted aloft, and leaving it to rot.

In 1837, in Van Diemen's Land, four years after hanging in chains, along with public dissection of murderers, was abolished in Britain, the body of John McKay, hanged for murder, was strung up in chains from a gibbet near Hobart. The body remained there until a friend of the victim, horrified by the sight of McKay's rotting corpse, demanded that it be taken down.

In the preceding dozen years, while the number of capital crimes fell to just 16 in Britain, more than 360 people – almost all of them white male convicts – have been sent to the gallows in New South Wales. Those were busy years for the hangman, with a yearly tally of executions higher than that of England and Wales combined. By 1838, however, the rate has declined significantly. The colony has belatedly – and often grudgingly – adopted British reforms, removing the death penalty for many crimes. Only in Van Diemen's Land are people still executed for rape, carnal knowledge and sodomy.

With cattle theft, nonviolent burglary, forgery, smuggling, slave trading and certain kinds of theft no longer designated capital crimes in New South Wales, public execution is now a fate reserved only for murderers and rapists, and thus, for the masses, a rare relief from toil and tedium.

These are such enlightened times.

From around eight o'clock on the morning of Tuesday 18 December, crowds begin to gather at The Rocks, outside the rear walls of Sydney Gaol. Seven men are to hang this day, and a public execution is akin to a festival or a fete. It's a family outing, and the children among the crowd are noisy and restless, eager to be entertained. Not everyone will be allowed within to watch the dance of death, and the jostling has already begun.

A public hanging is a stage-managed affair with its own particular etiquette and moral universe. For the condemned person, the authorities' intention is to intensify the severity of the punishment by a theatrical exhibition of shame and disgrace. For the crowd watching the gruesome spectacle, the intention is to engender fear and respect for the law.

Some here today have come in hopes of celebrating news of a last-minute reprieve by the governor. Indeed, many believe it possible, even probable. The ultimate responsibility for granting mercy for capital crimes excluding murder and treason lies with the governor. In cases of murder and treason he could grant a temporary respite while referring the case to London, but although pressure to do so has persisted into the early hours of Tuesday, Governor Gipps has remained unmoved by petitions for mercy and press campaigns pleading for the convictions to be overturned. With that in mind, he has arranged for a strong presence of armed troops in case of violence. There is cause for concern that those among the mob who look upon the killers as heroes might attempt to rescue the condemned men.

As a further precaution, the number of people allowed inside to witness the executions has been limited to those who applied the previous day. *The Sydney Gazette* reports, 'This arrangement no doubt gave offence to many persons who applied for admission, but the good effect was apparent by preventing the rush of the rabble usual on such occasions.'[3]

Usually, if the crowd expresses displeasure – often with hissing and booing, occasionally with riotous behaviour – it's not out of pity for the prisoner but out of scorn for the ineptitude of the hangman. A misplaced knot, for example, means a lingering, choking death for the condemned man rather than a swift snap of the neck. Getting it wrong spoils the show.

At nine o'clock, the seven condemned men – Kilmeister, Hawkins, Johnston, Parry, Foley, Oates and Russell – are brought into the yard. Three clergymen accompany them – two Protestant ministers for Kilmeister, Hawkins, Johnston and Parry, and a Catholic priest for Foley, Oates and Russell.

'They seemed greatly dejected,' a reporter for *The Sydney Gazette* notes, 'and Russell was much agitated, that he was obliged to cling to the priest's coat for support.'[4]

After the High Sheriff has proclaimed the warrant of execution, Foley, the youngest of the prisoners, asks permission to embrace the others. His request is granted, and the condemned men, eyes streaming with tears, hug and shake hands, bidding each other farewell before mounting the scaffold.

On the gallows, they fall to their knees in prayer while the hangman makes his final preparations. That done, the clergymen descend the scaffold, and, as the men cry to the heavens for mercy, the hangman releases the trap and drops them into oblivion.

The *Gazette* observes, 'Throughout the whole of the time they remained in the yard they appeared to pay much attention to their devotions, and although they expressed no contrition for the crime for which they were to suffer, their behaviour showed that they deeply felt contrition in their hearts. The crime for which they were executed was almost without a parallel, and the punishment the greatest that could be inflicted, and we sincerely hope that it may strike a terrible warning among those who, like these men, consider themselves out of the reach of the law.'[5]

One man who witnessed the hangings wrote to a friend in England, 'I have just returned from seeing the seven men all launched into eternity at the same moment. It was an awful sight and has made me feel quite sick. I shall never forget it.'[6]

The day after the hangings, Governor Gipps writes to Lord Glenelg, 'It is now my painful duty to inform your Lordship that seven of the perpetrators of this atrocious deed, having been convicted on the clearest evidence, suffered yesterday morning the extreme penalty which the law affords for the crime of murder.'

After giving an account of the massacre – in greater detail than in previous despatches – Gipps concludes: 'The eleven persons apprehended by Mr Day all arrived in this country as convicts, though of some of them, the sentences have expired. The twelfth man, or the one who has escaped, is a freeman, a native of the colony. It will be satisfactory to your Lordship to hear that the smallest doubt does not exist of the guilt of the men who have been executed or of their all having been actively engaged in the massacre. The whole eleven would indeed, I have reason to believe, have pleaded guilty at the first trial, if not otherwise advised by their counsel.

'After condemnation, none of the seven attempted to deny their crime, though they all stated that they thought it extremely hard that white men should be put to death for killing blacks. Until after their first trial, they never, I believe, thought that their lives were in jeopardy.'[7]

Gipps also informs Glenelg that he has dismissed Robert Scott as a magistrate. He explains:

Connected with the trial of the men whose execution for murder I have reported in my despatch of yesterday's date, No. 200, there are some circumstances which I think it right to bring separately to your Lordship's knowledge. The apprehension of so many as eleven men for the murder of the blacks, and the determination of the Government to bring them to trial, created an unusual sensation in the colony, and a meeting was held at Patrick's Plains, a place on the Hunter River about 30 miles above Maitland, at which the sum of, I believe, about £800, was subscribed to defray the expenses of defence.

The person who presided at this meeting was Mr Robert Scott, a magistrate of the territory, who, from his property, family connections, and the prominent part usually taken by him in public affairs, may be considered a person of note in the community. At this same meeting, a petition or memorial was adopted, which was subsequently presented to me by a deputation, of which Mr Scott was the leader. In all this, I saw nothing to find fault with. I could not be displeased that the accused should have counsel employed for their defence. The meeting at Patrick's Plains was held before the whole atrocity, which marked the murders, was known to the public. The persons who attended it might reasonably have supposed that the accused had only acted in defence of their masters' property against the aggressions of the blacks, and the memorial addressed to myself asked for nothing more than equal justice to both parties. I cautiously therefore avoided expressing in any way disapprobation of Mr Scott's proceedings. The case however was altered, when a few days afterwards the Attorney-General reported to me that Mr Scott had visited the eleven men in prison and, in the presence of the gaoler, advised them not to split among themselves, saying that there was no direct evidence against them, and that, if they were only true to each other, they could not be convicted.

Mr Scott happening to call upon me so soon after this occurrence, I thought it right to inform him of the report which had been made to me by the Attorney-General, telling him, however, that, until the trial of the men should be over, I was determined to say or do nothing more in the matter on this occasion. Mr Scott fully acknowledged that he had visited the men in prison, and spoken to them the words which been reported to me. He said, however, that when he did so, he did not know the full extent of the case against them, not having then read the depositions taken before Mr Day, and that after reading the depositions he was sorry for what he had done. From that moment, I supposed that Mr Scott would at least have ceased to take any personal part in the defence of the men, and it was therefore with the greatest surprise I subsequently learned that he was seated in court at their trial, close to the bar, and by the side of their attorney, thus making himself a party to their defence to the very last.

The governor tells Lord Glenelg he will soon be issuing a new list of commissions for magistrates, 'and I have to report to your Lordship that Mr Robert Scott's name does not appear in it'.

He concludes, 'I will only further express to your Lordship my opinion that the proceedings of Mr Scott did materially interfere with, and have in part prevented the due administration of justice. His appearance at the first trial contributed, I have no doubt, to a verdict from the jury directly against the evidence.'[8]

Yintayintin saw it all. From his hiding place behind a tree, the young man the whites call Davey watched the butchers go about their bloody business at Myall Creek. Now, he may be the last hope to bring justice to the four horsemen not included in the second trial for lack of evidence – John Blake, James Lamb, George Palliser and Charles Toulouse.

Yintayintin and his young brother Kwimunga, called Billy, are Kamilaroi youths of the Goonoo Goonoo clan. They hail from the plains by the Calala, which the whites call the Peel River (near present-day Tamworth, 400 kilometres north of Sydney).

Yintayintin is 19 years old, speaks good English and, according to Thomas Hobbs, his former employer at Myall Creek station, would make a competent witness if given sufficient instruction. Denny Day, who took a deposition from Yintayintin, is convinced that in the case now pending against Blake, Lamb, Palliser and Toulouse, the young black station hand would be a vital witness for the prosecution.

Attorney-General Plunkett agrees, and announces that at the trial of the four men he will 'bring forward the native lad Davey, aged 19 years, who witnessed the whole transaction, and who in the meantime he would take care to be instructed as to the nature of an oath'.[9]

Plunkett is hopeful that putting Davey on the witness stand could not only secure a conviction but test the legal waters on allowing Aborigines to give evidence in court – a cause he has taken to heart. But it's not to be – Davey is nowhere to be found. The trial is postponed and the prisoners remanded in custody while attempts are made to find the missing eye witness, but when two months pass with no sign of him, the case is dropped and, in February 1839, the prisoners walk free.

History loses sight of Lamb, Palliser and Toulouse. John Blake, in 1852, commits suicide by cutting his own throat. And Yintayintin, known as Davey, is never seen again. There are whispers that a prominent landowner had something to do with his disappearance, but no evidence comes to light to support the rumour.

Chapter 24

Seeking John Henry

The Flemings, like many other early Hawkesbury settlers, had moved on to greener pastures on Hunter's River and beyond, leaving behind them land scoured by years of unchecked clearing.

Increased run-off had eroded riverbanks, streams were silted up, grazing sheep and cattle had destroyed the native grasses, and floods had stripped the topsoil and spread weeds downstream.

On the Liverpool Plains, the country between the Big River and the ranges was ideal for cattle runs. There was ample water, even in time of drought, and the mountains on three sides formed a natural barrier. On the only open side, fronting the river, where cattle from different runs could mix, the cattlemen cooperated to sort them out. They were all friends on the Big River – the Halls, Glennies and Ogilvies, Richard Wiseman, Archie Bell and Robert Scott. The exception was the somewhat aloof Henry Dangar, who was not well liked by his neighbours.

The cattle country was hard won. At Hall's Bingara station, in 1836, a Kamilaroi attack left one convict stockman dead – speared when caught in the open while rushing to the shelter of a hut – and another stockman and one of the Hall brothers wounded. Other stations had similar tales.

In 1838, the Kamilaroi in the Big River territory are fewer in number and confrontations with settlers less frequent. When clashes do occur, however, they are as brutal as ever. For the whites, with no police or soldiers to protect them, and for the blacks, with protection under English law observed only in the breach, attack and reprisal have become a way of life.

The second Myall Creek trial, conviction and execution of seven of the killers creates deep resentment among Big River settlers of what they see as government interference in the frontier way, and drives a rift between the Myall Creek station cattlemen and their neighbours. If only Hobbs and Anderson had kept their big mouths shut and left well enough alone, 'Hall's Jemmy' – described by his master at the trial as quiet and inoffensive – and the rest, would still be alive and useful.

Matthew Henry Hall, of Bingara, declares that British law 'won't go down in this country',[1] and on the family's Hawkesbury holdings, William Hall shuns his brother-in-law and neighbour William Johnston, who was a jury member on the second Myall Creek massacre trial, and builds a boundary fence between their two properties. The Halls are related to the Flemings, and William will one day wed his cousin Elizabeth Fleming, John Henry's sister.

According to John Henry's own version of events, as told to his family, and since retold by his apologists, he and his men were on the trail of Myall blacks who had speared cattle and had attempted to spear the stockmen minding the cattle. They were incensed to find that some of the beasts wounded by spears had been left to die in agony, and by the sheer ingratitude of the blacks, to whom generous local settlers often gave meat to feed their families.

John Henry quickly realised that the blacks camped at Myall Creek were not the ones who had speared the cattle, but reasoned that perhaps leading his captives around for a while, and making a lot of noise about it, might flush out the real culprits who, inexplicably, would be hiding nearby and show themselves. When it became clear that this ploy was not going to work, John Henry fired at one of the Aboriginal men, intending not to hit him but to frighten him into revealing where the cattle killers were hiding. An instant later, to John Henry's horror, his men opened fire on the captives, and kept firing until all of them were down – some dead, some wounded.

In shock and alarm, he spurred his horse and rode away, and took no part in the atrocities that followed. He headed for the Hawkesbury, where he could find shelter and protection with relatives at St Albans, Wilberforce and Ebenezer, stopping at Invermein on the way to borrow a fresh horse from a friend.

A contrary version of Fleming's escape has it that all that happened that day was done at his command, and that he rode his horse almost to death that night, hoping to put as much distance between himself and Myall Creek as possible to give himself an alibi.

According to the inevitable conspiracy theory, John Henry was tipped off by the Mounted Police commander, Lieutenant George Pack, who was in the pay of influential landowners. To make sure Fleming avoided arrest and got clear away, a fast horse was delivered to him, and Pack made sure that the posse returning south with the prisoners travelled as slowly as possible. This unfounded smear of Pack's character is made more preposterous by the accusation that to avoid any suspicion of corruption arising from his sudden wealth he claimed to have found a bushranger's hoard. Pack, who died suddenly three years later, left an estate consisting of the remainder of his army pay, totalling eight shillings and sixpence.

Yet another version of events has John Henry Fleming provided with a relay of pony-express mounts by Bosney Nowen, the mail contractor at Muswellbrook. Riding like the wind, with fresh horses along the way, Fleming makes it to the port of Newcastle in time to board a ship bound for Van Diemen's Land.

Then again, local lore has him galloping into Thomas Simpson Hall's 'Dartbrook' station, halfway between Invermein and Muswellbrook, as if all hell is hot on his heels, on a horse so skittish that it requires three men to hold the animal while Fleming dismounts. Just what spooked the horse depends on who is telling the tale. Some say it was a desperate dash through a hail of spears as Kamilaroi warriors gave pursuit. Others insist the horse was drunk; that in order to keep his mount running at full tilt, Fleming wrapped a whisky-soaked rag around the horse's bit. The story goes on to claim that John Henry left the addled animal tied to a hitching rail at Maitland, which somehow gave rise to the rumour that he had escaped to Van Diemen's Land. Or to America. Or to parts unknown.

Chapter 25

Too dark to tell

At Merton Courthouse, on the rim of the upper Hunter Valley, in April 1839, Denny Day finally comes face to face with Major James Nunn, who led the Mounted Police attack at Waterloo Creek, along with Lieutenant George Coblian, Sergeant John Lee, Corporal Hannan and 'Major' Fitton, a stockman at Hall's Big River station, all of whom have now had plenty of time to get their stories straight – almost.

Nunn, who in light of Day's reputation after Myall Creek is no doubt wary of him, swears in a deposition that on being ordered to the frontier to suppress outrages by the blacks, he and his troop arrived at the Namoi River to be told that 'the blacks were at that time assembled in great numbers at a place lower down the Namoi.

'After marching all night, we came upon a tribe of blacks on the river bank,' Nunn says. 'After disposing of my men so as to prevent the escape of the blacks and giving them orders not to fire at all, but if necessary to defend themselves with their swords, I succeeded in capturing the whole tribe without any violence.

'With the assistance of a black boy who went with us, I communicated to the tribe that they were charged with murder, spearing cattle and all manner of outrages, and demanded that the actual perpetrators of these acts of violence should be delivered up to me.'[1]

Nunn tells Day that 15 of the band of about 100 were pointed out to him as the guilty parties, including two men said to have murdered a stockman from Hall's Big River station some time earlier. The 15 men were taken into custody, and the rest 'set at large and treated kindly by me, so much so that they remained with the party until evening'.[2]

According to Nunn, the troopers returned to their camp with the captives before sundown. There, the two men accused of murder, who were handcuffed, somehow managed to slip their cuffs and attempted to escape. One got away, and the other was shot dead by a sentry. 'The other 13 prisoners were subsequently liberated, all except one, who I retained with me as a guide,' he says.

Nunn does not explain why he set the 12 men free, despite them having been charged with 'all manner of outrages'.

Moving on to Cobb's station on the Big River, where two station hands had reportedly been killed by blacks, Nunn found 'everything in the greatest confusion; the shepherds and people all afraid to leave the vicinity of their huts.

'Lamb, the superintendent at the station, informed me of the particulars of the murder of the two men by blacks at the station, and told me the blacks had taken off eight and 20 sheep and some articles from the station.'[3]

If Nunn is aware that this is the same James 'Jem' Lamb, who was one of the four who escaped conviction for the Myall Creek

Massacre after the Aboriginal eye witness Davey conveniently disappeared, he gives no indication.

'On hearing this information,' he says, 'I considered it my duty to pursue the tribe who had committed these outrages, and, having provisioned the party for 15 days, I began my march.' Two days later, at Waterloo Creek, the troop rode into an ambush. Corporal Hannan was speared in the leg, Nunn heard shots fired ahead of the column, and his men suddenly 'charged and separated in such a manner that I was perfectly unable to collect them at the moment'. He insists that had Hannan not been wounded no shots would have been fired, and repeats his claim that only four or five blacks were killed. He does, however – perhaps inadvertently – confirm the rumour that Jem Lamb rode with him that day. 'Lamb recognised a tomahawk and a knife, which were found in the blacks' camp, as some of the articles that were taken from his master's station when the two men were murdered there,' Nunn says. 'From this and other circumstances I have no doubt whatever of this tribe having been guilty of the outrages at Mr Cobb's station.'[4]

Sergeant Lee, under oath, echoes his commander's version of events, with the notable exception of his own assessment of how many blacks were killed. 'From what I saw myself, I should say that from 40 to 50 blacks were killed,' he says.[5]

Corporal Hannan tells Day he could easily have shot the warrior who speared him, but did not do so because Major Nunn had told him never to fire except in self-defence. As for the death toll, he claims that after he was speared, 'the pain in my wound was so great that I cannot speak of anything that occurred'. He's certain, however, that no shot was fired before he was speared.[6]

The stockman 'Major' Fitton, who was back with the packhorses 'when the troopers went after the blacks, after Hannan had been wounded', swears he heard Nunn order his men to take prisoners but not to open fire.

Lieutenant Coblian, in a long and at times confusing statement, seems uncertain as to whether the shooting began before or after Hannan was speared. On the vital question of how many blacks were killed, he says, 'I only saw three or four bodies', but by then it was getting dark – too dark to tell.[7]

In the aftermath of the Myall Creek convictions, the implicit threat to Governor George Gipps from the frontier settlers, via *The Sydney Herald*, was that if he failed to use his powers of clemency to save the condemned men from the gallows they would ignite a war of extermination against the blacks.

Gipps, to his credit, did not cave in under pressure. However, given the opportunity to apply the Myall Creek precedent to the Waterloo Creek massacre, he loses his nerve and backs off, leaving the slaughter of up to 300 people to go unpunished.

The governor's sudden attack of faintheartedness must surely be galling to Denny Day, who on 9 April sent copies of the depositions taken at Merton to the Colonial Secretary. He has heard nothing since, and now he knows why.

In the aftermath of another clash of cultures, an ocean away, Vicente Filisola, an Italian-born general in the Mexican army, stands in the still-smoking courtyard of an abandoned Spanish mission in Bexar (now San Antonio) in the Mexican province of Tejas. The mission, called the Alamo, was the scene last night of terrible slaughter, when vastly outnumbered revolutionaries fighting for an independent state of Texas were wiped out by the forces of President Antonio Lopez de Santa Anna.

It is the morning of 7 March 1836, the day after a desperate, bloody battle in which some 260 defenders, led by William Travis, Davy Crockett and Jim Bowie, repulsed wave after wave of attack until overrun, yet Filisola takes little pride in the victory. In later reflections on the battle, he recalls:

Finally, the place remained in the power of the Mexicans, and all the defenders were killed. It is a source of deep regret, that after the excitement of the combat, many acts of atrocity were allowed which are unworthy of the gallantry and resolution with which this operation had been executed, and stamp it with an indelible stain in the annals of history.

These acts were reproved at the time by those who had the sorrow to witness them, and subsequently by the whole army, who certainly were not habitually animated by such feelings, and who heard with disgust and horror, as becomes brave and generous Mexicans who feel none but noble and lofty sentiments, of certain facts which I forebear to mention, and wish for the honour of the Mexican Republic had never taken place.

In our opinion the blood of our soldiers as well as that of the enemy was shed in vain, for the mere gratification of the inconsiderate, puerile and guilty vanity of reconquering Bexar by force of arms, and through a bloody contest.

The massacres of the Alamo, of Goliad, of Refugio, convinced the rebels that no peaceable settlement could be expected, and that they must conquer, or die, or abandon the fruits of ten years of sweat and labour, together with their fondest hopes for the future.[8]

In March 1839, Henry Dangar is back in court, this time being sued by William Hobbs, his former overseer at Myall Creek station, for unpaid wages.

Hobbs claims Dangar owes him £200 for work done after the Myall Creek trials. Dangar insists he owes him no more than £30, which he has paid into the court. In the convoluted language of the law, 'The defendant is a grazier and the plaintiff entered into an agreement to act as superintendent over his stock establishment, at Myall Creek, at the rate of £70 per annum, and £10 more at the end of the 12 months if the defendant was satisfied with his conduct. The agreement, which was put in and proved was dated the 3rd of October, 1836, and at the expiration of that time the defendant solicited the plaintiff to continue a year or two, when the plaintiff agreed for a second year at £100 per annum, but this agreement was only a verbal agreement. The plaintiff accordingly stopped in the defendant's service for another year, and in the month of October last, the defendant gave notice that he should not require the plaintiff's services any longer; but this notice was not given until after the plaintiff had entered on his third year, as appeared from a letter dated the 12th of October, nine days after the term of the agreement had expired, and the defendant required the plaintiff to muster the cattle which were spread over a large tract of country, which the plaintiff attempted to do, and remained some time after the notice to perform but failed to do in consequence of their being scattered during his absence in attendance as a witness on the trial of the men for the murder of the blacks, at Mr Dangar's station, at Myall Creek.'[9]

In plain English, Hobbs says Dangar hasn't paid him for rounding up the cattle that strayed from the station while he was away at the trials, on the excuse that the work was done after he had been fired.

Dangar's defence is that 'the plaintiff had neglected his duty and had suffered the cattle to go astray, for want of common attention. A person named Cook, who superseded the plaintiff as superintendent, stated that when he took charge there were 500 head of cattle short; but it also appeared that the plaintiff was prevented from collecting them by illness, and by having to attend at the prosecution of the men for the murder, and as he had received no notice from the defendant, he did not conceive that he was bound to expend a month or two to collect cattle which had been suffered to stray, without any remuneration for his services.'[10]

In other words, Hobbs was perfectly willing to return to Myall Creek to round up the strays, but he wasn't prepared to do it for nothing. The court finds in favour of William Hobbs, with damages of £11, 17 shillings and 8 pence, plus the £30 Dangar paid into court.

After William Hobbs appeared as the main Crown witness at the massacre trials, no one in the pastoral industry would employ him. He was appointed Chief Constable at Wollombi and McDonald River from 1847 to 1850, then Chief Constable at Windsor from 1850 to 1864, gaoler at Windsor from 1864 to 1865, and was the gaoler at Wollongong from 6 September 1865 until his death on 8 April 1871.

Chapter 26

The scourge

The Duchess and the Queen both enjoy a juicy piece of gossip – the more salacious the better. Anna Maria Russell, Duchess of Bedford, is Queen Victoria's Lady of the Bedchamber – the female equivalent of Groom of the Stool – and a lifelong friend.

Malicious gossip has got them both into trouble in the past. In a particularly scandalous example, the Duchess heard a whisper that Lady Flora Hastings, a lady-in-waiting to the Queen's mother, the Duchess of Kent, had consulted the court physician, Sir James Clark, complaining of abdominal pain, and that the doctor had informed her she was pregnant. Because Lady Flora was unmarried, her situation was hushed up, except by Duchess Anna and the Queen, who spread the rumour, naming Sir John Conroy as the father. Victoria detested Conroy, who was suspected of being her mother's lover.

When Lady Flora's supposed pregnancy turned out to be liver cancer, and she died soon after being diagnosed, at 33, both duchess and monarch came under severe public criticism for ruining the reputation of an innocent woman.

Both were suitably chastened, and now, in 1840, when Victoria comes to call, Anna treats her not to tittle-tattle but to tea and cake. Dinner in the nineteenth century is served between 7 pm and 8.30 pm, and lunch is a very light meal. Tired of feeling famished by dinnertime, the Duchess has invented another meal between lunch and dinner – a snack of cakes or sandwiches with Darjeeling tea. Her Majesty is amused, and afternoon tea is on its way to becoming a British tradition, even in the far-flung corners of the empire.

High tea is yet to catch on in the colonies, but Christmas has come a little early this year for the people of Wallis Plains. Patrick Grant has resigned as police magistrate to run for parliament, and Denny Day is back. It is November 1840.

For too long, Grant has been spending more time in Sydney than at his post in Maitland. The type of urgent business that so often required his presence at the colonial capital is instanced in a despatch from Governor Gipps to Lord Glenelg.

Gipps writes:

I have the honour to forward herewith, for the purpose of being presented to Her Most Gracious Majesty, an address of congratulation on Her Majesty's happy accession to the Throne of Her Ancestors, numerously and respectably signed by the inhabitants of Maitland, a flourishing and loyal town in the colony.

The address was placed in my hands by Mr Patrick Grant, a Police Magistrate of the District, with a request that I would entreat your Lordship to present it to our Most Gracious Sovereign.[1]

Grant, who made no secret of his belief that his humble position in the colonies was beneath him, accompanied Lady Jane Franklin, wife of the Governor of Van Diemen's Land, Sir John Franklin, on her visit to Maitland in 1839, during one of her many overland journeys. The remarkable Lady Jane, explorer, social reformer and political mover and shaker, was less than impressed with Grant, whom she described as seeming 'non compos, and appeared to be under the influence of liquor'.

Grant kept Lady Jane and her companions waiting an hour for dinner, arriving late and with a 'doleful look' before boring her to distraction by incessantly repeating the same topic.[2]

Grant's departure and Day's return brings welcome relief to the people on Hunter's River, who resented Grant spending his time swanning around Sydney salons sucking up to nobility when he should be out chasing bushrangers. The joy and relief at Day's return to Maitland as police magistrate is short-lived, however. He's not long back when he, too, resigns, determined yet again to be a success in business.

It's a scourge – a veritable scourge. There are more bushrangers in New South Wales, some say, than there are pickpockets in London.

By the 1830s, the term 'bushranger', which had previously referred to escaped prisoners, is generally applied to highwaymen. These are not all men 'made mad by bad treatment', as Ned Kelly would one day claim.[3] Unlike runaways, who seldom cause trouble for those around them, men making a dishonest living by armed robbery and stock theft, roaming far and wide and evading capture by sheltering in the wild bush, have created a state of fear and insecurity.

The Hunter's River district is so overrun with bushrangers that it is not uncommon for armed robberies to tally one per day. Thus far, the Mounted Police have a lamentable record in capturing outlaws, and those they do manage to catch escape with remarkable regularity. To be fair, police ineptitude is not entirely to blame – in the mid-1830s, two of the district's police bases have only one working pistol and one working musket between them.

The larger outlaw gangs rule the roads, but many bushrangers work alone or in small groups, skulking through the bush to kill a sheep or two for food, steal a horse, snatch a shepherd's rations, pilfer cash from mail bags, or hold up lonely travellers for their cash, valuables, weapons, or even their clothing.

By the late twentieth century, the shame of the 'convict stain' would be replaced by a romanticised view of convicts transported to Australia as essentially decent people driven by poverty to petty crime, and, indeed, many of those sent out in the early days of settlement had been convicted of trifling offences. By the 1830s, however, as Britain's penal laws became more humane, convict ships carry fewer victims of cruel circumstance and greater numbers of hardened criminals.

The story is told of a young woman – the daughter of First Fleet convicts – who, when asked if she would like to go to England, replied, 'No, because that is where all the thieves come from.'[4]

Captain Horsley wakes to the sound of his dogs barking – again. Twice so far during the night his sleep has been disturbed by their barking, and twice he has gone out onto his verandah to see what was causing the clamour but found nothing amiss. This time, when he steps outside, three men appear from out of the darkness. Captain Charles Henry Horsley, Hunter's River farmer, late of the 52nd Regiment of Foot and a veteran of Waterloo, is not one to shrink from a fight, but with three pistols aimed at his head he has no choice but to surrender.

He is ordered back to his bedroom where he is made to lie on the bed beside his terrified wife, Annie, and put a pillow over his face. The Horsleys are told that if they move they will be shot, and the men ransack the house, bundle up all the valuables and weapons they can find, then melt into the night.

It is 1 December 1840, and Charles and Annie Horsley have been paid a visit by Teddy Davis and the Jewboy Gang.

Edward Davis, a Jewish Londoner, was just 16 when he was convicted in 1832 of stealing from a shop at Brentford a till worth two shillings and the five shillings it contained.

At his trial at the Old Bailey, a neighbour who grabbed a boy running from the shop swore it was Davis. Davis, who protested his innocence, told the court, 'A lady in Gravel Lane missed her son for a fortnight, and sent me to look for him at Brentford. I heard an alarm, and saw the lad run out of the shop. I immediately pursued, and was taken.'[5]

The judge didn't believe him, and sentenced him to transportation to New South Wales for seven years – one year for every shilling stolen.

A description of Davis in 1833 reads: 'Age 18; able to read and write; religion, Jew; single; native place, Gravesend; trade, stable boy; tried at Middlesex 5th April, 1832; sentenced to 7 years; former convictions 7 days; height 4 feet 11 inches; complexion, dark ruddy and much freckled; hair, dark brown to black; eyes, hazel; particular marks or scars, remarks, nose large; scar over left eyebrow.'

Davis also had cryptic tattoos. On his left forearm was 'EDHDM love' and an anchor. On the inside of his left forearm was 'MJDBM' and there were five blue dots between the thumb and forefinger of his left hand.[6]

In Sydney, he was assigned to work at the military barracks but escaped. He was soon captured, another year was added to his sentence and he was sent to work on a farm west of Sydney. Undeterred, he absconded from the farm, was again captured and had yet another year added to his sentence. Assigned to a farmer on Hunter's River, he ran off, was caught, and two more years were added to his sentence. In July 1838 he escaped for the fourth time, but managed to avoid capture, and the following summer formed a gang and launched his career as a bushranger. Davis – very short and very freckled – may not have been physically imposing, but he was clever and inventive, with a theatrical flair, and a born leader.

In the wild valleys and on lonely roads between the Hawkes-bury and Hunter's River, and on the Liverpool Plains, a two-year reign of terror began. From their hide-out in a cave on Pilcher's Mountain, near the tiny Hunter Valley settlement of Upper William (now Dungog), the gang rode out to raid towns and sta-tions, and hold up travellers on the Great North Road. Davis cultivated an image of himself as a latter-day Robin Hood, robbing from the rich and giving to the poor, but although that reputation won him many sympathisers in the bush, there is scant evidence that he kept the second part of the bargain.

A story – probably put about by Davis himself – that he once flogged a notoriously tyrannical landowner on the public triangle with a cat-o'-nine-tails, endeared him to the convict community, and caused *The Sydney Herald* to complain that 'the Davis gang was doubtless helped by convict servants, as they showed great knowledge of the robbed establishments and families.'[7]

It was also said of Davis that he rounded up a chief constable and his posse, who were pursuing the gang, and, having 'yarded them like a mob of cattle', stole their money and their horses and rode away.[8] That tale, too, is probably apocryphal.

For a while, the gang varied in numbers as escapees from iron gangs and other runaways joined for a short period, then, on discovering little romance and much hardship in the outlaw life, gave themselves up and took their 50 lashes – the price of returning to the relative security of penal servitude. Others were captured and hanged, or sent to punishment stations such as Norfolk Island or Cockatoo Island. By 1840, however, the gang had seven core members: John Shea, John Marshall, Edward 'Ruggy' Everett, Robert Chitty, Richard Glanville, an as yet unnamed member, and Davis himself – all men in their twenties and thirties, and all of them escaped convicts.

They considered themselves knights of the road, were chivalrous to ladies while relieving them of their jewellery, and dressed to impress in gaudy clothes, broad-brimmed Manilla hats with the brims turned up at the front, satin neckerchiefs, brooches, rings and watches, and tied pink ribbons to their horses' bridles.

By 1839 the outlaw gang's crime spree was the talk of the colony. *The Sydney Gazette* reported:

The country between Patrick's Plains and Maitland has lately been the scene of numerous outrages by bushrangers. A party of runaway convicts, armed and mounted, have been scouring the roads in all directions. In one week they robbed no less than seven teams on the Wollombi Road, taking away everything portable. They also went to Mr Nicholas' house, and carried away a great quantity of property after destroying a great many articles which they did not want. Mr McDougall, late chief constable of Maitland [he had resigned as district constable], and a party of volunteers set out in pursuit. The Wollombi district constable is a tailor by trade, and he refused to leave his work to accompany the party on the plea that it would not pay him.[9]

On 9 June 1839, the gang raided 'Balickera', William Caswell's estate near Maitland. Caswell, a former British navy lieutenant debilitated by wounds received in the War of 1812, refused to stand and fight when challenged. One of the bushrangers went to shoot him regardless, but as he took aim, Caswell's wife Susan leapt forward and knocked the barrel of the gun up as he fired, saving her husband's life. Another of the outlaws knocked Susan to the ground, and the gang proceeded to rob the couple of some £400 in cash and valuables. So much for chivalry.

A week later, settler Joseph Fleming – elder brother of Myall Creek massacre fugitive John Henry Fleming – received a curious note. It was from the bushranger Teddy Davis himself, ordering Fleming to have horses ready for the gang to take the next morning. Outraged by such impudence, Fleming armed his stockmen and prepared to fight. When the outlaws rode in, Joseph Fleming and his men opened fire, and, after a fierce gun battle, drove them off.

On one occasion, two of the gang held up a bullock driver named Budge. When the outlaw guarding him turned to speak to his comrade who was looting the dray, Budge seized the opportunity to grab his pistol and knock him to the ground. He then disarmed the other man and made them both stand in the roadway, hoping some traveller would soon come along to help him deliver his captives to the nearest lock-up. An hour went by, then another, until Budge had no choice but to let them go. He took their weapons – two muskets and four pistols – and their saddles and went on his way, leaving behind two benighted bushrangers with a good deal of the flash out of them.

Budge, who was widely commended for his courage and quick thinking, was already well known in the district due to a macabre tale of some years earlier, when he was one of seven or eight convicts who escaped into the bush. The runaways planned to head north until they reached Dutch Timor, unaware that it was an island. After three days trudging through unknown country, with no food and the constant fear of Aboriginal attack, Budge turned back to Hunter's River, and was found starving and close to death by a stockman. Of his companions, who journeyed on, nothing was known until explorers pushing northward came upon their bleached and scattered bones. On inspection of the remains, it was evident that in desperation the men had turned to cannibalism. And even though one of their number had been killed and eaten to save the lives of the others, the rest died anyway.

Teddy Davis showed no hesitation in robbing a fellow Jew. In November 1840 the gang raided Henry Cohen's Shamrock Inn, at Black Creek – a brazen act on one of the busiest roads in the country – and proceeded to ransack the place while 26 men – almost all of them convicts – calmly looked on. A correspondent for *The Sydney Herald* noted that the bushrangers were on friendly terms with the convicts and bullock drivers, most of whom were ticket-of-leave parolees. 'On their arrival they shook hands with them, treated them to brandy and enquired after acquaintances, both male and female, and in fact showed such an understanding between the parties that Mr Day cancelled two of their tickets. The rest being unfortunately free, nothing could be done to them.'[10]

Denny Day is a private citizen, on a visit to Muswellbrook, when he hears of the robbery at Captain Horsley's. He resigned to try his hand at farming, but the venture was doomed almost before it began. He only avoided having his estate seized because the chief creditor, William Charles Wentworth, refused to sign the papers.

Wentworth, a statesman, lawyer and landowner famed for making the first crossing of the Blue Mountains, in 1813, with Gregory Blaxland, William Lawson, four servants, four horses and five dogs, was among those who decried the trial and execution of the Myall Creek murderers as judicial murder. Yet it seems he held the man who brought the killers to justice in some regard – or at least that he took pity on him.

Maitland's chief constable, George Wood, is laid up in bed after being shot in the arse by a convict who claimed to have mistaken him for a bushranger in the dark. The real bushrangers, meanwhile, are making their way north, robbing and looting as they go.

With no police magistrate at Muswellbrook at present, Denny Day knows it's all up to him. He has been told also that the outlaws have raided the nearby station of his friend Francis Forbes, so there is no time to waste. He assembles a posse of Mounted Police and volunteers and the chase is on.

The posse sets out before dawn, and further up the valley

will be joined by other men. They include: Dr John Gill, son of a veteran of Day's first regiment, the Red Feathers; publican Edward White; Muswellbrook chief constable William Shinkwin; ticket-of-leave men Peter Dawe, Martin Kelly, William Evans, William Walker and John Doran; an assigned servant named Martin Donahue; an unnamed Aboriginal tracker; and Henry Dangar's brother Richard. For Richard Dangar, there will be tragic news along the way.

Chapter 27

The carnival

Behind the counter at Thomas Dangar's store, in Scone, John Graham stands waiting, nervous as a cat, a pistol at the ready. He watched through the store window as the men rode into town, and knew immediately who they were; he could tell by their gaudy dress. He watched while most of the gang burst into the inn across the street, and now he can see that two of the gang are headed his way. He hears the ringing of spurs, then the door swings open. John Shea and John Marshall enter the store.

For reasons no one will ever know, John Graham, 24 years old, recently arrived from Inverness, Scotland, snatches up the pistol and fires at one of the outlaws. The shot misses its mark and he dashes out the door and onto the street, running in the direction of the police lock-up. John Shea runs after him, gives chase for about 20 metres then stops, draws his pistol and fires. Graham is hit, staggers, but then runs on. Shea moves closer, takes careful aim and shoots John Graham in the back. He falls to the ground, and, after lingering a few minutes, dies.

Teddy Davis, who has been busy robbing the St Aubin Arms, did not see the killing but rushes outside when he hears the shots. Davis, who has repeatedly warned his men never to shoot except in self-defence, has considered it a point of pride that in all their daring exploits the gang has never killed anyone. Now, seeing the young Scot lying dead in the dust, he knows the game has changed. Something tells him that somewhere, sometime soon, they will reap what they have sown. Some witnesses will later claim that he said, 'I would give £1,000 that this had not happened, but as well a hundred now as one.'[1]

Others will swear he said, 'Now, as we have commenced murdering, it matters little what may follow, as our lives are at last forfeited.'[2]

The outlaws hurriedly gather their loot and ride off into the ranges, shaken by the realisation that everything has changed forever, and it all happened in less than 20 minutes. Not so distracted by grief that they neglect the practice of their profession, the gang hold up a couple of drovers in the ranges, robbing them of their money and weapons, and at Atkinson's White Hart Inn at Page's River – an inn they had robbed three weeks earlier – they stop long enough to water and groom their horses, have a drink, rob the inn again, then head out onto the plains, bound for Doughboy Hollow (now Ardglen), about ten kilometres away.

The hollow is a regular stock route camp for drovers and teamsters, but for the past dozen or so years it's also been a haunt of bushrangers. Davis expects they will be followed there, but because sympathisers at stations along the way have provided them with fresh horses, he is confident they have left their pursuers far behind.

Rising to a canter as they near Doughboy Hollow, the outlaws are still a colourful sight in their flash outfits and pink ribbons, but the mood no longer matches the carnival clothes. And Everett, making it plain, has replaced the ribbons on his hat with a black kerchief.

It was one of station hand George Downes' duties to ride from Black Creek (now Branxton, 18 kilometres north-west of Maitland) to Patrick's Plains three times a week to collect the mail. In his diary, Downes writes:

The post town was seven miles away, the town consisting of Benjamin's stores, a public house and forge, and a few other buildings. Chain gangs were employed building the new road. It was there that I first saw the Jew Boy and his gang serving out the contents of the stores to the inhabitants. I was not seen by them as the horse track led through the town to the front of the stores. That morning they had made a raid on Maitland. They did not stay long as they expected the Police Magistrate, Denny Day, would be after them.[3]

Early in December 1840, Downes was one of ten men droving a mob of cattle from Black Creek to Page's River (Murrurundi), 150 kilometres to the north.

'On reaching Glennie's Creek we heard more of bushrangers,' he writes. 'Since leaving the farm we had heard of little else but now we saw some of their handiwork. We came across four drays despoiled of their contents. The Jew Boy had left that morning after destroying nearly all the cases of liquor which were on the drays. There was nothing left but broken cases and bottles and drunken drivers and their mates. There was nothing else talked of but the Jew Boy and his gang.'[4]

The drovers arrived at Muswellbrook to find that the bushrangers had been there two days earlier and were thought to be still in the district. Wherever the drovers went they were asked, 'Have you seen the bushrangers?' and, 'Do you know in what direction they are?'[5]

While camped next night at an 'accommodation house' near the Burning Mountain, they are told by the landlord of the house that the outlaws had been seen that morning, and that a visit from them was likely. 'One of us made the answer that we did not care for them as we were well armed. At the time, we were cleaning half-a-dozen Queen Bess muskets and vying with each other to see who could get them the brightest. Having cleaned them to our satisfaction, they were packed on the dray.

'We made an early start next morning to get up the range before the heat of the day, but we had no sooner crossed the foot of the range than the Jew Boy and his gang were upon us. They were wearing gaudy silk handkerchiefs and were heavily weighted with firearms – more than they found time to use, as was seen the same evening.'[6]

Downes was by the bullock dray, where two of the gang were covering the bullock driver and his mate. Luckily for the outlaws, the driver was not Budge. One of the bushrangers, John Marshall, asked, 'What are you, free or bond?'

Both answered, 'Bond.'

'What sort of master have you got?'

'Very good,' both men replied.

George Downes' turn was next. 'Free,' he answered.

What Marshall said next shocked him. 'Get up on that dray and hand down them muskets you were cleaning yesterday evening for the bushrangers.' Every word the drovers had spoken at the Burning Mountain camp was repeated to them by the gang. On how that might have happened, Downes doesn't speculate. Presumably, at least one of the gang, or one of their many sympathisers, was in earshot that night.

'Ruggy [Edward Everett], the most repulsive-looking man of the gang, ordered me to hand down the muskets, which I refused to do. He at once rode up to me and rammed a large horse pistol into my ear with the words, "You cur! I will send you to eternity where I sent Graham, the storekeeper at Scone this morning!"'[7]

Given that it was John Shea who shot Graham, either Downes' recollection here is faulty or Everett said this to frighten him.

'The bullock driver's mate, seeing the turn things were taking, jumped on to the dray and handed the muskets down, which some of the gang were in favour of breaking over the wheel. The Jew Boy, as captain of the gang, ruled otherwise, as where we were going we would need them as protection against the blacks. So our ancient firearms were saved and stood to us in after years as our best duck guns.

'After seeing most of our firearms, they were satisfied with a pair of rifle pistols, half a dozen silk handkerchiefs, and a compass. In return they gave us two small pepper-box pistol revolvers, a very large compass and two knocked-up horses, the whole of which we returned next day to the Police Magistrate, Denny Day.'[8]

'Come, lads,' cried Davis, 'we shall have a bloody mob after us.' And with the stolen silk handkerchiefs tied to the barrels of their guns, the outlaws rode off, up into the ranges, looking, according to George Downes, 'more like a troop of mountebanks than dangerous men, with the exception of perhaps one man, the murderer Ruggy.'[9]

Three hours later, as the drovers were climbing the range, they spotted Denny Day's posse passing near the top of the range, hot in pursuit. This was the 'bloody mob' Davis mentioned.

'When we arrived at Page's River we found that the pursuers had left for the Liverpool Range, close on the heels of the bushrangers. We passed Page's River and pitched camp for the night and soon after our arrival we could hear shots being fired in the direction of Doughboy Hollow, some distance ahead of us.'[10]

Chapter 28

A reckoning

Barely an hour into their journey, Denny Day's posse is crossing Hunter's River north of Muswellbrook when a man from Scone rides up to tell them of the events in the town that morning. For Richard Dangar, the news that a young man died needlessly, defending his brother Thomas Dangar's property, hits hard, but Richard will play his part in a reckoning before the day is out.

Day picks up the pace, pressing on northward to Scone, where he allows the men and horses only half an hour's rest while he goes to the courthouse to seek assistance from the police magistrate, John Anderson Robertson. Inexplicably, Robertson is less than helpful. He offers no information that might assist the pursuers, and will not even provide fresh horses.

Leaving Scone, the posse heads into the Kindon Ponds valley, and at about 5 pm reaches Atkinson's White Hart Inn at Page's River to find that the outlaws left there only 40 minutes earlier. It is raining heavily and the men are drenched and weary, but Day orders that they can rest only as long as it takes to dry and reload their wet firearms. That done, they ride on up the valley to a narrow pass where the northern road crosses the ranges, and, just before dusk, arrive at the top of a steep slope looking down on Doughboy Hollow. It's a pretty spot with a small stream running through it, tethered horses grazing by the stream, and – some gathered around a cooking fire and others casting musket balls – the Jewboy Gang.

The outlaws, having wrongly assumed that their stolen thoroughbreds could easily outpace the posse's Walers, are relaxed and careless; no one is keeping lookout. Teddy Davis planned to break camp at sunset and move on, but he has waited just a little too long. Denny Day tells his men to draw and check their weapons and to each select a target from among the bushrangers and make straight for that man. They steady their mounts, Day yells the order to charge and they plunge down the slope at full gallop, cheering and whooping, with Day at the lead, shooting from the saddle.

The outlaws, taken by surprise, leap to their feet, grab their guns and a desperate firefight begins. Shea and Ruggy clamber up a hill and fire down on the attackers. Others run for cover and open fire from behind trees. Denny Day makes straight for Davis, who runs to the other side of the gully, finds cover and shoots at Day but misses, then fires again, grazing Day's ear. 'I heard a whistling noise in the air of slugs or balls,' Day will later recall.

Denny Day returns fire, hitting Davis in the shoulder, then reins in, dismounts, throws down his gun and grapples with him. He strikes Davis with the butt of the outlaw's own pistol, and Davis falls to the ground. Shea and Marshall are wounded, two manage to escape into the scrub, and the rest, seeing their leader taken, lose heart and surrender. For Teddy Davis and the Jewboy Gang, the game is up.

Early next morning, at a drovers' camp on Page's River, Denny Day and his men ride in with five bedraggled bushrangers in tow. One of the two who escaped, Richard Glanville, is trailed by the Aboriginal tracker and soon captured.

Drover George Downes, in his memoir, recalls: 'We supplied the police with tea and damper, which they seemed to enjoy very much. Their prisoners went hungry and were chained to nearby trees while the policemen had their meal.'[1]

Later, at the White Hart Inn, where Day has locked up his captives, Downes enters the room in which the outlaws are chained. Davis, recognising him, says, 'You were the young fellow who refused to hand down the muskets yesterday.'[2]

Downes tells him he was, and asks what he had done with the pistols that were stolen. 'He told me that when we arrived at Doughboy Hollow, to turn to the right, and some distance up from the road I would see a tree at which they had been firing. A little to the left of that was a large gum tree, where he had taken shelter from the police. He said that he had thrown them down there.

'From the directions given to me I found one of the pistols, the other having been found by a drayman who was camped in a hollow of the range. He gave the pistol up to us, so that we lost nothing but the handkerchiefs.'[3]

The stolen handkerchiefs, which the bushrangers had tied to the barrels of their guns, were now on their way south, attached to unloaded muskets. 'Denny Day made the bushrangers carry them on muskets to Maitland, an arrangement they did not approve,' Downes writes. 'The Police Magistrate, however, said that as previously they had flashed them for their own pleasure, they would now carry them to Sydney for his.'[4]

The gang's loot consists of a little over £70 in bank notes, gold and silver, a few trinkets, 11 muskets and 20 pistols, for which there is no ammunition. Yet a legend persists that hidden in a cave on Pilcher's Mountain is the fabulous treasure of the Jewboy Gang, waiting to be discovered.

The bushrangers are first taken to Scone, where on 23 December an inquest is held by police magistrate John Robertson into the death of John Graham and the prisoners are charged with murder and robbery. Denny Day, who will never forgive Robertson for his obstructive behaviour during the pursuit, refuses to sit with him on the bench, and insists that the outlaws be committed for trial at Muswellbrook rather than at Scone.

Accordingly, on Christmas Eve, 1840, at Muswellbrook, the outlaws are committed for trial, then taken to Maitland where a party of Mounted Police is waiting to escort them to prison in Sydney. On the journey south, no ribbons or silk handkerchiefs are displayed.

In Sydney, the same newspaper that campaigned to spare the lives of the Myall Creek seven is now baying for the blood of the Doughboy Hollow six.

'The scoundrels who have so long infested the districts of the Hunter are at length safely lodged in Sydney Gaol,' says *The Sydney Herald*, 'thanks to the activity of Mr Day. As desperate diseases require desperate remedies, we think the crimes of these vagabonds have been so notorious that a special commission should be issued to try them, and if found guilty they should be, with as little delay as possible, executed near the spot where they murdered Mr Graham. They should not be kept in gaol until the ordinary sessions, but, while all men's minds are directed to the atrocity of their crimes, they should hear that the punishment due to those crimes has overtaken the miscreants who committed them.'[5] Cooler heads will ensure that the course of justice proceeds in the usual way.

The next day's issue of the *Herald* lavishly praises Denny Day but is scathing in its assessment of Scone police magistrate John Robertson's behaviour:

'We have received nearly 20 accounts of the capture, and there is not one that does not reflect upon Mr Robertson for his supinences. To allow a police magistrate belonging to another district to scour that part of the country which it was Mr Robertson's especial duty to keep in order, and not to proffer to assist the gentleman who was obviously doing that which he ought to have done himself, was conduct which, we have no doubt, before this the Governor has demanded an explanation of. Want of energy and decision we imagine are faults not likely to find much favour in the eyes of Sir G. Gipps. There is another point too on which all the communications agree: and that is in praising Mr Day, whose activity, courage, and perseverance have often been shown, but never so conspicuously as on this occasion. "Fortunate indeed," says one correspondent, "are we to possess one magistrate on the Hunter who has judgment to guide him, and courage to act in time of need." With this sentiment we entirely agree, and we are glad to find that the settlers at the Hunter are about to present Mr Day with some token of their esteem. We hope it will be of a value proportionate to his services and their wealth.'[6]

Chapter 29

'We have not reigned a day'

In a courtroom packed with sympathisers, on 24 February 1841, the gang faces judge and jury. Chief Justice Dowling is on the bench, Attorney-General John Plunkett is prosecuting and defence attorney William Purefoy is representing Teddy Davis. None of the other outlaws have counsel, and file into the dock in prison garb, unlike Davis, who is dressed in a smart new suit. The lawyer and the suit have both been paid for by members of Sydney's Jewish community – probably not out of 'a sentiment of solidarity with Davis', according to a Jewish historian writing more than a century later, but rather 'to spare the community the disgrace of seeing for the first time in the history of the colony a Jew hanged in public in Sydney'.[1]

John Shea is indicted for the wilful murder of John Graham, and Davis, Marshall, Everett, Chitty and Glanville are indicted for aiding, abetting and assisting in the murder, and with being accessories to murder. All plead not guilty.

The Attorney-General, on informing the jury that all the defendants had been assigned convicts, makes the dubious claim that the assigned servant system 'had assured them a leniency and kindness unknown to the law except in modern times'. And yet, these ingrates had conspired to 'keep the whole country, from the sea coast to the Liverpool Ranges, in a state of terror and confusion'.[2]

Turning to the matter of guilt for the murder of John Graham, Plunkett points out that regardless of who fired the shot that killed Graham they are all equally guilty as aiders and abettors. Whether or not Graham had fired the first shot made no difference, he says, 'for when a party of men leave their service and go out on an expedition of this kind they are beyond the pale of the law, to this extent, that every man is armed with authority to apprehend a bushranger, and to do so has all the authority of an officer of justice'.[3]

Denny Day, when called to the stand, recounts the capture of the gang in his usual matter-of-fact manner:

'I reside at Maitland. Shortly before then I was police magistrate at Muswellbrook. On the 21st of December I was at Muswellbrook on my own private affairs. I received information on Sunday evening of a party of bushrangers being out and took steps to collect a party and go in pursuit. I started about seven next morning. I had ten mounted men and a black boy.

'I took the direction of Scone, and passed through it. I continued in pursuit until six that evening. I came up about 50 miles from Muswellbrook with the bushrangers at a place called Doughboy Hollow.

'About half a mile off the road we saw some drays encamped and some smoke. There were some horses tethered and some men in their shirt-sleeves making a rush for the opposite side of the gully where the encampment was. I saw about six or seven.

'We galloped in amongst them; a great many shots were fired on both sides. I can speak positively to Davis having fired at me.

Davis rushed from the gully, evidently to get behind a tree. Whilst he was running I fired; he turned and fired at me. I was not more than 20 yards from him, he then ran towards a tree, and, resting the gun in the fork of the tree, fired at me through the branches. I returned the shot, and wounded him through the shoulder.

'Five prisoners were taken in less than five minutes after we charged them. Shea, Marshall, Everett, Davis and Chitty were the men. They had arms – there were ten or 11 guns and a great many pistols, and seven horses. Glanby [Richard Glanville] was taken next morning.'[4]

Day tells the court, 'A good deal of conversation took place between the prisoners. They were very communicative. Davis and Marshall kept us awake all night telling stories. I did not hold out any inducements to them. As they came out, I asked their names – they gave a history of all their proceedings without my inducing them to do so.

'Shea said there need nothing more be said about it; it was he who shot Mr Graham and no one else.'

Day testifies that Richard Marshall told him he would shoot any man who attempted to resist, and that, in the presence of the others, he said of John Graham, 'He was a very foolish young man, and could not expect anything else in firing among so many armed men.'[5]

John Shea told Day he would shoot his father if he attempted to shoot him, and some of the others said that until that morning, in all their robberies, they had done nothing that would have risked their lives.

Davis told Day that during the gunfight he had fired four shots. Shea admitted to six, Marshall four, Everett two, and Chitty would not say. All of them seemed proud that they had put up a good fight, and said they would cheerfully have shot the two gang members who ran away. Some also told him they would rather go to the gallows than be sent to the dreaded Norfolk Island penal colony for life.

Day commends to the court the men of his posse for their bravery, adding that the ticket-of-leave men behaved admirably. 'There was no shirking whatsoever,' he says.

Under cross-examination by William Purefoy, Day tells the court that Shea confessed to the murder about an hour after being captured, and that Davis told him he had always opposed the shedding of blood, for he knew that if they committed a murder they would not reign a week. As he said this, he looked right and left and said, 'As you see, we have not reigned a day.'[6]

Several witnesses add detail to the timeline of events at Dangar's store and the inn, completing the case for the prosecution.

In an eloquent address in defence of Davis, William Purefoy contends there is no evidence that warrants his client being found guilty of aiding and abetting Graham's murder, and calls on the jury to give Davis the benefit of the doubt.

John Plunkett, in turn, counters Purefoy's argument by reminding the jury that it is a principle of British justice that if a group of people go out to commit a crime, and another crime is committed by one of the people who went out to commit the first crime, then, in the eyes of the law, the others are equally guilty as accomplices unless they can prove they had no hand in committing the second crime.

The judge, summing up, adds his weight to the point raised by the Attorney-General, but nonetheless advises the jury that, should they have any serious doubts as to the guilt of any of the prisoners, they should give them the benefit of it. At 6.15 pm, when the jury retires to consider its verdict, Davis, Shea and Marshall, who have been laughing and chatting all throughout the trial, seemingly convinced that acquittal is a foregone conclusion, become quite raucous, calling out to friends and well-wishers among the crowd. Ignoring calls for silence in the court, the festive mood lasts until 7.30 pm, when the jury returns with a verdict of guilty against all five defendants. The crowd howls in outrage, Davis bursts into tears, his face contorted with horror, and his erstwhile loyal compatriots instantly turn on him – blaming him for leading them to their doom, threatening to kill him.

When at last the pandemonium subsides, Judge Dowling places the black cap on his head. He reminds the prisoners that they told Denny Day they would rather hang than be sent to Norfolk Island, and tells them their wish has been granted. Addressing each man in turn, he sentences them all to death.

Davis has friends who hope to be able to save his life, and some of these friends have friends in high places. 'The Hunter River bushrangers who are under sentence of execution were warned by the sheriff not to entertain the smallest hope that the order for their execution would either be deferred or rescinded,' *The Australian* reports. 'The Executive Council, which sat relative to this case, on receiving the judge's report, were unanimously of the opinion that the extreme sentence of the law ought to be carried into effect upon each individual culprit. Towards Davis, public sympathy seems to be a good deal excited. The culprits have been attended for several days past by the ministers of their respective persuasions. We learn that a very urgent appeal has been made to the Executive Council particularly on behalf of Davis. The friends of this unhappy criminal relied mainly on the point adduced in evidence that he was adverse to the shedding of blood, but the Council, in having their attention addressed to the point, immediately referred to the evidence of Mr Day, who swore that Davis placed a musket in the fork of a tree, and took deliberate aim at him twice to take his life.

'We hate public executions, but the question arises whether the public justice of the country would be satisfied by foregoing the judge's sentence. For the present we forgo answer.'[7]

The minutes of the Executive Council – an advisory body of officials appointed by the governor – reveal that the 'very urgent appeal' was initiated by Davis himself, and that it was brought to the Council's attention by no less a personage than Governor George Gipps.[8]

Still, the Council is unmoved. The Minute concludes, 'The Council, after an attentive and mature consideration of the cases of the several prisoners and of a petition from one of them, Edward Davis, which was laid upon the table by His Excellency advised as follows. John Shea, convicted of the wilful murder of John Graham, and John Marshall, Edward Everett, Edward Davis, Robert Chitty and Richard Glanville convicted of being present, aiding and abetting the murder, all sentenced to suffer death, that the sentence of the law be allowed to take its course.'[9]

Curiously, the minutes are undated and do not list the names of the councillors at the meeting, only a note, 'Members present not given.'[10] It seems that even though the Council has only a few members and everyone knows who they are – Attorney-General John Plunkett is one, for example – they baulked at putting their names to what is effectively a death warrant based on the dubious assertion that because Teddy Davis shot at Denny Day he was somehow guilty of murdering John Graham.

*

Lower George Street, at the rear of the jail, is a sea of excited people, pushing and shoving, trying to get as close as possible to where the scaffold has been erected, over the footpath in Harrington Street. Many have been here since 8 am, more since even earlier, to jostle for a prime position. And a select few, who happen to know the jailer, have an unrestricted view from the base of the gallows. It's expected there will be a great many of the bushrangers' associates and sympathisers among the crowd, so additional troopers are on guard in case of a riot or rescue attempt.

As the church bells chime nine o'clock, the condemned men appear – Marshall, Everett, Chitty and Glanville accompanied by Reverend Cowper, Shea by Father Murphy, and Davis by Mr Isaacs, reader of the synagogue. The men are as they appeared in court: Davis in a dark suit; the others in prison dress.

There is no bravado today; no flash; each man a study in penitence. Each man, that is, except for Teddy Davis. There is no contrition to be read on his face, only an awful, heaving sorrow as his eyes dart back and forth across the crowd as if desperately searching for a familiar face. Instead, he sees above him six nooses, and below him six coffins.

The deputy sheriff reads the warrant, and one by one the outlaws mount the platform, Davis being the last to step up. On the scaffold, Chitty, Marshall and Glanville burst into song – an old hymn from *The Book of Common Prayer*:

Awake my soul, and with the sun,
Thy daily stage of duty run.
Shake off dull sloth and joyful rise
To pay thy morning sacrifice.

Everett, who until now has been silent but increasingly agitated, suddenly kicks off his boots, sending them flying into the crowd, shouting that he did so to make a liar of his mother, who always said he would die with his boots on, meaning he would be hanged.

As the others murmur prayers, Teddy Davis quietly thanks Mr Isaacs for his kind attention, then all fall silent as hoods are placed over their faces, the nooses are tightened and the bolt is pulled.

It is 16 March 1841. The carnival is over.

It had long been supposed that the six bushrangers were buried in an unmarked common grave in Sydney's Devonshire Street Cemetery. The cemetery was closed in 1867 and the bodies exhumed and relocated, and the site now occupies the city's Central Railway Station. However, in 1955 a plan of the Jewish section of the cemetery was discovered by workmen under the vestibule of Sydney's Great Synagogue. On the plan is marked the grave of Edward Davis, buried alone in the Jewish section, in a corner of the graveyard.

On the west wall of St Luke's Church, Scone, a tablet reads: 'Sacred to the memory of John Graham, of Inverness, Scotland, who was cut off on 21st December 1840 at the early age of 21 years by a lawless gang of seven bushrangers who maliciously shot him whilst in the conscientious defence of his master's property, Mr Thomas Dangar of this parish. Six of these unhappy men suffered for their unhappy crime the extreme penalty of the law in Sydney, 16th March, 1841.'[11]

Chapter 30

Silver dishes and gamebirds

At a dinner held at Maitland on 5 April 1841, Denny Day, once again Maitland's police magistrate after some injudicious business deals fell through, is presented with a silver service plate inscribed, 'Presented to Edward Denny Day Esq., Police Magistrate at Maitland, by some residents of the district of Scone, as a testimonial of their admiration of the promptitude and gallantry he displayed in following and capturing a band of bushrangers which had for some months infested the Hunter. February, 1841.'[1]

It is a Sheffield Plate silver entrée dish made by James Dixon and Sons. *The Australian* reports that 'the service of plate, which is to be presented to E.D. Day Esq. is on view at the establishment of H. Lamb and Co, Jewellers.'[2]

John Plunkett is awarded a similar but more modest silver dish, made in China. It is inscribed, 'Presented to John Hubert Plunkett Esq., M.C. Attorney-General by the people of New South Wales as a token of respect for his public character and esteem for his private worth. Sydney, March, A.D. 1841.' Plunkett's dish is now in the collection of Sydney's Powerhouse Museum.[3]

Denny Day's dish passed into the hands of Dr James Watson, a collector of Australia memorabilia, and in 1982 was bought by an unnamed Sydney private collector. The dish is now held at Maitland Gaol museum but is no longer on display.

Late in 1841, Denny Day receives a copy of a circular from Caroline Chisholm. He knows of this extraordinary woman by reputation – social reformer, champion of women's rights, fearless advocate for female and family immigration. Born Caroline Jones, the sixteenth and last child of a four-times-married Northampton pig farmer, she is the wife of Archie Chisholm, a former officer of the East India Company army. A convert to Catholicism, some say she is a living saint.

Her letter begins: 'Sir, I am endeavouring to establish a home for female immigrants, and, as my first object is to facilitate their obtaining employment in the country, I shall feel obliged if you will favour my intention (should you approve of the same) by giving me the information I require regarding your district, and any suggestion you may think useful will be considered a favour.'

Chisholm became increasingly concerned that unaccompanied young women arriving in the colony too often found themselves alone and destitute on the mean streets of Sydney, where they were lured into prostitution. She became a familiar sight on the water-front, jostling with the pimps and spivs, taking immigrant girls and women into her own home until suitable employment could be found for them. She convinced Governor Gipps to help her establish an immigrants' home in Sydney, and was soon taking in not only single women but also unemployed single men and entire families.

Lately, her concern is that her women's quarters have become seriously overcrowded because women are fearful of leaving the safety of Sydney to take up work in the country – hence the circular to civil and religious authorities through the colony. Many refuse to help, suspecting that Chisholm, being Catholic, is intent on seeding the population with followers of the Church of Rome. Others, uninfected by sectarian bigotry, offer their support. Denny Day is one of them.

So, early in 1842, Caroline Chisholm and 40 young immigrant women arrive at the river port of Morpeth on the steamer *Rose*. On the overnight voyage from Sydney they were granted reduced fares and free baggage but no cabins, and so slept on deck huddled under blankets.

When the tall, russet-haired woman and her young charges enter Maitland their way is blocked by a delegation of concerned citizens determined to send these Popish interlopers back whence they came. It's a delicate situation that could easily turn ugly, but that doesn't happen. A burly man in a well-worn frock coat pushes his way through the protesters to greet the arrivals warmly, offering to escort them to the cottage in Smith's Row that has been arranged for their accommodation. The protesters know better than to take on Denny Day, and meekly turn tail.

Within two days, 32 of the 40 women Caroline Chisholm brought to Wallis Plains have found employment. Single men and families will follow, and while prejudice will continue, Hunter's River will forever benefit from their presence.

There has been a death in the family. The sad news reaches the Day household that Margaret's brother-in-law, Arthur Kemmis, has died suddenly in Melbourne, leaving her sister Aphra and her six children destitute. His estate has been declared insolvent and apparently he left no will. Aphra has returned to Sydney and is staying with their parents, James and Aphrasia Raymond.

Arthur Kemmis, like Denny Day, was the son of a Church of Ireland clergyman and a member of the Anglo-Irish ascendancy. His landed family harked back to a companion of William the Conqueror, but, as a second son, with no entitlement to his father's estate, Arthur had to make do with a bequest of several thousand pounds. With cash in his pocket, he sailed for New South Wales, sure to turn his legacy into a fortune.

It didn't happen. He bought a whaling ship that was wrecked on its first venture, and, despite having been granted land south of Sydney, failed to make it prosper. It was at about that time that he met Margaret Day's sister Aphrasia – named after her mother but known to family and friends as Aphra.

Arthur and Aphra were married in 1831, and took up land in the Bathurst district. It was soon apparent that Arthur's second attempt to establish a working farm would be as unsuccessful as his first – a situation made worse by separation, with Arthur away on the farm at Bathurst, and Aphra in Sydney, staying with her parents, sinking into a melancholy compounded by the deaths of two of her children.

Arthur Kemmis, staring failure in the face, found no solace in letters from Aphra, exhorting him to 'be a man, my Arthur'.[4]

By 1839, however, he had turned fate on its head. Realising that life on the land was not in his cards, he pulled up stumps and moved to the Port Phillip district (Melbourne), where he spent what was left of his legacy to set himself up as a merchant. Within two years he had built a thriving mercantile business and a grand house, said to be one of the finest in Melbourne. He founded a steamship company, carrying passengers and cargo between Melbourne and Sydney on a steamer he named the *Aphrasia*. Now a wealthy man about town, he was a member of the exclusive Melbourne Club and, of course, a magistrate.

Fate wasn't long in twisting, however. By the end of 1841, economic depression had hit the merchant trade hard, and serious irregularities had been found in the books of his steamship company. Arthur Kemmis was a very worried man when, in February 1842, he came down with a heavy cold and took to his bed. Seven days later he was dead at just 36 years old.

His obituary in *The Port Phillip Gazette* dubbed him the 'Founder of Steam Navigation' at Port Phillip, adding that 'despite the conclusions which have been drawn against his management of the local company's affairs, from the want of success which latterly attended their operations, we are prepared to protect his talents against the shafts which could only in ignorance have been pointed at his conduct in this important affair.'[5]

Whether or not they ever met, Denny Day would surely have found in Arthur Kemmis a man after his own heart. Apart from their similar origins, they shared heaped measures of grit and determination. Day might have even been a little envious of Kemmis, who had, for a while at least, been spectacularly successful in business. A celebrated frontier lawman Denny Day may be, but his business ventures have been dismal failures.

A year passes, with a reminder that fate doesn't always favour the bold. On Boxing Day, 1843, Denny Day happens upon a group of men gathered in a circle by the roadside on the edge of town.

He knows from experience that this is a cockfight, a blood sport banned in New South Wales since 1835, along with dogfighting, bull-baiting and bear-baiting, but still popular.

In a ring surrounded by the crowd, cheering and making bets, feathers fly as two gamebirds, tormented to make them aggressive, attack each other with their beaks and with razor-sharp steel spurs attached to their feet. The spurs cut deep as the frenzied birds grapple, and the fight would have continued until one bird was dead or too injured to go on, but Day bursts into the ring and stops the fight.

His attention is drawn to a man named Robert Turner 'who was very busy, was betting and noisy, and appeared to be the prime mover'.[6]

When told by Day that he will 'have him before the bench',[7] Turner lets fly a torrent of abuse. Day then takes hold of both gamebirds and Turner, who slips from his grasp and punches him repeatedly. The two men fall to the ground, and, after a tussle, Turner starts to choke Day, forcing him to release his hold, and runs off, leaving Day with a bloodied lip and a cut to the back of the neck.

A week later, Robert Turner finds himself before the bench at Maitland Court, charged not with the relatively minor offence of illegal gaming but with assaulting the police magistrate. Found guilty, he is sentenced to pay a £5 fine or go to prison for two months, and is bound over to keep the peace for 12 months.

As for the gamebirds seized by Denny Day, their fate is unknown, although Margaret Day was reputedly a good cook.

Chapter 31

Miracles and wonders

Colonials devour news from the old country. Epoch-making or trivial, it is all the stuff of fascination and envy. Steampower is increasingly replacing windpower, waterpower, horsepower and manpower, and almost every day brings revelations of wonders and curiosities.

In London, outside the Polytechnic Institute in Regent Street, a Mr Bain has built a large illuminated clock that runs day and night without stopping or slowing because it is powered by electricity. Some say electric lighting is bound to replace gas some day soon, but then again, what would become of London's 380 lamplighters? The same was said of Mr Beningfield's patented electric gun, which was supposed to replace powder and shot. In experiments last year, the weapon was said to have fired five-eighth-inch bullets at the rate of a thousand a minute, yet it hasn't been heard of since.

A certain Mr Whishaw has demonstrated a device he calls a Telakouphanon, or speaking trumpet, that can carry the voice for at least three-quarters of a mile. It's made of gutta-percha, a natural plastic made from the sap of palaquium trees, and is all the rage in England these days. More and more things usually made of India rubber, such as raincoats, cricket balls and fillings for teeth, are now being made of gutta-percha.

They say that the planet Jupiter, as seen through Lord Rosse's new telescope – the largest ever built – looks like a coach light. And the tube is so high and wide that the Dean of Ely, as a jolly jape, walked through it with his umbrella up.

It's been announced that a railway bridge to be built across the Mersey at Runcorn will be so gigantic that it is an engineering feat never before attempted. Things just keep getting bigger and bigger.

What promised to be the marvel of the age, however, has disappointed all but cartoonists and satirists. In 1843, John Stringfellow and William Henson, makers of equipment for the lace industry, announced to the world the launch of the Aerial Transit Company. Their promotional material showed an 'aerial steam carriage which is intended to convey passengers, troops and government despatches to China and India in a few days'.[1] But although it caught the public's imagination, the venture didn't get off the ground – literally. After being ridiculed in parliament and mercilessly lampooned in the press, not only did Stringfellow and Henson fail to find financial backers but their aerial steam carriage simply wouldn't fly. Since then, the absurd notion of flying machines carrying people and things here and there has been all but forgotten. It was just another nine-day wonder.

At an inquest into the death of a Tralee weaver named Connell, the coroner, Justin Supple, heard evidence that the man had three children, the youngest being four and the eldest 13, who, along with a mother-in-law aged 70, he was trying to support. For the past few weeks all five had survived on a penny's worth of bread.

Connell was found dead in a tiny, squalid room, in a filthy and neglected state, his children beside him and the old woman on a bed of putrid straw, unable to walk or crawl. The eldest child crept outside yesterday to beg for food for the others, but no one has even a morsel to spare, so the children and their grandmother are sure to die soon. The coroner and jury made up the price of a coffin for Connell, and recorded a verdict of death by starvation.[2]

Sir Edward, who owns most of Tralee, will not raise the rents or evict tenants who can no longer pay, as so many other Irish landowners have done. He simply refuses, and he refuses because he believes such an act would be evil. Rather, he has slashed his tenants' rents and is providing whatever practical help he can to ease their hardship. Sir Edward Denny, 4th Baronet, of Tralee Castle, is the eldest son of Sir Edward Denny and Elizabeth Day, and cousin to Edward Denny Day. He is unmarried and will remain so all his life, and is a follower of the Plymouth Brethren, an evangelical Christian movement.

Sir Edward's tenants in County Kerry have been afflicted by two deadly blights. The first is a bug – a strain of the fungus *Phytophthora infestans*, which arrived in Ireland in 1845 from Mexico's Toluca Valley and has spread throughout the island, devastating the potato crops; infecting the plant and leaving it shrivelled and inedible. Already, people are starving, dying, fleeing the country in rotting coffin ships to North America and Australia. Millions more will follow, and millions more will perish.

The second blight, and equally as virulent, is an English civil servant named Charles Edward Trevelyan, who, as Assistant

Secretary to the Treasury, is in charge of all famine relief for Ireland. Trevelyan, yet another son of an Anglican clergyman, harbours a pathological hatred of the Irish, and believes the famine has been sent by God to teach them a lesson. 'The real evil with which we have to contend is not the physical evil of the famine,' he proclaims, 'but the moral evil of the selfish, perverse and turbulent character of the people.'[3]

Cold-bloodedly defining famine as a means of reducing surplus population and encouraging emigration, Trevelyan believes starvation is God's vengeance on Irish Catholics for the heresy of popery, and accordingly has provided little or nothing in the way of famine relief.

In 1848, for his complicity in the deaths of 1.5 million people, he will be knighted by Queen Victoria and his salary doubled.

In her memoir *More Recollections*, celebrated journalist and social activist Mary Gilmore relates a story her grandmother told her of a 'bushwack' at Richmond, on the Hawkesbury, in 1846, just before her mother, Mary Anne Beattie, was born.

'Among the sports of the military officers and landed gentry, was hunting the blacks. Grandmother told me they went out after them with packs of dogs "just as they hunted foxes in Ireland. It was just like fox hunting," she said, "for when it was over they made a feast and had a ball."

'I forbear to give the description she gave of those hunts, or the names of those who took part in them. But once, not long before my mother was expected, a hunt was arranged, and on that day my grandfather had to go to Sydney as a witness in a law case. Before he left he loaded the gun for her and said on no account was she to venture out of doors or the dogs might tear her to pieces.

'After he was gone she began to make some scones (she was famous as a scone maker). As she mixed up the dough she heard the dogs, the shouts of the horsemen, and the cries of the hunted who were being driven to the river. It was not the first time, and she went on with her work.

'Suddenly the door was pulled open and a girl of about 12 rushed in, fell at her feet, clutched her skirts, and with agonised eyes and broken words pleaded for protection.

'There was nothing that could be done, for immediately "two gentlemen" entered the room, dragged the girl out and beat in her head at the door. The blood was still there when grandfather came home.'4

He had nowhere else to run, so he has made his way back to Wallis Plains, back to the only place where he was treated kindly. William McGill is dying. His lungs are burning and a terrible weariness tells him his bones will carry him no further. Somehow, he finds his way to the hospital at Maitland, only to be told that it is against the rules to admit ticket-of-leave holders. Instead, they send for the man whose assigned servant he was until six months ago – the police magistrate Denny Day – who takes him home to care for him.

William McGill is a farm labourer from Nottingham, England. In 1827, at 18 years of age, he was convicted at Downpatrick, in the north of Ireland, of stealing a horse, and transported to New South Wales for life. By 1832 he had been granted a ticket-of-leave, but it was cancelled that same year when he was convicted of forgery and sentenced to six months on the iron gang. A year later, he escaped from the iron gang but was soon captured.

After four more years of toil in leg irons, he was assigned to a settler on the Liverpool Plains, then, in late 1844, Denny Day took him as his assigned servant for 12 months. Day, who had seen McGill on a number of occasions in his court, apparently recognised something in the man that belied his record as a horse thief, forger and runaway.

Denny and Margaret make him comfortable in a hut beside their home and do the best they can for him, but it's all too late. On Saturday 27 May 1846, at 10 pm, William McGill dies. At a coroner's inquest held the next day at the Blue Bell Inn, Dr Edye, who performed a post-mortem, states that McGill died of inflammation of the lung, and that from the extent of the disease death was inevitable. The doctor refuses to speculate on whether or not the man's life could have been saved if he had been admitted to the hospital, and the jury returns a verdict of death from natural causes.

Chapter 32

Mal de mer

You board at eight in the evening, dodging stray dogs and pick-pockets at the northern end of George Street, before stepping onto the dock at Campbell's Wharf. The lights of ships off Port Jackson are dancing on the water and you hear the chimes of Eight Bells. On the wharf, you join the crowd of people waiting to board the steamer and others who have come to wave farewell. Some are fussing about, lugging trunks and carpet bags, chattering or fidgeting impatiently; some are standing quietly, staring out to sea.

At last you're up the gangplank and on deck, bustling past other passengers, and sailors hurrying to and fro as the formidable Captain Biddulph strides from stem to stern and port to starboard, barking orders as he goes.

You find your cabin at last. It's a snug but elegant berth with a comfortable bed, a drawing room with a horsehair couch, polished mahogany tables and a steward's buttery. Satisfied, you return on deck to watch your ship pull away from the dock.

The steam whistle blows, the paddles begin to churn and you're on your way down the harbour and out through the heads.

When the novelty of sky above and sea below wears off, which doesn't take long, you return to your cabin, remembering with a smile the accommodation on your first trip some years ago – not so much a cabin as a cramped nest of double bunks, and in the bunks an assorted bunch of cabin mates – eating sandwiches, drinking brandy, wheezing, snoring, farting and heaving with seasickness as the steamer pitched and rolled, rolled and pitched.

Not this time. Lucky enough to be unafflicted with mal de mer, you crawl into your bunk and the cadence of the ship's movement rocks you to sleep.

Next morning, you're on deck as Nobby's Head – the sentinel of Newcastle harbour – comes into view. You see that the pier connecting the island to the mainland, begun by Macquarie all those year ago, is finished at last. After 38 years, some said it would never be completed – the government kept running out of money and the convict labourers kept getting swept off the rocks and drowned.

As you steam down the harbour towards the mouth of Hunter's River, you note that everything people used to say about Newcastle is no longer true. For many years it was all but a ghost town – no longer a penal station but not yet a town – and from seaward seemed all but deserted, with a few ragged streets of charmless, dilapidated houses winding up a hill. Now, along the harbour foreshore, the rotted remnants of convict stockades, packs of starving dogs and knots of idle men are gone, replaced by busy wharves, bond stores and bustling stevedores. Not so long ago, it was true to say that if Newcastle were not the seaport for Maitland there would be no need for it to exist. Now, as your steamer butts into dock, it's not hard to imagine that some day this town might be bigger even than Maitland.

And when you arrive at the town wharf and step ashore, there are encouraging signs that the coal trade is burgeoning here and could well be the making of this place. The best evidence of that is a set of iron tracks running down the hill to a coalmine. It's Australia's first railway line.

After an excellent breakfast of beefsteak and eggs at one of the dockland inns, you're in no hurry to leave when the ship hoists the blue peter.

Heading upstream, the river is sometimes narrow and heavily wooded on each side, and at other times wide with clear views of the hills beyond. There is little in the way of civilisation to be seen along the way until you arrive at Morpeth, the river port of Wallis Plains, just a short carriage ride from Maitland, and as you disembark you tell yourself there is surely no finer mode of travel. That is, of course, unless the riverboat is the *Sophia Jane* and your name is Denny Day.

In 1847, Day famously and publicly clashes with Edward Biddulph, captain of the *Sophia Jane*, a paddle steamer plying between Maitland and Sydney with goods and passengers. Captain Biddulph, a former lieutenant in the Royal Navy, saw action against the French and Spanish. In 1831, he retired on half-pay, bought the *Sophia Jane* and took up a land grant at Wallis Plains.

There's no disputing Biddulph's reputation as a skilful and brave skipper. He was commended in 1832 for bringing the *Sophia Jane* to the rescue of the sloop *Glatton* in foul weather off Newcastle, and, as a passenger on the steamer *William IV* when she was wrecked off that same port in 1839, his heroic efforts saved many on board from drowning. However, he also has a reputation as a bully and a troublemaker.

The captain's short temper and haughty manner have sparked all manner of disputes with settlers and merchants over the years, and he seems incapable of keeping convict servants for long. Margaret O'Toole absconded from his service. So did George Allen, Thomas Coll, William Dolby and William Poulton. Julia Birmingham was charged with insolence, as was Peter Sullivan, who was sentenced to two months on the treadmill for using grossly insulting language to Biddulph. James Morley was charged with public nuisance after lurking around Biddulph's home hoping to see assigned servant Ann Assett, and Assett was given 14 days' solitary confinement. Sarah Mee robbed him, and a nine-year-old boy was charged with attempting to steal a sail from the *Sophia Jane*. Mary and Robert Langan were charged with breach of agreement after they refused to work for Biddulph, after which Mary Langham threatened to burn down his house. And an unnamed convict was sentenced to 50 lashes for stealing tallow from the captain's engine shop.

Denny Day has taken offence at a speech Biddulph made at a public meeting on convict transportation, in which he referred to the police and police magistrates as 'nothing more than spies'.[1]

The captain, unrepentant, goes public. In an open letter to Day in *The Maitland Mercury*, he writes:

This forenoon your friend Captain Button [Charles Fitzacry Button, an old army comrade of Denny Day] called upon me, and presenting *The Maitland Mercury* of the 14th November

1846, said you were exceedingly angry at reading the report of my speech at the public meeting on the Transportation System, and demanded a denial of that part which alluded to the police, or to give you a meeting. Being thus peremptorily called upon, without reading the paragraph, I immediately acknowledged it as my sentiments, and I refuse to retract, and I refuse your challenge, because I believe what I said, and because I have a right to express my sentiments at a public meeting, on a public question, and upon the conduct of public servants, and I shall do it upon every occasion, whether the police magistrate is angry or pleased, and because I think Mr Edward Denny Day has no right to set himself up as the champion of the police.[2]

Three days later, Day replies:

Sir, I have only a single observation to make in reference to your communication of the 2nd instant, just handed to me by Captain Button. In that you admit having used language which I feel reflects most calumniously on my private character, and you refuse either to retract that language or to give me the meeting I have demanded from you, I therefore have no alternative left but to brand you, in plain terms, as a cowardly poltroon who has uttered a great falsehood, which you have not the spirit to defend. I shall make use of your communication, and this will make your conduct in the matter, and my sentiments in reference thereto, extensively known in this neighbourhood.[3]

Captain Biddulph, who prefers to duel with printer's ink than with gunpowder, publishes Day's letter in the *Mercury*, along with his response:

I have this instant received your letter, which is so gross, but I will not descend to use the foul language you have, but will content myself with publishing your letter.

You, Mr Denny Day, have entirely mistaken your man – the Celt cannot bully the Saxon.[4]

With that, this particular Saxon warrior abandons the field.

Captain Biddulph has form. He was a party in a similar exchange of insults by post, back in 1832, which ended up in court after Biddulph laid assault charges against two men *The Sydney Gazette* described as 'gentlemen of respectability, moving in a circle of life far above the common'.[5] The men were prominent landowners John Woolley and Robert Scott – the same Robert Scott who six years later would chair the defence fund for the Myall Creek murderers, the Hunter's River Black Association.

After a dispute over freight charges led to a feud by mail between Scott and Biddulph, Robert Scott, being equally as hot-headed as the captain, challenged Biddulph to a duel. When Biddulph declined to meet him on the field of honour, Scott, incensed, branded the captain a coward and a blackguard. It came to a head when the *Sophia Jane* was docking at the port of Newcastle, with Scott and Woolley among the passengers.

Biddulph told the court that when he boarded a boat ferrying passengers ashore, 'I immediately heard the defendant Scott say, "That is the captain, damn him! Throw him overboard!" when I was seized backwards and thrown down. Scott had hold of me and struck me. Woolley also struck me – I both saw and felt him. I struggled with them as hard as I could; the other passengers gave me no assistance – on the contrary, assisted the defendants. In a few seconds I was thrown overboard. I caught hold of the thwarts of the boat and seized a stick from Mr Abbott, with which I struck Mr Scott as hard as I possibly could. While holding by the boat, Mr Woolley bit my hand.

'When I regained the boat, Mr Scott again threw me overboard, and if I had not been picked up by the pilot's boat, I swear I think I should have been drowned.'

Passengers who had witnessed the incident told a different version of events, testifying that Scott had been hurling abuse at Biddulph while still aboard the *Sophia Jane*, and that as the boat taking the passengers ashore pulled away, Biddulph leapt into the boat in a furious rage. He knocked Woolley to the deck then threw a punch at Scott, grabbed a stick and began to beat him savagely. It was then that Scott yelled, 'Throw him overboard!'

The jury, after retiring for half an hour, returned to declare John Woolley not guilty and Robert Scott guilty, with a plea to the bench to pass the most lenient sentence possible. Accordingly, Robert Scott was fined £15, which he paid on the spot, and was immediately discharged.

Denny Day and Robert Scott, while poles apart on the issue of justice for Aborigines and much else, nevertheless have one thing in common – an intense dislike of the captain of the *Sophia Jane*.

Chapter 33

No *turning back*

On the morning of Friday 5 October 1849, Denny and Margaret Day and their children board the steamer *Ross*, bound for Sydney. The *Sophia Jane* was never an option. Day has been appointed superintendent of police for Sydney, and, as the press reports, he's getting quite a send-off.

'A good muster of inhabitants of Maitland, on horseback and in gigs, proceeded to Morpeth, and three hearty cheers were given as the party went on board, Captain Pattison replying by discharges from a cannon.'[1]

There's no turning back now. They've cut all their ties, sold everything they can't take with them – a Stanhope gig with harness, a riding horse and pony in foal, two cows, two carts and a water cart – as well as some things the children have outgrown, including a whirligig and a toy horse.

At a public meeting on Thursday, a deputation of local gentlemen was appointed to present Denny Day with a testimonial 'of respect and esteem for the services he has rendered to Maitland

and the district in his capacity of Police Magistrate, and for his impartial and upright conduct on the bench'.

The Catholic parish priest, Dean Lynch, reminded those present that Day had risked his life in the performance of his duty, and thanked Margaret Day for her work in establishing Maitland's new hospital.

The deputised gentlemen made their way to the Days' home at Government Cottage, where resolutions of respect and esteem were read aloud, and Denny Day was presented with 'a purse containing the sum which had been raised as a testimonial'. Donated by the good folk of Wallis Plains, it amounted to £130, a substantial sum.

Overcome by emotion, Day said there was no higher gratification for a public officer than the appreciation of those he had served. The simplest expression of approval, coming from the people, would have been sufficient for him, he said, adding that he was a happy man for having lived for so many years in their company.

'But the people of Maitland had done more,' *The Sydney Herald* reported. 'They had given him a proof of esteem which his children would inherit, and hold as an inducement for their future guidance. He need not say with what regret he left them – nothing indeed would have induced him to have removed but that there was an uncertainty whether the office he had so long filled would be continued.'[2]

The editorial of *The Maitland Mercury*, while asserting that in appointing Denny Day as Sydney's superintendent of police the government had chosen the right man for the job, seems to suggest that without Day on the bench there is a risk Maitland might once again lapse into its wilder ways. The district, the newspaper says, has lost a man whose conduct was 'marked by a strong desire to administer the law uprightly, impartially and strictly – whose vigilance and energy in the management of the police has afforded general security to the community – and whose zeal and ability in the discharge of his functions has kept the public business of the district in a well-ordered and credible state.'[3]

There were those, however, who had been whispering lately that Denny Day had lost his edge. A few weeks before Day's departure for Sydney, two bushrangers, sentenced the previous June to ten years on the iron gang for robbing the Singleton mail coach, escape from Maitland Gaol.

When a turnkey, distracted by other prisoners in the exercise yard, forgot to secure their leg irons, James Davidson and William Smith grabbed the chance to slip away. Placing prisoners' rolled-up beds – left out for airing – on top of each other, they scaled a wall at the end of the exercise yard, passed unobserved through the general yard, climbed onto the roof of the cookhouse and, although they were then spotted by guards who raised the alarm, climbed down a rope and disappeared into the dense scrub on the southern side of the jail.

Denny Day raised a posse and gave chase, but when, after two days, no trace of the bushrangers could be found, some said that Day gave up too easily; that the Denny Day of old would have pursued the fugitives to the ends of the Earth.

On 24 September, Davidson was captured at 'Bundobah' station at Port Stephens, a popular haven for escaped convicts, about 45 kilometres north of Newcastle. While crossing to Bundobah on the Sawyer's Point ferry, the fugitive caught the attention of a young local pastoralist, Charles McArthur King. A grandson of Philip Gidley King, the third governor of New South Wales,

Charles King would one day be police magistrate at Milparinka, in outback New South Wales, during the 1870s goldrush, and he had the sharp eye and suspicious mind suitable for the role.

King noted that the man who said his name was Young, then later called himself Cook, fitted the widely circulated description of the bushranger James Davidson: a tall, thick-set, determined-looking man aged between 40 and 50, with a weather-beaten, sparsely whiskered face without a savage or ferocious expression. Shortly after arriving at Bundobah, convinced the man was indeed Davidson, King confronted him and called on him to surrender. Davidson refused and fled towards a creek, tripped and fell into the creek. King, hot on his heels, also tripped and fell into the creek, where the two grappled in the water. The bushranger, although he had the advantage of being on top of King as they struggled, had the misfortune of bringing a knife to a gunfight. As he scrambled onto the creek bank, King drew his pistol and shot him in the hand, and, though he tried to flee, he was slowed down by a painful back injury sustained when dropping over the prison wall, threw his hands in the air and surrendered.

Davidson, while being escorted back to Maitland by King and two constables, kept insisting they had arrested the wrong man. He was still denying his identity when, at Raymond Terrace, the party boarded the riverboat to Morpeth. Unfortunately for James Davidson, there happened to be someone on board who could identify him – Denny Day.

James Davidson died six months later at Sydney's Cockatoo Island prison. His partner in crime William Smith, who parted company with him shortly after their escape, was never seen or heard from again.

*

A decade on, the deep social and political divisions caused by the Myall Creek trials remain. Back in 1838, immediately after the trials, Attorney-General John Plunkett failed in his first attempt to have a law passed allowing Aborigines to give evidence in court. A second attempt also failed, denounced by members of parliament as sentimental nonsense. William Charles Wentworth infamously compared Aboriginal evidence to 'the chatterings of the orang-utang'.[4]

In 1849, after yet another attempt is defeated, by one vote, members rise to condemn the hanging of seven of the Myall Creek killers as judicial murder.

In a blistering reply, Plunkett begins by reminding the House that these men were indicted for the murder of a child, and subsequently for the murder of that child's father; that although the evidence presented in the first trial made it clear all 11 of the accused men were guilty, they were acquitted as the result of a conspiracy by influential pastoralists to pervert the course of justice.

Members of the jury, by threats and persuasion, had been induced to vote not guilty regardless of how convincing the prosecution evidence might be. Many of those called for jury duty did not show up for the trial, having been advised that for the sake of their continued good health they should make themselves scarce. All the jurymen were challenged by the defence, and the courtroom was stacked with creatures of the conspirators.

Referring to the second trial, in which seven of the 11 were convicted and sentenced to death, Plunkett asked honourable members to consider whether any government in the civilised world would have refused to let justice take its course. He reminded them, too, that each of the seven, before his execution, admitted his guilt and justness of the sentence.

Loud as the outcry against him might be, Plunkett declared, he would be ashamed of himself as a man, and as a public officer, if he had taken a different course.

May 1850 finds Plunkett leading the prosecution of three soldiers charged with shooting 'at an aboriginal native with intent to do him some grievous bodily harm'[5] during a raid on the York's Hollow camp on the outskirts of Brisbane. The raid by troops of the 11th Regiment was in response to a rumour that the Turrbal people camped there were preparing to launch an attack on the town. It was a false alarm, as the troops discovered after surrounding the peaceful, sleeping camp, yet although no order was given, some of the troops opened fire.

Plunkett's closing remarks to the jury are memorable:

'A black man's camp is as much his castle as a white man's house and if he found it invaded at night by an armed and hostile force, he would be justified in throwing a boomerang. He would have been highly culpable if he had neglected to institute this prosecution. If offences like these could be committed upon the blacks, with impunity, it must be conceded that an armed military force might be called out to any place where large numbers of white people were assembled – to the race course for instance, into one of the tents where numbers of people might be assembled, drinking, and perhaps intoxicated, and that they might fire upon those people. Who was there present who would not shudder – the hair of whose head would not stand on end at such a monstrous proposition? When he had placed the evidence before the jury he should have done his duty, and no doubt the jury would do theirs.'[6]

The jury finds only one of the three men guilty – of common assault – and recommends mercy. The judge complies and sentences the man to six months' jail.

*

In 1850, transportation of convicts to New South Wales is abolished. After many years of divisive debate, the system officially ends on 1 October. Opposition to transportation among free settlers has increased in recent years, not because they believe it to be inhumane or draconian, but because they believe it's not punishment enough. From now on, accusations of governments being too soft on crime will be standard fare in Australian populist politics.

Chapter 34

Shame and redemption

For Denny Day, no longer a frontier lawman, such is the daily grind on the Sydney bench:

Donald Leech, for stealing an axe, three months' hard labour; Mary Lambert, for stealing a nightgown, three months' hard labour; Samuel Osborne, for embezzling £30, 18 months' hard labour; Susan Webb, theft of four £1 notes, found not guilty, prisoner discharged; John McEnerny, for 'robbing a Chinaman', two years' hard labour.

Billy, an Aborigine, for stealing a basin, found guilty with a recommendation of mercy, hard labour for one month; James Harper, indicted for burglary and larceny but found to be insane, to be kept in safe custody at the governor's pleasure; Michael Ryan, for stealing a mattress, 12 months' hard labour; Catherine Wright, for keeping a disorderly house, 12 months' imprisonment and a £50 fine; John War, theft of a brush, three months' hard labour; George Jones, for stealing 12 brooms, three months' hard labour; Mary Roach, for stealing a bucket, three months' hard labour; William Hope, theft of a shawl, three months' hard labour; Catherine Williams, for stealing five £1 notes, 10 shillings and a purse, found not guilty and discharged; David Morrow, stealing a saddle, found not guilty and discharged; Margaret Walsh, theft of a shawl, found not guilty and discharged; John Day and Philip Kedley, for assaulting a police constable, each found guilty with a recommendation of mercy, each sentenced to three months' hard labour; William Durham, for obtaining money under false pretences, three months' hard labour; Alice Harpur, for stealing a boot from a shoemaker, three months' hard labour.

William Carney, for passing a counterfeit coin, found not guilty and discharged; Michael Cassidy, theft of a hat, found not guilty and discharged. All grist for the mill.

Occasionally, but only very occasionally, something out of the ordinary comes along to break the monotony, such as the case of John Warrington. The charge against Warrington, of Surry Hills, is that on land belonging to him he has dumped '1,000 loads of night soil [human faeces] and other filth, where the air was corrupted, infected and impregnated with filthy and unwholesome smells and stenches, to the great damage and common nuisance of all the liege subjects of our said Lady the Queen then and there residing'. Warrington is also charged with 'continuing the nuisance'. The case wears on until 6 pm as 24 witnesses testify for the prosecution, and the court is adjourned until the following morning, when Warrington, who offers no defence, is fined £50 and ordered to remove the ordure within three months or be sent to prison.[1]

Then, after less than a year in the job, in *The Sydney Morning Herald*, this:

'Some surprise was created yesterday by the announcement that Mr E.D. Day had been removed from his office of Superintendent of Sydney Police, and that Mr McLerie, keeper of the gaol, had been appointed to succeed him. We understand that Mr Day was reported to have been intoxicated on the night of the Mayor's Fancy Dress Ball, and that an inquiry into the circumstances of the case before the Executive Council on Monday resulted in his removal from office.'[2]

William Augustus Miles, superintendent of Sydney police from 1841, was sacked in 1848, charged with corruption and being drunk on duty. His successor, Joseph Innes, was dismissed the following year for corrupt activities. Now Denny Day has become the third Sydney police chief in three years to be fired.

Why did he take to the bottle? Perhaps he was bored and jaded after so many years of laying down the law to an endless parade of the pitiful and the pitiless. Perhaps, after so many years on the frontier he was having difficulty adjusting to life in Sydney. And perhaps, after all he'd done in the cause of law and order, he was deeply offended by sneers and innuendo that he was riding on the coat-tails of his father-in-law, such as this article in *Bell's Life in Sydney*, titled 'Colonial nepotism':

Again we find Postmaster-General James Raymond, his son Mr James Raymond, accountant in the same department, his son Mr Robert Peel Raymond, clerk in the same department, his son Mr Samuel Raymond, chairman of quarter-session, his son-in-law Mr Edward Denny Day, superintendent of police, his cousin Mr O'Dell, postmaster at Windsor. The whole of these gentlemen are well-known to the public as 'most efficient' officers in their respective departments. Let those who wish to ascertain the pounds, shillings and pence extent of this peculiar patronage refer to the estimates of the last and many preceding years. The curious in such matters will there find ample gratification, and 'rich' food for thought.[3]

Then again, maybe he couldn't stand the mayor, and couldn't face socialising with him sober. Big, bluff George Hill, the son of convicts, is a self-made man – butcher, slaughterhouse owner, publican and landowner. A gambler, glad-hander and big spender, Hill, being mayor, is also a magistrate, and occasionally sits with Day on the Sydney bench. Openly critical of the organisation of the police force, he has made many vague promises to reform it, and might well be regarded by Day as a dilettante and a pain in the arse.

The mayor's fancy dress ball, at the Victoria Theatre, is the highlight of Sydney's social season, an absolute must for anyone who is anyone, and much lampooned by the hoi polloi who delight in pricking the pomp and pretentiousness of it all. Bawdy poems have been written in dishonour of the occasion, and broadside ballads such as 'The Lord Mayor's Fancy Dress Ball', which mocks the shameless toadying to the governor and his lady by the colony's would-be aristocracy, ending with:

And majors and captains attended the muster,
Their scarlet coats brightening the glittering cluster,
And groups of fair ladies their faces unveil
And sparkle like the stars in her ladyship's tail.[4]

'The civic reign of Mr George Hill is fast drawing to a close, but it has been a most brilliant one,' gushes the *Herald*. 'Full well has his Worship maintained throughout his reputation for liberality, and the gorgeous fete of Thursday night, which will in all probability be the last great festivity of the year, will long be remembered by all who attended it.

'There were, we should suppose, from 1,100 to 1,200 persons present, of whom at least one-half were at all times on the floor of the ballroom, while the remainder rested from the fatigues of the dance in the surrounding boxes.

'At most fancy dress balls there are found a large sprinkling of Hamlets, Othellos, Romeos, princesses, nuns, and the like. It was not so here. There were, indeed, a couple of Hamlets, and it is possible that there might have been some other doubles which escaped our notice, but in general the assemblage was free from this defect.'

When, at 10 pm, Governor FitzRoy arrives at the theatre, he and his military escort are forced to run a gauntlet of lesser mortals jeering and pelting them with rocks. Curiously, though, the *Herald* claims the angry crowd 'was drawn together from motives rather of curiosity than mischief'.

Safely inside, Sir Charles Augustus FitzRoy, Knight of the Royal Hanoverian Guelphic Order, is welcomed with hearty hurrahs and serious fawning. The *Herald* reports: 'His Excellency the Governor and the civil and military officers were, as usual, in uniform. The Mayor appeared in his official robes. The aldermen and most of the city councillors appeared in civic uniform. The Lady Mayoress wore a most becoming and minutely correct costume of the last century.

'The company did not begin to separate at all until after two o'clock, but a very large proportion remained there until the morning was far more advanced – in fact, until the approach of day warned them that it was time to seek repose.

'The whole affair passed off with a degree of harmony and smoothness, which struck us as affording a most complete answer to those who would wish it to be thought that we at the Antipodes were deficient in these courtesies which form the charm of English society.'

The report then lists the names of the more than 1000 guests, and the costumes they wore, except for the gormless few who forgot to give their calling cards to the flunkies at the door.[5]

Although the list specifies the costumes worn by many of the guests – those who came as Henry VIII, Marie Antoinette, a Chinese mandarin, Ophelia, and a pirate, for example – it lists some, including Denny Day's costume, as simply 'fancy dress'. The only clue to what he wore – and it's a cryptic clue – is in *Bell's Life in Sydney* of 24 August:

> Fancy Ball casualty – The charger of the Superintendent of Police indulged so freely in the early part of the evening as to throw his rider in the vicinity of the theatre. The only serious scrape likely to result from the accident is that upon the animal's knees.[6]

Surely Denny Day didn't attend the mayor's fancy dress ball in a pantomime horse costume! More likely, he was so drunk that on leaving the ball he fell off his horse. It's worth noting that the list of guests doesn't include Margaret Day. This is unusual, particularly since her father and brother Samuel were there – James as an officer of the Royal Horse Guards, Samuel as George II. It's possible there had been some falling out between Denny and Margaret, perhaps over his drinking.

History loses sight of Day until January 1853, when he is listed among new police appointments, much to the disgust of *The Empire* newspaper, which snorts:

It will be remembered that one gentleman among the late recipients of government favour was dismissed from a similar office, within the last few months, for inebriety. The English people have an old-fashioned Roman way of thinking that those whom they trust should be 'above suspicion'. A something of indignation, very natural under the circumstances, was undisguisedly manifest by many on learning that Mr Edward Denny Day had been appointed Provincial Inspector of Police, in the face of his late ignominious dismissal from the office of superintendent. It was felt that he was not exactly a model for a wife of Caesar.[7]

The newspaper strongly implies that Day's appointment, among others, is a case of what later generations will call 'jobs for the boys'. And that assessment could be close to the truth. The governor who sacked Day, Sir Charles FitzRoy, is the same governor who appointed him police superintendent of Sydney, most probably on the recommendation of his predecessor, Sir George Gipps, who held Day in high regard.

FitzRoy, like Day, is a British Army veteran, and by all accounts a man of tolerance and humanity. So it's not unlikely that he found it in his heart to offer the old frontier lawman a chance to redeem himself.

In reality, the grand title of Provincial Inspector of Police meant being posted to Port Macquarie, a former penal colony 420 kilometres north of Sydney. The district has been open to free settlers for about 20 years but has been in decline since the late 1840s, hit hard by economic depression and the removal of convict labour. Port Macquarie, despite its beautiful coastal setting, is a backwater.

For the next seven years, at Port Macquarie, history pays scant attention to the doings of Denny Day, apart from noting the birth there of his son Sydney Borden Day. The full complement will be eleven – John Nodes Dickinson Day, Sydney Borden Day, Maitland Tyrell Day, Phoebe Margaret Day, James Raymond Day, Edward Denny Day Junior, Henry Day, Aphrasia Charlotte Day, Agnes Raymond Day, Margaret Day and Justina Day.

In the obituary column of *The Sydney Illustrated News*, on 10 December 1853, the praises are sung of Colonel Kenneth Snodgrass, who has died of gout in the stomach at his estate on Hunter's River.

Mention is made of 'this distinguished officer's courage' in leading British troops to glorious victories against the French during the Napoleonic Wars. 'He was no less distinguished for his social qualities, his unbounded hospitality and goodness of heart, than for military acquirements. He was well-known in the colony as commander of the forces and originator of the Mounted Police during the desperate bushranging period.'[8]

The colonel's obituary omits to mention that a place in northern New South Wales is named after him. At Waterloo Creek, the spot where innocent blood stained the water is called Snodgrass Lagoon.

In August 1858, on the retirement of the police magistrate at Maitland, Day returns to the bench at Wallis Plains once again, and this time he's back to stay. He's now 47 years old and Maitland is no longer a wild frontier town, but his adventures aren't quite over yet.

*

Caroline Carleton, an Adelaide cemetery curator's wife, is perusing the advertisement columns of *The Adelaide Advertiser* of 1 October 1859, when the following catches her eye:

> A prize of ten guineas open to South Australia is offered by the Gawler Institute for the words of a patriotic song, to be entitled 'The Song of Australia', copyright of words to which the prize may be awarded to become the property of the Gawler Institute.
>
> Competitors are free to adopt any treatment of subject or rhythmical measure, so long as the composition is in accordance with the title and suitable for musical expression.[9]

The institute, an adult education foundation in Gawler, 45 kilometres north of Adelaide, also offers a ten-guinea prize to the composer whose music best suits the winning lyrics.

Caroline Carleton, between tidying graves, sets to and pens a poem that begins:

> There is a land where summer skies
> Are gleaming with a thousand dyes
> Blending in witching harmonies, in harmonies,
> And grassy knolls and forest heights
> Are flushing in the rosy light,
> And all above is azure bright –
> Australia, Australia, Australia.

And she wins. Her 'Song of Australia', with music by Carl Linger, the winning composer, is judged the best out of 96 entries, and, while it is criticised as a little too flowery, with odd references to pigment ('a thousand dyes'), many believe it should be enshrined as a sort of trans-colonial anthem – a national anthem for a continent not yet a nation. The idea is embraced for a while but soon fades.

Nineteen years later, on a Sydney bus, a Scottish-born school teacher named Peter Dodds McCormick will write the first verse of 'Advance Australia Fair'. McCormick will never say whether or not he had been inspired by Caroline Carleton's 'Song of Australia', but there is cause to suspect his use of a certain arcane word owes a debt to an even earlier candidate for a national anthem – 'Australian Hymn', written in 1825 by Presbyterian minister John Dunmore Lang.

McCormick's line: 'Our home is girt by sea', and Lang's line: 'Our sea-girt isle', are surely too similar to be mere coincidence.

Chapter 35

Holy war

'The charge which I prefer against Popery is that it is largely impregnated with heathen elements.'[1] On 29 March 1860, in Maitland, Wallis Plains, those words were never spoken.

'Disgraceful riot at Maitland,' shrieks *The Empire*'s headline of 31 March. The nub of the story is that a certain firebrand Presbyterian minister and his brother were attacked and severely beaten by a rioting crowd of Catholics, while the police magistrate, Denny Day, stood idly by and let it happen.

It all began with an advertisement in *The Maitland Mercury* announcing a lecture by the Reverend William McIntyre entitled, 'The Heathenism of Popery, proved and illustrated'.[2]

Scottish-born William McIntyre is the cousin of the late Peter McIntyre, whose complaint of land-grabbing by Henry Dangar back in 1827 led to Dangar being sacked as a government surveyor. William, 55, is married to his cousin Mary, Peter's sister, almost 20 years his senior and the inheritor of Peter McIntyre's vast wealth and string of pastoral properties. Po-faced Reverend

McIntyre – though ruthlessly ambitious, abrasive, narrow-minded and unpopular with clergy and community alike – is quite possibly the richest parson in Australia.

A strict Calvinist, he led a group that in 1846 split from the mainstream Presbyterian Church to form the Presbyterian Church of Eastern Australia, and later opened a church of the new denomination, and a high school, in Maitland.

That church by the school was to be the venue for McIntyre's controversial lecture, but when, with his brother Donald, he arrived in his carriage at 6.30 pm, hundreds of outraged Catholics were there to meet him.

An eye witness told the presumably partisan *Wesleyan Record*:

'The enemies of Protestantism assembled from all country parts of the surrounding district at a little past five o'clock pm, and they stationed themselves in the yard surrounding the church, taking observations. They were informed by one of the trustees of the property that they were intruding on private property – that the place would not be open to the public until seven o'clock, but this only excited murmurs, and threats that he had better take care of himself.'

William McIntyre was pushing his way through the crowd when 'he was closed in on by the Popish rabble, his hat was struck off his head once or twice but, it falling rather away from the crowd, tended to release him from them. He replaced his hat each time, but a severe blow was struck on the left side of his forehead, after which the crowd left him to assail someone else, and he escaped into the high school.'

When Donald McIntyre, following close behind, grappled with one of the men who struck his brother, all hell broke loose.

'"Hit him! Hit him!" sounded from all sides until down came

the sticks on his devoted head, so thick and fast that they actually formed a shield of defence for him by striking each other. I came out of the high school at this moment, and, not knowing who was attacked, immediately went for the constabulary.' Donald McIntyre escaped with a bloodied head but luckily his skull was not fractured.

'The mob had increased from five to six hundred persons and was still swelling. The police now began to arrive but attempts to restrain them or disperse them seemed futile. The police magistrate, Mr Day, stationed himself on the step of the front door, but they broke the windows and destroyed the paling [fence] in his presence. He called on the police to do their duty but the mob laughed at him and his police, and it is said by some of the bystanders that many of the police laughed at the rioters. The Riot Act was not read, which most certainly ought to have been done, by Mr Day.'

The correspondent goes on to claim that the crowd then rampaged through the town until about 10 pm, attacking the homes of prominent Protestants, who barred their doors and closed their shutters in fear and alarm. 'The whole time, this wave of Popish heathenism was allowed to roll on unmolested, for Protestants were unprepared for such an exhibition of social disorder.'

He also claims that a Catholic priest, Dean John Lynch, incited his congregation to riot by telling them that a horde of Protestants from the Liverpool Plains was descending on the town to burn an effigy of the Virgin Mary, and that the priest posted a notice in his church declaring, 'Irish Catholics, every man is expected to do his duty on Thursday night.'[3]

The Sydney Morning Herald, however, heard it somewhat differently:

Mr Day, the police magistrate, was not close at hand during the actual assaults, although he had been for some time previously with the police about the locality, but he soon arrived on the spot, and exerted himself in trying to prevent further outrage. After the lapse of a considerable time, the crowd, which had been very noisy and threatening all the time, and whose number were computed at nearly a thousand (of whom only a portion appeared active), made an attack on the church. Some of the front palings were torn up, and a number of panes of glass in the two front windows were smashed with brickbats and stones. But Mr Day succeeded in preventing any forcible entry into the church by bursting the doors open, which some of the crowd tried.

After the lapse of some further time, during which an occasional stone was thrown at the front windows, Mr Day told the crowd that he was enabled to assure them that no lecture would take place, and ultimately, but we believe not till nearly ten o'clock, they left the spot.[4]

The lecture is postponed until 12 April, when it is delivered, without incident, in the open air before a crowd of 3000 faithful, according to McIntyre's count. In a transcript of the lecture, 'published by the unanimous request of the audience',[5] McIntyre admits ignoring Denny Day's warning that his actions risked causing a riot, but then accuses Day of making no arrangements 'for the preservation of the peace, though he was previously aware that a breach of it was likely to be committed'.[6]

Chapter 36

Quite a lady

On 14 February 1867, an anonymous letter appears in *The Maitland Mercury*:

On looking over your paper of Saturday last I find that Mary Ann Ward has been convicted by the Paterson bench, and sentenced by Mr Cory to three months' imprisonment in Maitland Gaol, for having a few yards of calico and a few yards of derry cloth in her possession, for which she could not satisfactorily account.

I have been credibly informed by a looker-on that this woman informed the bench that she purchased the property at the stores of Messrs. Wolfe and Gorrick, in West Maitland, and that upon enquiry there the truth of her statement could be ascertained. It appears that no opportunity was afforded to this woman of proving her statement, no subpoena was granted on her behalf, and no inquiries were made by the police as to the truth or falsity of her statement. This seems to me a case of gross injustice, and I trust the attention of the proper authorities may be directed to this matter. I am clearly of opinion that this woman is as illegally in custody now as when she was arrested and convicted under the Vagrant Act by a bench not many miles distant, on a charge of vagrancy, and subsequently discharged from Maitland Gaol by order of the Attorney-General. Seemingly the sins of Thunderbolt are visited on this unfortunate woman.[1]

There is much more to this woman's story than the alleged theft of a few yards of cloth, and the clue is in the letter's final sentence.

As police magistrate at Maitland, Denny Day is also the visiting magistrate for Maitland Gaol. This is appropriate, given that back in 1844 he laid the foundation stone for the prison, one of the colony's first penitentiaries. The penitentiary system, which began in Britain and was adopted in the United States, Canada and Australia, made imprisonment a punishment in itself. Previously, prisons were used only to hold felons until punishment could be administered, be that a fine, a flogging or the rope. On this day, in Maitland's forbidding stone fortress, the visiting magistrate climbs the stairs to the top landing of A Wing, where women prisoners are housed to keep them well away from the men. As he gets closer he hears the cries of mothers scolding their children, many of whom were born in the jail.

He has come to see the prisoner Mary Ann Ward, also known as Mary Ann Bugg, but widely known as the Captain's Lady. Mary Ann is a bushranger – the compatriot and lover of Fred Ward, the far-famed Captain Thunderbolt.

Mary Ann was born in 1834 at Berrico, near Gloucester, in the upper Hunter Valley. Her mother, Charlotte, was a Gringai woman of the Wonnarua nation, and her father was English ex-convict James Bugg, who had been transported for sheep stealing.

At five years old, Mary Ann and her three-year-old brother were taken from their parents by a clergyman, William Cowper, who took them to Sydney to 'elevate them above the barbarism of [their mother's] tribe' by teaching them the ways of their larcenous father's people.[2]

In Sydney, Mary Ann learned to read and write, and when, at ten years old, she was allowed to return to her family, she was easily familiar with the white man's social graces, a skill she would one day employ in armed robbery.

Married at 14, and by 25 a mother of four with three failed relationships behind her, Mary Ann met Fred Ward in 1860 at 'Cooyal' station, in central western New South Wales. Ward, a ticket-of-leave man and son of a convict, was a skilled horse-breaker, stockman and horse thief. The two became lovers and took to the bushranging life, he as Captain Thunderbolt and she as the Captain's Lady, and became the most successful bushrangers in Australia's history, ranging far and wide, robbing mail coaches, travellers, inns and stations.

Mary Ann, when not riding at Thunderbolt's side, dressed in men's clothing, pistols at the ready, was promenading through towns in bonnet and dress, scouting for likely places to rob. She also found the time to have two children by Ward.

By 1867, the outlaw life has taken its toll. When Denny Day meets the Captain's Lady in Maitland Gaol, although she has miraculously avoided arrest for robbery under arms, she has served time for vagrancy, and is now charged with petty theft.

On 4 January, on hearing that Thunderbolt and his lady had been spotted in the Paterson River district, Constable James Johnstone and a posse set off in pursuit. After two days' ride, they came upon Thunderbolt and Mary Ann and gave chase.

Thunderbolt and Mary Ann split up, riding hard in different directions. But while Thunderbolt, on his fine thoroughbred, easily evaded capture, Mary Ann, who was carrying a young child with her, could not outrun the posse. They caught up with her at Henry Jarrett's 'Allyn Vale' station, where she was arrested and charged with possession of stolen goods, namely, seven yards of calico, five and a half yards of derry (linen) and two lengths of tweed.

The police took custody of her horse, saddle and saddlebags, which were also presumed to have been stolen, and she was taken before Paterson magistrate Edward Gostwyck Cory and remanded in custody until she could prove the goods were not stolen. When she could not provide evidence she had purchased the goods legally – a difficult task when you're locked up – Cory, a notably bloodless arch-conservative, found her guilty and sentenced her to three months' imprisonment. Mary Ann petitioned the governor – the notably liberal Sir John Young – to examine her case, which is why Denny Day is standing in a prison cell looking down on a forlorn woman pleading her innocence but unable to prove it.

She needn't worry. Denny Day knows exactly what to do. He leaves the gaol, rides the short distance to Wolfe and Gorrick's store and returns to the gaol with a shop assistant named Edwards who identifies Mary Ann as the person who bought the cloth. Edwards' statement is sent off to the Colonial Secretary, and, with the stroke of a pen, Mary Ann walks free.

The Captain's Lady is surely grateful to Denny Day, but, from one living legend to another, no thanks are necessary.

*

Denny Day is attending his last execution. He has seen more than his share of hangings in his time, but never one with such a bizarre epilogue.

At Maitland Gaol on 26 April 1860, before Day, the sheriff, prison officials, clergy and the press, two men are to be hanged for rape and murder. The execution is within the prison walls – public hangings having been abolished eight years ago in New South Wales – and only about 60 people have come to watch. These days, witnesses to an execution must apply for approval. It is no longer a picnic.

The condemned men are a young Aboriginal man known as Jim Crow, and John Jones, a labourer. Crow has been convicted of the rape of a woman named Jane Delanthy, and Jones of the murder of his common-law wife, Rebecca Bailey.

The correspondent for *Bell's Life in Sydney* reports: 'Just before the men came forth of the cell, Bailey (the husband of the fallen and murdered woman) visited and shook hands with Jones, weeping copiously as he bade him farewell. The ill-fated men exchanged a parting salutation with the respited man, previous to leaving the cell. At about half-past nine o'clock Jones and Jim Crow came forth with their arms pinioned from the cell, clothed in white shirts and light trousers, and advanced to the fatal scaffold, upon the lower steps of which they knelt and prayed.'

With nooses adjusted and prayers concluded, the public executioner, Robert Elliott, slips the bolt. 'Jones appeared to suffer but little before life was extinct,' the *Bell's Life* reporter notes, 'but the Aboriginal struggled convulsively for a longer period. In a few moments the souls of the wretched men were in eternity, and the vengeance of the law was satisfied.'

Half an hour later, after the bodies are lowered to the ground, Elliott the hangman, on removing the nooses from around the men's necks, makes a coarse joke about how well he 'cooked them'.[3]

As the corpses are placed in coffins, the hangman, in accord with ancient tradition, kindles a fire in the prison yard and burns the ropes used in the execution. However, those observing this ritual would not be impressed by Elliott's performance had they read *Bell's Life* issue of 23 May 1857:

> Robert Elliott, hangman of New South Wales, was brought before the magistrates at the Central Police Court for drunkenness, and was fined 10 shillings. Being unable to pay that sum, he was sent to the cells for 24 hours. It appeared that Elliott, who was lately up at [Bathurst, for a double hanging on 12 May] brought down two pieces of the ropes he had used for their strangulation, and had been exhibiting them as relics at various public houses in the city, the landlords of which, in return, gave him so many nobblers that he was unable to take care of himself.[4]

The press report on the hanging of Crow and Jones concludes with a comment, rare for the times, on the barbarity of capital punishment: 'The sight is revolting, and the sensation sickening, but the whole affair is destitute of a sound human reason to recommend it as a final penalty for crime.'[5]

An additional report sets the scene for a macabre epilogue: 'Mr Hamilton, the phrenologist, obtained casts in plaster of Paris of the heads of Jones and Jim Crow after execution on Thursday. Doubtless the learned gentleman will afford the public of the district the result of his phrenological examinations on the skulls of these unhappy men.'[6]

*

It's well after dark when William House, the sexton of St Peter's Church and graveyard, makes his way to Finch's Inn, having received word that a guest there wishes to see him. The guest, to the sexton's surprise, is Professor Archibald Sillars Hamilton, the eminent phrenologist, who has come to town to lecture on the fascinating new science of determining character and intellect from measurement and features of the human skull.

The professor asks House if he happens to know where in the graveyard the two hanged men are buried. When House tells him they are in the corner near the gate, Hamilton offers him £1 to dig them up and cut off their heads. When House recoils in horror, Hamilton explains that the law against grave robbing doesn't apply to executed criminals. And besides, Denny Day himself had given him permission to remove the heads for scientific purposes, so everything was above board.

House, suspicious and stalling for time, tells Hamilton he's not well enough to dig at present but will get back to him in a day or two. He tells his story to the rector of St Peter's, John Greaves, who immediately reports the incident to Denny Day.

Day, who had attended one of the professor's lectures and was not convinced, and did not give him permission to exhume and decapitate the bodies, issues a summons for Hamilton's arrest.

Charged with inciting another to exhume corpses from a burial ground, the phrenologist argues that the law does not apply in this case. 'Referring to the fact that the bodies were those of a murderer and an Aboriginal, he stated that he believed them to be beyond the class of those whose burial in consecrated ground would constitute the act of their removal an offence.'[7] The court does not agree, and he is granted bail and committed for trial.

At his trial, the professor, conducting his own defence, enthrals the court with a long and detailed lecture on the benefits to humanity of phrenological science, with applications in criminology, education, mental health, social development and more. The judge is impressed, and advises the jury, 'The possession of human bones might be very important for the ends of science, and very desirable for the benefit of the public, but it was quite clear that in pursuing that science it must be done within legitimate bounds. Nothing must be done to injure another, nor in an illegal manner. There was nothing imputed particularly wrong, in a moral sense.'[8]

The jury, equally impressed, retires and returns 15 minutes later with a verdict of not guilty.

Because neither judge nor jury nor general public are yet aware that phrenology has been exposed as pseudo-scientific claptrap, and that Archibald Sillars Hamilton is not a professor but a sideshow entertainer, the skeletal remains of Aborigines will continue to be collected, displayed and disrespected by curio hunters, amateur anatomists and disciples of quackery.

More than 150 years later, Museum Victoria researchers working to identify and repatriate Indigenous artefacts are intrigued by an item in a collection donated by Archibald Hamilton's widow in 1889. It's a skull labelled 'Jim Crow', a common pejorative for black Americans and black Australians in the nineteenth century. After exhaustive investigation, they discover the skull is that of the man hanged at Maitland Gaol in 1860 and interred in St Peter's churchyard. It seems Archie found someone to do his dirty work after all.

Chapter 37

One of those days

William and Elinor Howells are fond of saying that their rambling Second Empire-style home at 37 Concord Avenue is by far the 'prettiest house in Cambridge'.[1]

Last year, on any number of crisp Massachusetts mornings, William could be found sitting out on the back porch of the prettiest house in town, casting a critical eye over the manuscript of a friend's latest work – a children's book.

William Dean Howells, author, literary critic and editor of *Atlantic Monthly* magazine, read through his friend Sam's manuscript in his usual methodical way, and while he was enthusiastic about the story there were a few changes he believed would improve it, so, as usual, he wrote suggestions in the margin in pencil. First and foremost, he suggested the story should be promoted not just as a children's book but as specifically a boys' book. William knew Sam would resist this, but he was sure it would sell better on that basis. His other suggestions included:

In a passage in which a dog disrupts a church service, William suggested deleting a line describing how the dog 'went sailing up the aisle with his tail shut down like a hasp'. In the margin he wrote, 'Awfully good but a little too dirty.'

In the margin of a page where a schoolgirl discovers in a teacher's anatomy book 'a picture of a human figure, stark naked', William cautions Sam, 'I should be afraid of the picture incident.'

The revised copy went to the printers today, and when William gets to read the book – and there is no doubting that he will – he will note that the dog is still sailing up the aisle with his tail shut down like a hasp, and that although Sam agree to delete the words 'stark naked', he later changed his mind and replaced them. Nor did he take up William's suggestion to promote the novel as a boys' book.

But none of that matters, not to these two old friends. William Dean Howells, as self-appointed arbiter of literary taste and decorum, will keep on suggesting changes. But there will always be days when Samuel Clemens, now better known as Mark Twain, will blissfully ignore his suggestions, and today is one of those days. Regardless, *The Adventures of Tom Sawyer* will become a timeless classic.

No fewer than eight special excursion trains will run on the Great Northern Line today to bring spectators to the championship footrace at Maitland.

The tipster for *The Newcastle Herald* has predicted that 'thousands of anxious spectators will be seen making the best of their way to the convincing ground, to witness for themselves who has the best and undoubted right to the proud title of champion sprint runner of the Australian colonies.'

The competitors are 'that wonder of the age' Frank Hewitt, 'the Champion of Old England', and his opponent, local lad Robert Fletcher Watson. Until Watson 'made his mark in the pedestrian area of New South Wales', the tipster says, 'the man that would have the temerity to try and wrest the laurels from [Hewitt's] brow would have been looked upon as little less than a madman'.[2]

While early betting favoured Hewitt, Watson is now the punters' as well as the sentimental favourite. 'The fate of a nation could hardly beget more interest in some circles than this spin between these crack peds,' says the *Herald*.[3]

The town is full of visitors from upcountry, come to see the 200-yard dash for £400 and sporting glory, but not all the strangers in the street are here for the race. Some are passing through, fever in their eyes and shovels on their backs, on their way to the Barrington rush. In the deep gorges of the high country, the recent discovery of a seven-ounce nugget and some fine gritty gold has so far drawn 200 or more hopefuls to the diggings at Back Creek, on the Barrington River (near Gloucester, 220 kilometres north of Sydney).

The gold there is hard won. It's remote, rough country, freezing in winter, prone to sudden snow flurries, and already word is trickling back that the narrow streams are all but played out already. Some say working with pans and sluice boxes will get you nowhere slowly; that the serious colour is hidden in reefs on the ridges; that the mother lode is out there somewhere, and that it will most likely be hard-rock miners who find it.

Apart from the odd few who strike pay dirt, the only man guaranteed to make a fortune at Back Creek is 'an enterprising storekeeper who has, we are told, commenced putting up a building, to enable him to meet the requirements of diggers'.[4]

Still, the dreamers will keep heading north out of town until the inevitable day when they come shuffling back through, backs and hearts broken, headed south. They say the cure for gold fever is equal doses of hard work and hard luck, but it's a desperately slow cure, and there are days when the cure is as cruel as the disease. Today is one of those days.

At his home on Stockade Hill today, with Margaret and some of his many children at his side, Denny Day, long since retired due to failing health, died. It is Saturday 6 May 1876.

Three days later, his obituary in *The Maitland Mercury* begins:

'A gentleman who has been withdrawn for many years from active life by sickness died at his residence in East Maitland on Saturday Morning last. Mr Edward Denny Day was, previous to an attack of paralysis, and after the attack till increasing feebleness compelled him to resign his public duties, police magistrate of Maitland, and had occupied that responsible office for so long a time that his name was historical in connection with it.'

Making no mention of Day's role in bringing the Myall Creek killers to justice, the obituary continues:

'At one period of his life, Mr Day made a considerable figure in the public eye by a gallant capture of a noted bushranging gang who had established a reign of terror in the district of the Upper Hunter.

'Mr Day was admirably fitted for the duties of the magisterial bench. He possessed a keen intelligence, an active mind, and a very wide practical knowledge of the law. By some people he was charged with harshness and tyranny, and it must be admitted that in his administration of the law he made it a terror to evildoers. That is rather a virtue than a failing in the dispenser of justice. His stern manner detracted materially from the estimation in which he was held by people generally, but although he made a few mistakes, his decisions on the bench were almost invariably distinguished by strict equity.

'He held office at a time when rigour was specially called for from a magistrate, and when a stern enforcement of the law was essential to social security. He was a faithful public servant, always doing his duty honourably, and if the manner of an older and worse Day was sometimes a little too rugged for the improved state of society in his later time, we can pardon it for the sake of such conspicuous fidelity.'

The obituary concludes:

'Mr Day leaves a widow and a large family, all grown up and settled in life. He was one of the old school of officials, which almost every year now sees reduced by death, and he was one of the best in his sphere.'[5]

The *Australian Town and Country Journal*, likewise, omits any reference to Myall Creek:

In 1840 bushranging was at its height in New South Wales, and no man then residing in Australia more prominently distinguished himself in the capture of the desperadoes and the extermination of the crime than Mr Day.

For several years he has been bedridden and suffered a good deal of pain with patience and fortitude. He was throughout this period most tenderly nursed by his devoted wife, and firmly attached friends often visited his bedside. He died at his residence in East Maitland, on the 6th of this present month of May, at 75 years of age. His funeral was in all respects a strictly private one, being only attended at his especial request by members of his family, and his two most intimate friends and associates, Mr. J. M. Saunders and Mr. E. M. Close.

In the cemetery of East Maitland lies now one of the oldest residents of that district, a man of iron nerves and integrity of purpose, and a staunch supporter of the creed to which he belonged, that of the Church of England. By some he was considered an austere and severe man, but no one ever questioned his strict impartiality and justice, whilst those who knew him best were well aware of his unostentatious charity distributed wherever deserving. As a thorough Christian and an upright honourable gentleman, the name of Mr Edward Denny Day will be long remembered in the Hunter River district.[6]

So, the old frontier lawman is in the ground and the process of collective disregard can begin. It's safe now for some to say – after a respectful period, of course – that he was the right man for his times but his times were over long ago. And you couldn't say he was at all likeable – he didn't seem to care whether people liked him or not. Oh yes, he was certainly brave, no doubt about that, but he was also, what's the word? Irascible? Tetchy? Sometimes he could be downright rude! Of course, one shouldn't normally speak ill of the dead, but there are certain times when that is quite acceptable, and today is one of those days.

Chapter 38

Finding John Henry

He did not run off to Van Diemen's Land, America or parts unknown. John Henry Fleming, who led the killers at Myall Creek, then abandoned them to their fate, fled to his father's home in the village of Macdonald (later renamed St Albans) on the Macdonald River, about 90 kilometres north-west of Sydney. There, he hid in plain sight, sheltered by family and friends.

In 1840, at Wilberforce, a village on the western bank of the Hawkesbury, he married Charlotte Dunstan, and by the 1850s had moved to Wilberforce where he became a prominent farmer of the district and a pillar of the community.

In 1859, during the building of St John's Church, he donated the stained-glass window on the south wall, near the chancel.

He was appointed a church warden in 1862, a trustee of the Church of England burial ground in 1889, a trustee of the town common in 1874, served on the committee of the Benevolent Society, and in 1882 – in a grand irony – was made a magistrate, and remained on the bench until his death on 20 August 1894. He and his wife Charlotte had no children.

At his funeral at St John's Church, attended by almost the entire community, the cortege was met by an honour guard of local schoolchildren, marshalled by their headmaster, and many wreaths were laid upon the coffin to the sombre strains of 'The March of Saul'.

His obituary in *The Windsor and Richmond Gazette* reads:

After a long illness, attended by much suffering, an old and respected resident of Wilberforce, Mr John Henry Fleming, passed away on Monday. Born at Pitt Town, early in life he engaged in squatting pursuits in Queensland. He ultimately settled down at Wilberforce, and for many years followed a farming life, where he acquired a comfortable competency. He was a member of the Committee of the Hawkesbury Benevolent Society for many years, and the old folks lose a kind-hearted sympathiser by his death. He was appointed a Justice of the Peace about ten years ago. Deceased used to tell some stirring stories of the early days of settlement in the colony, and the trouble he had with the blacks. Mr Fleming had been gradually declining during the past few years, and added to this he lately had a severe attack of influenza. For weeks past he has been undergoing much suffering, but through all his pain he was remarkable for his patience. As a resident he will be much missed for his kindness of heart and generosity to the poor; he was never known to refuse to anyone in want. Deceased was 78 years of age, and was a brother to Mrs William Hall of Cattai. His remains were interred in the Church of England Cemetery, Wilberforce, on Tuesday last. Deceased leaves a widow, but no family.[1]

Revelation 12:7-9: 'And there was war in heaven: Michael fought and his angels fought against the dragon, and the dragon fought and his angels, and prevailed not; neither was their place found any more in heaven. And the great dragon was cast out, that old serpent, called the Devil, and Satan, which deceiveth the whole world: he was cast out into the earth, and his angels were cast out with him.'[2]

John Henry Fleming's stained-glass window in St John's Church depicts an obscure story from Christian apocrypha – St John and the Poisoned Chalice at the Temple of Diana at Ephesus.

According to non-biblical texts, in 1 AD, when the Greek city of Ephesus was part of the Roman Empire, and the temple of the goddess Diana was one of the wonders of the ancient world, St John the Evangelist, author of the Book of Revelation, was in Ephesus working miracles.

Hoping to stop this Christian upstart poaching his flock and to reveal him as a charlatan, Aristodemus, high priest of the temple of Diana, challenged St John to drink from a poisoned chalice. To prove the cup was poisoned, Aristodemus forced two criminals to drink from it, and both immediately fell dead.

St John blessed the cup, whereupon a dragon emerged from it and flew away. He then drank from the cup, with no ill effects, and proceeded to bring the two criminals back to life. Aristodemus, mightily impressed, converted to Christianity on the spot.

The stained-glass window, which shows St John holding the chalice with the dragon, is believed to symbolise the triumph of Christianity over paganism. That suggests Fleming donated it to the church not as an act of contrition but of triumphalism. If that is so, Revelation 6:8 would be a fitting epitaph for John Henry Fleming:

'And I looked, and behold a pale horse, and his name that sat on him was Death, and Hell followed with him.'

Chapter 39

Free at last

Two elderly women are standing on a ridge overlooking creek flats where cattle are grazing. There seems nothing special about this place – nothing that meets the eye, anyway. Myall Creek could be anywhere in rural Australia, but to these women, and others with them today, 10 June 2000, this is the time and the place for healing an old and still painful wound.

The two women, Sue Blacklock and Beaulah Adams, take each other by the hand, tentatively at first, but then, on looking into each other's eyes, they embrace and break into tears. Now, they are clinging tightly to one another, as if determined to never let go.

The taller of the two, Sue Blacklock, is a Wirrayaraay woman from Tingha, a small town near Inverell, 630 kilometres north-east of Sydney. She is a descendant of John Munro, who as a boy was one of the fortunate few who managed to escape into the bush when John Henry Fleming's band of killers rode into Myall Creek station on 10 June 1838.

Beaulah Adams, frail and clearly nervous, is a white woman from the nearby town of Glen Innes. Recently, while researching her family history, she discovered that she is a descendant of Edward Foley, one of the Myall Creek murderers.

She had been anxious about coming here today, unsure of how the Aboriginal descendants might react. But in the end she decided it was the right thing to do, and here she is, face to face with a woman who shares a tragic history.

At last, Beaulah Adams finds the courage to speak. Choking back tears, she says to Sue Blacklock, 'I just want you to know how truly sorry I am for what happened here and how ashamed I am that my family was involved.'[1]

'We can forgive but never forget,' Sue Blacklock tells her, still holding her close. 'We have to talk to each other to acknowledge these things happened.'[2]

Adams, who has lived all her life in Glen Innes, says she had always wondered why her grandparents avoided talking about the family's history.

'My husband and I checked the family history through the records a few months ago,' she says. 'First we found that my great-grandfather, John Foley, was a convict sent out from Ireland for life with his brother, Edward, after setting fire to haystacks.

'Then we discovered Edward was one of those hanged for the Myall Creek massacre. I felt shame, absolute shame. Even though it had nothing to do with me and I am not responsible for it, I still felt a great sense of shame.

'It is a terrible feeling. At first I thought it couldn't be true. Even though it happened more than 150 years ago, I felt just as shocked as if a member of my family was involved in something like that today.'

In 1998, Sue Blacklock organised a small remembrance ceremony by Aboriginal people at Myall Creek. She and others are here today in advance of the dedication on 10 June of a permanent memorial to the massacre.

It's been a long time coming. In 1965, a Bingara resident, Len Payne, who had written extensively on the massacre, proposed that a memorial be erected on the site. His proposal was opposed by many local people, who believed such events were best forgotten, and while Payne never gave up hope, and laid a wreath at the site every 10 June, he didn't live to see his dream realised. Len Payne died in 1993.

Motivated by the modest 1998 ceremony, Sue Blacklock, Uniting Church minister John Brown and others began lobbying for a permanent memorial. At last, government funding came through, the Bingara and Gwydir shire authorities lent their support, and the memorial was built.

Looking down from the ridge, Sue Blacklock points to where her ancestor ran to warn others of the coming of the horsemen.

'My family have always talked of what happened down there,' she says. 'We have always known, even when white people didn't want to know. I think Beaulah should get a medal for having the courage to come forward to say sorry for what her family did. It is a step in the right direction for reconciliation.'

She has no wish to venture below the ridge. 'We weren't allowed on the property where the massacre actually happened, but I don't want to,' she says. 'You can imagine what happened there and I don't want to stand on it. It is best to have the monument on the hill.'

Blacklock's daughter-in-law Margaret, who has joined her today, says she feels shivers when she goes anywhere near the site. 'I can't even see cattle without thinking my people were killed for those beasts,' she tells Walker. 'They thought Aboriginal people were killing cattle, so they tried to exterminate them.'[3]

Also here today is Des Blake, a retired bank manager from Lennox Head, a coastal town in northern New South Wales. Blake learnt a few years ago that he is a descendant of John Blake, one of the four men who avoided prosecution for the massacre.

'It came as a huge shock,' Blake says. 'We had no idea. We didn't even know our ancestors were convicts. No one ever mentioned it. One of my relatives was doing a family tree and made this discovery. John Blake was the only married man among the gang. He might have got off, but reading the records it is clear he was guilty as hell. He slit his own throat when he was 41, so maybe he felt guilty.'[4]

Des Blake says meeting Sue Blacklock and other Wirrayaraay descendants didn't make him feel personally guilty. 'But I certainly felt sorrow, and I think it is a sorrow felt by most people in Australia.

'I don't think my ancestors were doing anything more than acting in the behaviour of the time. They were feted as heroes by other whites. I will be saying I am sorry at the ceremony for what my ancestor did. If any member of my family did something like that, I would say I am sorry. I am not personally responsible, but I am sorry my people have done this thing.'

Blake says his many years as a bank manager in country towns have convinced him that racism is alive and well in Australia. When he has told people what his ancestor did, some have replied, 'He should have got them all.'[5]

Early on the morning of 8 June 2000, amid worldwide media attention, the Olympic torch, on its journey to Sydney from Greece for the 2000 Olympic Games, arrives by plane at Uluru and is passed to a group of Anangu people, traditional owners of the area.

Just after 10 o'clock the same morning, amid no media attention, Colin Markham, parliamentary secretary and Member for Wollongong, gets to his feet in the New South Wales parliament and moves that the House 'recognise the significance of Myall Creek as an example of the treatment of Aboriginal people and of justice being done; recognise the importance of sharing the whole truth of Australian history; and commend the Myall Creek Memorial Committee, and all the Aboriginal and other Australians who have worked together in a spirit of reconciliation to acknowledge the shared truth of our history.'

Markham tells the House: 'This Saturday on 10 June at Myall Creek near Bingara in north-west New South Wales a ceremony will be held to dedicate a memorial to the 1838 Myall Creek massacre. That event needs to be remembered as an appalling example of the treatment of Aboriginal people on colonial frontiers. Myall Creek can also be celebrated as an early example of Australian justice and of reconciliation in action. After all, there can be no reconciliation without justice.'

After recounting the story of the massacre, Denny Day's investigation and the trials, Markham concludes, 'Relatively few non-indigenous Australians have much to do with Aboriginal or Torres Strait Islander people in their day-to-day lives. A lack of first-hand information provides fertile ground for simplistic or false perceptions. Myall Creek is a very important part of New South Wales and Australian history, and the memorial should be given every support. The memorial commemorates not only the massacre and the fact that justice was done, it is testimony to the true history of Australia.

'The memorial is an initiative of the Myall Creek Memorial Committee, led by Kamilaroi elder Lyall Munro Senior and Dr John Brown of the Uniting Church. Indigenous and non-indigenous community members were also involved, including descendants of the Aboriginal people who were massacred and descendants of the white stockmen who were hanged. This is a true sign of reconciliation.'[6]

In the very chamber that once echoed with cries of 'Hear! Hear!' whenever honourable members heaped scorn and derision upon the recalcitrant blacks, member after member from both sides of the House rises to support the motion, and it is passed unopposed.

'Very soon we will all take a journey together,' noted artist and former Bingara resident Paulette Hayes tells the large crowd gathered at Myall Creek on 10 June 2000. 'We will walk up the hill and along the serpentine path together, and as we walk down towards the rock, we will read about the massacre that happened 162 years ago today. And as you walk, I ask only this of you. Think about those who died, speak to them, say a prayer for them, remember them. And as you return back along the path, take a stranger by the arm and walk back in peace, knowing that today you have taken a very big step towards justice, truth and reconciliation.'[7]

Visitors follow a 500-metre winding gravel path – past markers providing a timeline of events leading up to and following the massacre – to a large stone monument inscribed with the words:

In memory of the Wirrayaraay people who were murdered on the slopes of this ridge in an unprovoked and premeditated act in the late afternoon of 10 June 1838. Erected on 10 June 2000 by a group of Aboriginal and non-Aboriginal Australians in an act of reconciliation, and in acknowledgement of the truth of our shared history.

We remember them.

Ngiyani winangay ganunga.

In 2005, after vandals damaged the plaques along the memorial walk, attempting to obliterate the words 'murder', 'women' and 'children', the New South Wales government reacts by calling the act an appalling and insulting crime.

Addressing his remarks to the vandals, Aboriginal Affairs Minister Andrew Refshauge says, 'Defacing this memorial is disrespectful and insulting to the people who were murdered, and their families. The reconciliation of Aboriginal and non-Aboriginal people in the region is already a powerful movement. Join it, don't trash it!'[8]

In 2008, to provide protection against further acts of vandalism, the federal government declares the memorial a national heritage site.

The purpose of the smoking ceremony, Aboriginal elder Colin Isaac explains to the hundreds gathered at the memorial on 10 June 2015, as the scent of eucalyptus and sandalwood, and the hum of a bullroarer fill the air, is to 'purify the souls of the people that come through, and shut out the evil. At the same time, it is a cleansing ceremony to call the good spirits and allow them to mingle with you,' he says.[9]

Voices are raised in a solemn vow, as hundreds of people pledge:

'We are here today to commit ourselves again to the hard work of reconciliation between our peoples. We remember the past so that we may understand the present. We commit ourselves to the task of the present so that our children and grandchildren may have a better tomorrow.'

'I get emotional every time I see it,' Sue Blacklock says. 'I can't explain in words how I feel when we come here every year, and to see different people and to meet different families – there are no words to express how I feel.

'I know that my ancestors are free that we are finally recognising that they are free. Their spirits are free to wander now and to be at peace.'

She is delighted that attendance at the ceremony grows larger each year, and that so many children come. 'It was very lovely to have them here with us and to know and teach them our language and teach them our culture,' she says. 'This is their culture too, not only mine, and it's helping them to respect their culture, letting them never forget where they come from and keep walking in the footsteps of their elders.'

Uniting Church minister John Brown, who played a large part in establishing the memorial, thanks those who have come from near and far – some from as far away as Western Australia – 'to remember this largely untold part of our history, and it is important that be acknowledged as we move on, not in order to grovel in the sins of the past, but in order that we bring all our people together, acknowledging the truth of our history.

'I'm very happy about what we have achieved,' he says. 'I hope that we get a good result from the referendum [on recognising Indigenous Australians in the Constitution] that is to come, and that we end some of the other things that are going on. I am surprised that some people still want to remove Aboriginal people from their traditional lands and resettle them on the fringes of towns. That makes no sense,' he says. 'That is crazy stuff, so I hope we can put all of that aside.'[10]

For Sue Blacklock, the most intense and abiding memory of Myall Creek is that of the first remembrance ceremony in 1998.

She recalls: 'When they were dancing all these white cockatoos just rose up and flew. I'd never seen so many white cockatoos and I believe after they did that dance, the people that were massacred, their spirit was free, and every year after that it rained and we said that our ancestors were crying tears of joy that they are now free.'[11]

Afterword

The stockyard at Myall Creek station, no longer used, fell into disrepair. For a long time only the gatepost remained, and eventually that, too, rotted away. For many years, stockmen refused to corral cattle there, believing the scent of blood would drive the beasts wild, and children from the homestead eventually built at the station would never go anywhere near the old yard. Having been told the story of what happened there, they were too afraid.

On the downward slope of a hill, in the well-kept cemetery at Wilberforce, is the marble vault where lie John Henry Fleming and his wife Charlotte. The most imposing in the graveyard, the vault stands on the western edge, away from the main area of graves.

Charlotte Fleming's plaque, which tells us she died in 1908, in her ninetieth year, faces the rising sun, in accordance with old Christian tradition, in anticipation of the second coming of Christ on Judgement Day. John Henry's plaque faces the setting sun, and the ground beneath that side of the vault has collapsed, leaving a gaping hole.

Above the altar at St Peter's Church, Maitland, is a stained-glass window depicting the ascension of Christ into heaven. Dating from 1887, the dedication reads: 'To the Glory of God and in memory of Edward Denny Day of the 62nd Regiment who fell asleep 6th May 1876.' The window is also dedicated to Margaret Day, who died three years later.

And in the Old Glebe Burial Ground, the headstone of Denny and Margaret Day's grave has toppled, and lies face down on the ground.

There's a tale they tell around old Wallis Plains. Some swear it's true, and some say that if it's not it ought to be. So the story goes, sometime after Denny Day died – no one can say exactly when – an Aboriginal man made his weary way up Stockade Hill to the Days' cottage and knocked at the front door.

When Margaret Day opened the door, the man swept off his hat and asked, 'Excuse me, Ma'am, may I see Mr Day please?'

Margaret couldn't reply; the words caught in her throat.

'Just tell him it's Davey,' the stranger said. 'Tell him they didn't get me. He'll understand.'

She sighed and slowly shook her head. 'I'm sorry, Davey,' she said at last, 'Mr Day has passed away. He's gone.'

Davey stood there on that doorstep for a full five minutes

without speaking a word, staring at nothing in particular, then he smiled at Margaret Day, said, 'But not forgotten,' turned and walked away.

They say Davey died not long afterwards, somewhere upriver, of nothing in particular – that he just sort of faded away.

No doubt, some would dismiss such a tale as mere folklore and fancy, and perhaps they'd be right. Still, there are yet places in this country where conflicts and concerns long forgotten elsewhere are still table talk, where yesteryear is yesterday, where history and legend are familiar bedfellows.

The old frontier is just such a place. There, you'll find people who speak of the wild days as if the memories were their own. And you're sure to find people who believe, or desperately want to believe, that on nights when the wind blows high and hard across the Old Glebe Burial Ground, the ghosts of Denny Day and Davey walk those yellow hills. Their shades are fated to walk there, side by side, so people say, until the winds that stir the grass are winds of change.

And that is why they walk there still.

Notes

Introduction

1 Boldrewood, R., *Old Melbourne Memories*, Heinemann, Melbourne 1969

2 *Census of New South Wales* 1828, Saintly, M., and Johnston, K. (eds.), Biographical Database of Australia, Sydney, 1980, revised edition 2008, bda-online.org.au

3 *Report of the Select Committee on Transportation, 1837–38*, vol. 22, pp. 22, 41

Chapter 1

1 Strype, J., *Ecclesiastical Memorials*, vol. 1, part 2, Oxford, 1822, p. 458

2 Kerry's History for the E-Reader, *The Dennys of Tralee Castle, their exceptional connections*, historytralee.wordpress.com

3 Ardfert and Aghadoe Census of 1821, *Encyclopaedia Britannica*, 8th ed., 1857

Chapter 2

1 Chisholm, C., *Voluntary Information from the People of New South Wales*, W.A. Duncan, Sydney 1845, quoted in Sidney, Samuel, *The Three Colonies of Australia*, Ingram, Cooke & Co, London, 1853, pp. 50–52

2 Ibid

3 Ibid

4 Tench, W., *A Complete Account of the Settlement at Port Jackson in New South Wales, Including An Accurate Description of the Situation of the Colony; of the Natives; and of Its Natural Productions*, G. Nicol and J. Sewell, London, 1793, p. 66

5 Ibid, p. 68

6 Collins, D., *An Account of the English Colony in New South Wales*, vol. 1, T. Cadwell Jnr and W. Davies, London, 1798, p. 330

7 Ibid

8 Ibid, p. 345

9 Ibid, p. 347

10 King to Banks, *Letter*, 5 June 1802, Sir Joseph Banks Electronic Archive, series 39.068, Mitchell Library, Sydney

11 Banks to King, *Letter*, Sir Joseph Banks Electronic Archive, series 39.076, Mitchell Library, Sydney

12 Macquarie to Bathurst, *Despatch*, 4 April 1817

13 *The Australian* (Sydney), 10 November 1825, p. 3

14 Ibid, p. 2

15 Walker, W., *Reminiscences (Personal, Social and Political) of a Fifty Year Residence at Windsor, on the Hawkesbury*, Turner and Henderson, Sydney, 1890, pp. 6–7

16 Bunbury, T., *Reminiscences of a Veteran: being personal and military adventures in Portugal, Spain, France, Malta, New South Wales, Norfolk Island, New Zealand, Andaman Islands and India*, vol. 2, Charles J. Skeet, London, 1861, p. 290

17 Walker, W., *Reminiscences (Personal, Social and Political) of a Fifty Year Residence at Windsor, on the Hawkesbury*, Turner and Henderson, Sydney, 1890, p. 9

18 Warner to Bourke, quoted in Turner, J., and Blyton, G., *The Aboriginals of Lake Macquarie*, Lake Macquarie City Council, Newcastle, 1995, p. 37

19 Bannister, S., *Humane Policy: or Justice to the Aborigines of New Settlements Essential to a Due Expenditure of British Money, and to the Best Interests of the Settlers*, Thomas and George Underwood, London, 1830, p. 7

20 Ibid, p. 240

Chapter 3

1 Becket, I. F. W., *Discovering English County Regiments*, Shire Publications, Buckinghamshire, 2003, p. 27

2 Macquarie, L., *Sydney Gazette*, 7 January 1810

3 Macquarie, L., *Diary*, Sydney, 10 April 1816

4 Ibid

5 Macquarie, L., *Instructions to the Military*, 9 April 1816

6 Macquarie, L., *Instructions for Capt. W.G.B. Schaw*, 9 April 1816

7 Macquarie, L., *Diary*, 4 May 1816

Chapter 4

1 National Army Museum, *62nd (Wiltshire) Regiment of Foot*, nam.ac.uk/research/famous-units/62nd-wiltshire-regiment-foot

2 Risvi, A., *The Other Sepoy Mutiny*, Bangalore Mirror Bureau, 1 June 2014

Chapter 5

1 *The Sydney Herald*, 28 August 1834, p. 2

Chapter 6

1 *The Australian,* 28 June 1826, p. 2
2 *The Sydney Monitor,* 23 September 1835, p. 3
3 Zouch, Lieut. H., *Report to Capt. Williams, Commandant of Mounted Police,* 7 December 1835
4 Ibid
5 Ibid
6 Ibid
7 White, C., *The Story of the Blacks, Bathurst Free Press,* 3 January 1890, p. 4

Chapter 7

1 *4 William IV,* Act No. 7
2 *The Sydney Gazette and New South Wales Advertiser,* 9 January 1836, p. 4
3 Ibid

Chapter 8

1 Department of Main Roads New South Wales, *Main Roads,* September 1949, p. 11
2 Darwin, C., *Letter to his sister Caroline,* 27 December 1835
3 Darwin, C. R., *Journal of researches into the natural history and geology of the countries visited during the voyage of H.M.S. Beagle round the world, under the Command of Capt. Fitz Roy, R.N.,* 2nd edition, John Murray, London, 1845, p. 433
4 Ibid
5 Ibid, p. 435
6 Ibid, pp. 444, 445
7 Ibid, p. 452
8 *The Sydney Gazette and New South Wales Advertiser,* 6 August 1836, p. 3

9 Ibid

10 Royal Archives, *Queen Victoria's Journal*, 20 June 1837

Chapter 9

1 Ogilvie, E. D. S., *Diary of Travels in Three Quarters of the Globe*, Saunders & Otley, London, 1856, vol. 1, p. 47

2 Breton, Lieut., R. N., *Excursions in New South Wales, Western Australia and Van Diemen's Land*, Richard Bentley, London, 1833, p. 90

3 Ridley, Reverend W., *Kamilaroi and Other Australian Languages*, 2nd edition, Thomas Richards, Sydney, 1875, p. 155

4 Ibid, p. 90

5 Ibid, p. 172

6 Telfer, W., *The Wallabadah Manuscript*, New South Wales University Press, Sydney, 1980, pp. 47, 48

7 Wood, W. A., *Dawn in the Valley*, Wentworth Books, Sydney, 1972, p. 220

8 Huey, A., *Diary: The Voyage of the 73rd Regiment of Foot*, State Library of New South Wales, Sydney, 1790, p. 24

Chapter 10

1 White, G. B., *Diary*, 4 May 1870

2 *The Sydney Gazette*, 10 June 1804, p. 2

3 *The Sydney Gazette*, 5 March 1803, p. 3

4 Ibid

5 Biggs, J. T., *Report of the Commissioner of Inquiry into the State of the Colony of New South Wales*, 1822, p. 117

6 *Threlkeld, L. E., to Colonial Secretary*, 31 December 1837, quoted in Gunston, N., (ed), *Australian Reminiscences and Papers of L.E. Threlkeld*, vol 1, Australian Institute of Aboriginal Studies, Canberra, 1974, p. 139

7 Threlkeld, L. E., *Journal*, 14 December 1825

8 *The Maitland Mercury*, 9 May 1876, p. 4

9 *The Sydney Herald*, 18 December 1837, p. 2

10 *The Sydney Herald*, 22 January, 1838, p. 2

Chapter 11

1 Watson, W., and Handt, J., *Report of the Mission to the Aborigines of New Holland, Wellington Valley*, 14 December 1833

2 Ibid

3 Threlkeld, L. E., *Annual Report of the Aboriginal Mission at Lake Macquarie, New South Wales, for 1835*, 28 June 1836

4 Ibid

5 Ibid

6 Ibid

Chapter 12

1 Cunningham, P., *Two Years in New South Wales*, vol. 1, Henry Colburn, London, 1827, pp. 33, 34

2 *The Sydney Herald*, 3 December 1835, p. 2

3 Macqueen, T. P., *Australia As She Is and As She May Be*, London, 1840, p. 12

4 *The Australian*, 14 January 1837, p. 2

Chapter 13

1 Paterson, A., *Report on Outrages by Aborigines on Namoi, Gwydir and Big Rivers*, 6 December 1837, quoted in *Historical Records of Australia*, 22 July 1839, p. 252

2 Nunn, J. W., *Deposition taken before Edward Denny Day*, 4 April 1839

3 Gipps to Glenelg, *Despatch*, 27 April 1838

4 Faithfull, G., *Letter to Lieutenant-Governor La Trobe*, 8 September 1853

5 Ibid
6 *Despatch from Sir George Gipps to Lord Glenelg*, 21 July 1838

Chapter 15

1 Hobbs, W., to Day, E. D., *Letter*, 9 July 1838
2 Various colonists, *Memorial to Governor Sir George Gipps*, Sydney, 8 June 1838, in *Copies of Extracts of Despatches relative to the massacre of various Aborigines of Australia in the year 1838, and respecting the Trial of their Murderers*, House of Commons, London, 12 August 1839, pp. 26–27
3 Thomson, E., *Letter to Philip Gidley King*, Sydney, 23 June 1838
4 *Despatch from Governor Sir George Gipps to Lord Glenelg*, 21 July 1838
5 *The Hobart Town Courier*, 20 July 1838, p. 2

Chapter 16

1 *Assistant Colonial Secretary Thomas Harrington to E.D. Day*, 9 July 1838
2 Day, E. D., to Plunkett, J. H., *Letter*, 8 September 1838
3 Evidence of A. Burrowes, New South Wales Aborigines Protection Society, *Extracts from the Papers and Proceedings*, No. 1, October 1838, p. 50
4 Day to Attorney-General, 8 September 1838
5 *The Sydney Herald*, 14 September 1838, p. 2

Chapter 17

1 *Unlawful Oaths Act 1797* (37 George III, c. 123)
2 Loveless et al, *A Narrative of the Sufferings of Jas. Loveless, Jas. Brine, and Thomas and John Standfield, four of the Dorchester labourers, written by themselves*, Leave, London, 1838, pp. 10–12

3 Evidence of Scott, R., *Report from the Committee on the Aborigines Question*, 1838, New South Wales Legislative Council, pp. 16–17
4 *The Australian*, 17 November 1838, p. 3
5 *The Australian*, 20 November 1838, p. 2

Chapter 18

1 *The Sydney Gazette*, 20 November 1838, pp. 2–3
2 Ibid
3 Ibid
4 Ibid
5 Ibid, pp. 3–4
6 Ibid

Chapter 19

1 Ibid
2 Ibid
3 Ibid
4 Ibid
5 Ibid

Chapter 20

1 *The Sydney Herald*, 14 September, 1838, p. 2
2 *Australian Dictionary of Biography*, adb.anu.edu.au/biography/burton-sir-william-westbrooke-1857
3 *The Australian*, 1 December 1838, p. 2
4 Ibid
5 Ibid
6 Ibid
7 Ibid
8 Ibid
9 Ibid
10 Ibid

Chapter 21

1 Genesis 9:6, *The Holy Bible*, King James Version, Robert Barker, London, 1611
2 Quoted in Roberts, J., *Massacres to Mining: The Colonisation of Aboriginal Australia*, Dove Communications, Melbourne, 1981, p. 19

Chapter 22

1 *The Sydney Herald*, 5 October 1838, p. 3
2 *The Australian*, 8 December 1838, p. 2
3 *The Sydney Herald*, 10 December 1838, p. 4
4 *Report on the Committee on the Aborigines Question*, New South Wales Legislative Council, 1838, p. 44, quoted in *The Sydney Herald*, 10 December 1838, p. 4
5 Ibid, p. 4
6 *The Sydney Gazette*, 4 December, 1838, p. 2
7 *The Sydney Gazette*, 11 December 1838, p. 2
8 *The Colonist*, 12 December 1838, p. 2
9 *The Sydney Herald*, 19 September 1838, p. 4
10 *The Colonist*, 10 October 1838, p. 2
11 *The Sydney Gazette*, 20 November 1838, p. 2
12 *The Colonist*, 12 December 1838, p. 2
13 *The Sydney Herald*, 14 November 1838, p. 2
14 Ibid
15 Bartlett, T., *New Holland*, Longman, Brown, Green and Longmans, London, 1843, pp. 65–66

Chapter 23

1 *The Murder Act 1751* (25 Geo 2 c 37)
2 Ibid
3 *The Sydney Gazette*, 20 December 1838, p. 2
4 Ibid

5 Ibid

6 Bannatyne, J. H., to Berry, O., *Letter*, 18 December 1838

7 Gipps to Glenelg, *Despatch No. 200*, 19 December 1838

8 Gipps to Glenelg, *Despatch No. 201*, 20 December 1838

9 *The Sydney Gazette*, 6 December 1838, p. 2

Chapter 24

1 Wearne, J. T., *Bingara 1827–1937*, Bingara District Historical Society, 1885, p. 9

Chapter 25

1 Deposition by Major J. W. Nunn, *Documents relating to Aboriginal Australians 1816–1853*, Mitchell Library, State Library of New South Wales, Sydney, p. 138

2 Ibid

3 Ibid, p. 139

4 Ibid, pp. 141–42

5 Ibid, p. 144

6 Ibid, pp. 146–47

7 Ibid, p. 165

8 Filisola, V., *Memorias para la Historia de la Guerra de Tejas*, Ignatio Cumplido, Mexico City 1849, trans. Gustavo Pellon, pp. 13–15

9 *The Sydney Herald*, 29 March 1839, p. 2

10 Ibid

Chapter 26

1 Gipps to Glenelg, *Despatch*, 18 March 1838

2 Russell, P. (ed.), *This Errant Lady: Jane Franklin's overland journey to Port Phillip and Sydney, 1839*, National Library of Australia Press, Canberra, 2002, p. 131

3 *The Age* (Melbourne), 9 August 1880, p. 3

4 Wood, W. A., *Dawn in the Valley*, Wentworth Books, Sydney, 1972, p. 308

5 *Old Bailey Sessions Papers*, 1831–2, p. 381

6 *Indent of Convict Ships*, 1832–33, pp. 171–72

7 *The Sydney Herald*, 8 December 1839, p. 2

8 Ibid

9 *The Sydney Gazette*, 3 April 1839, p. 2

10 *The Sydney Herald*, 23 December 1840, p. 2

Chapter 27

1 *The Sydney Herald*, 26 December 1840, p. 2

2 *The Australian*, 29 December 1840, p. 2

3 Diggles, M., *Extract from memoir of George Downes*, Royal Historical Society of Queensland, 1881

4 Ibid

5 Ibid

6 Ibid

7 Ibid

8 Ibid

9 Ibid

10 Ibid

Chapter 28

1 Diggles, M., *Extract from memoir of George Downes*, Royal Historical Society of Queensland, 1881

2 Ibid

3 Ibid

4 Ibid

5 *The Sydney Herald*, 30 December 1840, p. 2

6 *The Sydney Herald*, 31 December 1840, p. 2

Chapter 29

1   Australian Jewish Historical Society, *Journal and Proceedings*, vol. 4, part 5, Sydney, 1956, p. 229

2   Ibid, p. 230

3   Ibid

4   *The Australian*, 25 February 1841, p. 2

5   Ibid

6   Ibid

7   *The Australian*, 13 March 1841, p. 2

8   *Minutes of the Executive Council*, vol. 5 (1837–1841), Minute No. 6

9   Ibid

10 Ibid

11 *The Muswellbrook Chronicle*, 12 February 1937, p. 1

Chapter 30

1   *The Muswellbrook Chronicle*, 12 February 1937, p. 1

2   *The Australian*, 27 February 1841, p. 3

3   http://www.powerhousemuseum.com/collection/database/search_tags.php?tag=john+plunkett+entree+dish

4   Dargin, P., *The Kemmis Letters 1827–1844*, Development and Advisory Publications Australia, Dubbo, 2007, p. 84

5   *The Port Phillip Gazette*, 9 February 1842, p. 3

6   *The Maitland Mercury*, 2 January 1844, p. 2

7   Ibid

Chapter 31

1   Davy, M. J. B., *Henson and Stringfellow*, HMSO, London, 1931, p. 2

2   *The Cork Examiner*, 28 December 1846

3   Quoted in Smith, C. W., *The Great Hunger*, Penguin, London, 1991, p. 156

4 Gilmore, M., *More Recollections*, Angus & Robertson, Sydney, 1935, pp. 246–47

Chapter 32

1 *The Maitland Mercury*, 14 November 1846, p. 2
2 *The Maitland Mercury*, 2 January 1847, p. 2
3 *The Maitland Mercury*, 5 January 1847, p. 2
4 Ibid
5 *The Sydney Gazette and New South Wales Advertiser*, 13 March 1832, p. 3

Chapter 33

1 *The Sydney Morning Herald*, 9 October 1849, p. 2
2 Ibid
3 *The Maitland Mercury*, 9 October 1849, p. 2
4 Reece, R. H. W., *Aborigines and colonists: Aboriginal and colonial society in New South Wales in the 1830s and 1840s*, Sydney University Press, Sydney, 1974, p. 181
5 *R v Richard Bambrick, William Kearns & James Tredenick*, in Supreme Court, Criminal Jurisdiction, Brisbane, 1850, 9/6359 SRNSW
6 *The Morton Bay Courier*, 20 May 1850, p. 1

Chapter 34

1 *The Sydney Morning Herald*, 17 June 1850, p. 2
2 *The Sydney Morning Herald*, 4 September 1850, p. 3
3 *Bell's Life in Sydney and Sporting Reviewer*, 15 June 1850, p. 1
4 'The Lord Mayor's Fancy Dress Ball', *Sydney Punch*, 21 August 1844
5 *The Sydney Morning Herald*, 24 August 1850, p. 2
6 *Bell's Life in Sydney and Sporting Reviewer*, 24 August 1850, p. 2

7 *The Empire* (Sydney), 24 January 1851, p. 2

8 *The Sydney Illustrated News*, 10 December 1853, p. 5

9 *The Adelaide Advertiser*, 1 October 1859, p. 1

Chapter 35

1 McIntyre, W., *The Heathenism of Popery, proved and illustrated*, Henry Thomas, Maitland, 1860, p. 3

2 *The Maitland Mercury*, various issues, March 1860

3 *The Wesleyan Record*, reprinted in *The Morton Bay Courier* (Brisbane), 5 May 1860, p. 4

4 *The Sydney Morning Herald*, 2 April 1860, p. 4

5 McIntyre, W., *The Heathenism of Popery, proved and illustrated*, Henry Thomas, Maitland, 1860, p. 2

6 Ibid, p. 8

Chapter 36

1 *The Maitland Mercury*, 14 February 1867, p. 3

2 Cowper, W., to Dumaresq, H., *Letter*, 2 December 1837

3 *Bell's Life in Sydney and Sporting Reviewer*, 5 May 1860, p. 4

4 *Bell's Life in Sydney and Sporting Reviewer*, 23 May 1857, p. 3

5 *Bell's Life in Sydney and Sporting Reviewer*, 5 May 1860, p. 4

6 Ibid

7 *The Empire*, 30 July 1860, p. 5

8 *The Sydney Morning Herald*, 14 August 1860, p. 3

Chapter 37

1 Lynn, K. S., *William Dean Howells: An American Life*, Harcourt Brace Jovanovich, New York, 1970, p. 173

2 *The Newcastle Morning Herald & Miners' Advocate*, 4 May 1876, p. 2

3　*The Newcastle Morning Herald & Miners' Advocate*, 6 May 1876, p. 2

4　*The Newcastle Chronicle*, 1 July 1876, p. 2

5　*The Maitland Mercury*, 9 May 1876, p. 4

6　*Australian Town and Country Journal*, 27 May 1876, p. 13

Chapter 38

1　*The Windsor and Richmond Gazette*, 25 August 1894, p. 6

2　Revelation 12:7-9, *The Holy Bible*, King James version

3

Chapter 39

1　*The Sun-Herald*, 14 May 2000, p. 92

2　Ibid

3　Ibid

4　Ibid

5　Ibid

6　New South Wales Legislative Assembly, *Hansard*, 6 June 2000, p. 6894

7　*Friends of Myall Creek*, www.myallcreek.info/index.php/massacre-story

8　*The Sydney Morning Herald*, 31 January 2005

9　*ABC News*, 11 June 2015

10　*ABC News*, 11 June 2015

11　*ABC News*, 10 June 2012

References

ABC News

Ardfert and Aghadoe Census of 1821, *Encyclopaedia Britannica*, 8th ed., 1857

Assistant Colonial Secretary Thomas Harrington to E. D. Day, 9 July 1838

Australia in the year 1838, and respecting the Trial of their Murderers, House of Commons, London, 12 August 1839

Australian Jewish Historical Society, *Journal and Proceedings*, vol. 4, part 5, Sydney, 1956

Australian Town and Country Journal

Bannister, S., *Humane Policy: or Justice to the Aborigines of New Settlements Essential to a Due Expenditure of British Money, and to the Best Interests of the Settlers*, Thomas and George Underwood, London, 1830

Bartlett, T., *New Holland*, Longman, Brown, Green and Longmans, London, 1843

Becket, I. F. W., *Discovering English County Regiments*, Shire Publications, Buckinghamshire, 2003

Bell's Life in Sydney and Sporting Reviewer

Biggs, J. T., *Report of the Commissioner of Inquiry into the State of the Colony of New South Wales*, 1822

Boldrewood, R., *Old Melbourne Memories*, Heinemann, Melbourne, 1969

Breton, Lieut., R. N., *Excursions in New South Wales, Western Australia and Van Diemen's Land*, Richard Bentley, London, 1833

Bunbury, T., *Reminiscences of a Veteran: being personal and military adventures in Portugal, Spain, France, Malta, New South Wales, Norfolk Island, New Zealand, Andaman Islands and India*, vol. 2, Charles J. Skeet, London, 1861

Census of New South Wales 1828, Saintly, M., and Johnston, K. (eds.), Biographical Database of Australia, Sydney, 1980, revised edition 2008, bda-online.org.au

Chisholm, C., *Voluntary Information from the People of New South Wales*, W.A. Duncan, Sydney 1845, quoted in Sidney, Samuel, *The Three Colonies of Australia*, Ingram, Cooke & Co, London, 1853

Collins, D., *An Account of the English Colony in New South Wales*, vol. 1, T. Cadwell Jnr and W. Davies, London, 1798

Cowper, W., to Dumaresq, H., *Letter*, 2 December 1837

Cunningham, P., *Two Years in New South Wales*, vol. 1, Henry Colburn, London, 1827

Dargin, P., *The Kemmis Letters 1827–1844*, Development and Advisory Publications Australia, Dubbo, 2007

Darwin, C., *Letter to his Sister Caroline*, 27 December 1835

Darwin, C. R., *Journal of researches into the natural history and geology of the countries visited during the voyage of H.M.S. Beagle round the world, under the Command of Capt. Fitz Roy, R.N.*, 2nd edition, John Murray, London, 1845

Day, E. D., to Plunkett, J. H., *Letter*, 8 September 1838

Davy, M. J. B., *Henson and Stringfellow*, HMSO, London, 1931

Department of Main Roads New South Wales, *Main Roads*, September 1949

Deposition by Major J. W. Nunn, *Documents relating to Aboriginal Australians 1816–1853*, Mitchell Library, State Library of New South Wales, Sydney

Despatch from Governor Sir George Gipps to Lord Glenelg, 21 July 1838

Diggles, M., *Extract from memoir of George Downes*, Royal Historical Society of Queensland, 1881

Evidence of A. Burrowes, New South Wales Aborigines Protection Society, *Extracts from the Papers and Proceedings*, No. 1, October 1838

Evidence of Scott, R., *Report from the Committee on the Aborigines Question*, 1838, New South Wales Legislative Council

Faithful, G., *Letter to Lieutenant-Governor La Trobe*, 8 September 1853

Filisola, V., *Memorias para la Historia de la Guerra de Tejas*, Ignatio Cumplido, Mexico City, 1849, trans. Gustavo Pellon

Friends of Myall Creek, www.myallcreek.info/index.php/ massacre-story

Gilmore, M., *More Recollections*, Angus & Robertson, Sydney, 1935

Gipps to Glenelg, *Despatch*, 18 March 1838

Gipps to Glenelg, *Despatch*, 27 April 1838

Gipps to Glenelg, *Despatch No. 200*, 19 December 1838

Gipps to Glenelg, *Despatch No. 201*, 20 December 1838

Hobbs, W., to Day, E. D., *Letter*, 9 July 1838

Huey, A., (diary), *The Voyage of the 73rd Regiment of Foot*, State Library of New South Wales, Sydney, 1790

Indent of Convict Ships, 1832–33

Kerry's History for the E-Reader, *The Dennys of Tralee Castle, their exceptional connections*, historytralee.wordpress.com

King to Banks, *Letter*, 5 June 1802, Sir Joseph Banks Electronic Archive, series 39.068, Mitchell Library, Sydney

Loveless et al, *A Narrative of the Sufferings of Jas. Loveless, Jas. Brine, and Thomas and John Standfield, four of the Dorchester labourers, written by themselves*, Leave, London, 1838

Lynn, K. S., *William Dean Howells: An American Life*, Harcourt Brace Jovanovich, New York, 1970

McIntyre, W., *The Heathenism of Popery, proved and illustrated*, Henry Thomas, Maitland, 1860

Macquarie, L., *Diary*, Sydney, 10 April 1816

Macquarie, L., *Instructions for Capt. W. G. B. Schaw*, 9 April 1816

Macquarie, L., *Instructions to the Military*, 9 April 1816

Macquarie to Bathurst, *Despatch*, 4 April 1817

Macqueen, T. P., *Australia As She Is and As She May Be*, London, 1840

Minutes of the Executive Council, vol. 5 (1837–1841), Minute No. 6

National Army Museum, *62nd (Wiltshire) Regiment of Foot*, nam.ac.uk/research/famous-units/62nd-wiltshire-regiment-foot

New South Wales Legislative Assembly, *Hansard*, 6 June 2000, p. 6894

Nunn, J. W., *Deposition taken before Edward Denny Day*, 4 April 1839

Ogilvie, E. D. S., *Diary of Travels in Three Quarters of the Globe*, vol. 1, Saunders & Otley, London, 1856

Old Bailey Sessions Papers, 1831–2

Paterson, A., *Report on Outrages by Aborigines on Namoi, Gwydir and Big Rivers*, 6 December 1837, quoted in Historical Records of Australia, 22 July 1839

Powerhouse Museum

Reece, R. H. W., *Aborigines and colonists: Aboriginal and colonial society in New South Wales in the 1830s and 1840s*, Sydney University Press, Sydney, 1974

Report of the Select Committee on Transportation, 1837–38, vol. 22

Ridley, Reverend W., *Kamilaroi and Other Australian Languages*, 2nd edition, Thomas Richards, Sydney, 1875

Roberts, J., *Massacres to Mining: The Colonisation of Aboriginal Australia*, Dove Communications, Melbourne, 1981

Royal Archives, *Queen Victoria's Journal*, 20 June 1837

Russell, P. (ed.), *This Errant Lady: Jane Franklin's overland journey to Port Phillip and Sydney, 1839*, National Library of Australia Press, Canberra, 2002

R v. Richard Bambrick, William Kearns & James Tredenick, in Supreme Court, Criminal Jurisdiction, Brisbane 1850, 9/6359 SRNSW

Shakespeare, W., *The Famous History of King Henry the Eighth*

Smith, C. W., *The Great Hunger*, Penguin, London, 1991

Strype, J., *Ecclesiastical Memorials*, vol. 1, part 2, Oxford, 1822

Telfer, W., *The Wallabadah Manuscript*, New South Wales University Press, Sydney, 1980

Tench, W., *A Complete Account of the Settlement at Port Jackson in New South Wales, Including An Accurate Description of the Situation of the Colony; of the Natives; and of Its Natural Productions*, G. Nicol and J. Sewell, London, 1793

The Adelaide Advertiser

The Age (Melbourne)

The Australian

The Book of Common Prayer

The Colonist

The Cork Examiner

The Empire (Sydney)

The Hobart Town Courier

The Holy Bible, King James Version, Robert Barker, London, 1611

The Maitland Mercury

The Murder Act 1751 (25 Geo 2, c. 37)

The Muswellbrook Chronicle

The Newcastle Chronicle

The Newcastle Morning Herald & Miners' Advocate

The Port Phillip Gazette

The Sun-Herald

The Sydney Gazette

The Sydney Gazette and New South Wales Advertiser

The Sydney Herald

The Sydney Illustrated News

The Sydney Monitor

The Wesleyan Record, reprinted in *The Morton Bay Courier* (Brisbane)

The Windsor and Richmond Gazette

Thompson, E., *Letter to Philip Gidley King*, 23 June 1838

Threlkeld, L.E., *Annual Report of the Aboriginal Mission at Lake Macquarie, New South Wales, for 1835*, 28 June 1836

Threlkeld, L. E., to Colonial Secretary, 31 December 1837, quoted in Gunston, N., (ed), *Australian Reminiscences and Papers of L.E. Threlkeld*, vol. 1, Australian Institute of Aboriginal Studies, Canberra, 1974

Unlawful Oaths Act 1797 (37 George III, c. 123)

Various colonists, *Memorial to Governor Sir George Gipps*, Sydney, 8 June 1838, in *Copies of Extracts of Despatches relative to the massacre of various Aborigines of Australia in the year 1838, and respecting the Trial of their Murderers*, House of Commons, London, 12 August 1839

Walker, W., *Reminiscences (Personal, Social and Political) of a*

Fifty Year Residence at Windsor, on the Hawkesbury, Turner and Henderson, Sydney, 1890

Warner to Bourke, quoted in Turner, J., and Blyton, G., *The Aboriginals of Lake Macquarie*, Lake Macquarie City Council, Newcastle, 1995

Watson, W., and Handt, J., *Report of the Mission to the Aborigines of New Holland, Wellington Valley*, 14 December 1833

Wearne, J. T., *Bingara 1827–1937*, Bingara District Historical Society, 1885

White, C., *The Story of the Blacks*, Bathurst Free Press, 3 January 1890

White, G. B., *Diary*, 4 May 1870

Wood, W.A., *Dawn in the Valley*, Wentworth Books, Sydney, 1972

Zouch, Lieut. H., *Report to Capt. Williams, Commandant of Mounted Police*, 7 December 1835

4 William IV, *Act No. 7*

Acknowledgements

Great credit is due to my brother Dan Smyth for introducing me to Denny and Margaret Day in that old graveyard years ago, for his knowledge of the workings of the law and justice in the nineteenth century, and for his historical detective work. Thanks to my publisher, Alison Urquhart, for her unwavering support, and to my excellent editor, Virginia Grant. Research would have been frustratingly slow if not impossible but for the resources of the State Library of New South Wales, the Trove collection of the National Library of Australia, and British regimental histories and memoirs.

My particular thanks to Terry Maher for the invaluable gift of local knowledge, and to all those people of the Hunter, Hawkesbury and Liverpool Plains who helped put flesh on the bones of this story with oral histories, legend and lore.

Index